Jon Bell
Steven Elliott
Tim Forcade
Martin Foster
Phillip Miller
Greg Phillips
Gregory Pyros
Keith Seifert
Richard Sher
David Stinnett

3D Special Effects Studio

NRP
NEW RIDERS PUBLISHING

New Riders Publishing, Indianapolis, Indiana

3D Studio® Special Effects

By Jon Bell, Steven Elliott, Tim Forcade, Martin Foster, Phillip Miller, Greg Phillips, Gregory Pyros, Keith Seifert, Richard Sher, and David Stinnett

Published by:
New Riders Publishing
201 West 103rd Street
Indianapolis, IN 46290 USA

Printed in the United States of America 1 2 3 4 5 6 7 8 9 0

```
3D studio special effects / Jon A. Bell . . . [et al.].
       p.    cm.
    Includes index.
    ISBN 1-56205-303-5
1. Computer animation. 2 Autodesk 3D studio. 3. Computer
graphics.  I. Bell, Jon A. (Jon Allen), 1961-
006.6'869--dc20                                 94-32981
                                                    CIP
```

Warning and Disclaimer

This book is designed to provide information about the 3D Studio computer program. Every effort has been made to make this book as complete and as accurate as possible, but no warranty or fitness is implied.

The information is provided on an "as is" basis. The author and New Riders Publishing shall have neither liability nor responsibility to any person or entity with respect to any loss or damages arising from the information contained in this book or from the use of the disks or programs that may accompany it.

Publisher	Lloyd J. Short
Associate Publisher	Tim Huddleston
Product Development Manager	Rob Tidrow
Marketing Manager	Ray Robinson
Director of Special Projects	Cheri Robinson
Managing Editor	Matthew Morrill

Trademark Acknowledgments

All terms mentioned in this book that are known to be trademarks or service marks have been appropriately capitalized. New Riders Publishing cannot attest to the accuracy of this information. Use of a term in this book should not be regarded as affecting the validity of any trademark or service mark.

Product Director
Kevin Coleman

Senior Editor
Tad Ringo

Copy Editors
Sarah Kearns
Cliff Shubs
Janis Brown

Senior Acquisitions Editor
Jim LeValley

Technical Editor
Andrew Reese

Acquisitions Coordinator
Stacey Beheler

Editorial Assistant
Karen Opal

Publisher's Assistant
Melissa Lynch

Cover Designer
Roger Morgan

Book Designer
Roger S. Morgan

Graphics Image Specialists
Dennis Sheehan
Susan VandeWalle
Theresa Forrester

Production Imprint Manager
Juli Cook

Production Imprint Team Leader
Katy Bodenmiller

Production Analysts
Mary Beth Wakefield
Dennis Clay Hager

Production Team
Nick Anderson
Mona Brown
Aryrika Bryant
Kim Cofer
Elaine Crabtree
Mike Dietsch
Rob Falco
Brian-Kent Proffitt
Kim Scott
Susan Shepard
Karen Walsh
Dennis Wesner

Indexer
Bront Davis

Contents at a Glance

Table of Contents

Effect 1

- Simulate and animate high-quality, full-color shadows from transparent objects.

- Maintain a quality level comparable to 3D Studio's shadow-mapped shadows.

- Generate convincing color shadows and gain considerable speed flexibility over 3D Studio's ray-traced shadows.

Effect 2

- Use the Copy Tracks and Slide Keys features of 3D Studio to cause a number of objects to follow each other along an animation path.

- Animate a single object and copy its motions to other objects rather than relying on hierarchical linking

- Commonly used for commercials and the opening titles of television shows.

Effect 3

- Use an animated stand-in process.

- Build several similar items that would be very complex if done individually.

- Add detail and realism to a scene without any difficult modeling.

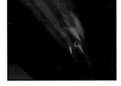

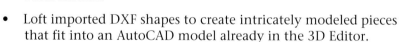
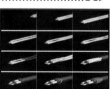

- Produce quicker, smoother, and more predictable results.
- Avoid the tedium associated with manually setting numerous keyframes and repeatedly aligning complex geometry.

Effect 16

- Create an effect often used in the titles and credits of movies and TV shows.
- Fade out the colors in an image to produce a uniform, low-contrast backdrop for foreground titles or objects.
- Have foreground objects or titles stand out from the background.

Effect 17

- Use IPAS routines to create smooth spline-based surfaces over cross sections of regular polygon geometry.
- Avoid common problems with polygon-based 3D packages when animating characters.
- Use the 2D Shaper and 3D Lofter tools to create complex characters with skinning across the joints of major limbs.

Appendix

- Unusual images
- Animation clips
- Use for direct application as any of 3D Studio's maps or masks.
- Use as points of departure to create your own custom effects.

Introduction

Have you ever seen a computer animation special effect and said to yourself, "How'd they do that? I want to do that in my animations!" *3D Studio Special Effects* shows you how.

3D Studio Special Effects is a collection of special effects and techniques from some of the world's most creative 3D Studio artists. Many of the artists have created award-winning animations in 3D Studio. Each special effect is described, step-by-step, by the artist and is illustrated with full-color screen shots and renderings.

The effects in this book cover all areas of 3D Studio, including modeling, materials and maps, keyframing, Video Post, IPAS, and even post-production video editing. All types of animators can benefit from these special effects. Whether you produce animations for network broadcast, multimedia presentations, games, architectural walkthroughs, industrial design, or just for fun, you will find this book is an excellent idea resource for spicing up your animations. Even veteran 3D Studio users will benefit from the techniques in this book.

Getting the Most from This Book

3D Studio Special Effects is written at a level for intermediate through advanced 3D Studio users. This is not to say that beginning 3D Studio users won't find useful information in this book. If nothing else, this book will inspire the beginner to dive deeper into 3D Studio. However, this book doesn't focus on teaching 3D Studio; it concentrates on teaching the artists' special effects.

You should have a general, well-rounded knowledge of 3D Studio in order to get the most out of the effects in this book. You should have completed the 3D Studio tutorials and thoroughly understand the concepts presented in them. You also should be familiar with the 3D Studio reference manuals and know where to find needed information. Last, but not least, you should have created several animations of your own ideas and designs.

What You Need to Use This Book

Many of the special effects in this book only require 3D Studio itself. However, to do all of the effects you will need several other applications as well. These other applications are standard parts to a 3D Studio animator's toolkit. These other applications include the following:

- **A 24-bit image editor.** Image editors are among the most often-used applications after 3D Studio itself and is a requirement for professional animators. Image editing programs are essential for creating and modifying bitmaps for materials, editing background images, and creating composite images. Adobe PhotoShop, Aldus PhotoStyler, and Ron Scott's HiRes QFX are the most popular image editing programs with 3D Studio animators. To create professional quality 3D Studio composite images, a program capable of reading and using alpha channel information is necessary. One such program is Altamira Composer. Many animators have several image editing applications, taking advantage of the strengths of each.

- **Autodesk Animator Pro.** This is another essential companion program for the 3D Studio professional. Animator Pro is used to create FLI files for animated materials and is a versatile 8-bit paint program. Often you do not need a 24-bit image editing program to create mattes, masks, bump maps, and opacity maps. These types of images are often just shades of gray. Animator Pro can only paint with 256 colors, but can be set up to paint with 256 shades of one color.

- **Third-party IPAS programs.** Although they are not required to produce animations with 3D Studio, third-party IPAS programs are extremely useful tools. There are third-party IPAS programs that simulate camera lens and filter effects, create realistic trees and plants, deform objects, simulate the qualities of old film, and automatically create skin over skeletal structures. New IPAS routines are released all the time. The

ASOFT forum on CompuServe is the best place for the latest information on IPAS programs for 3D Studio.

In addition to software, you also need some hardware to get the most out of this book.

- **A PC system.** Your animation system should be the fastest and most advanced system that you can afford. Although the examples in this book are designed to minimize system requirements, many of these effects, when used in real-world animations, require large amounts of processing power, RAM, and disk space.

- **A CD-ROM drive.** A CD-ROM drive is one of the most essential pieces of hardware for a 3D Studio animator after the PC system itself. Many resources for 3D Studio are only available on CD-ROM because of the size and quantity of the files. In addition to the World Creating Toolkit that ships with 3D Studio, third-party meshes, maps, and animations are available on CD-ROM. A CD-ROM drive is required to use the example files for the effects in this book and to access the bonus maps on the CD-ROM.

- **Video editing equipment.** For the most part, the effects in this book can be rendered to FLI files and edited in Animator Pro. One effect requires access to an A/B/C roll video editing suite.

Other Reference Materials

Besides 3D Studio's reference manuals, there are other books that can help you produce better animations. *Inside 3D Studio* from New Riders Publishing is an excellent and highly recommended extension to the 3D Studio manuals.

Other good resources for information are general books on animation, graphic design, video production, theatrical lighting and scene design, and, of course, computer graphics. Check out your local library or large bookstore. Operating 3D Studio is only half (or less) of the animation process.

There are also magazines with 3D Studio-specific and general computer animation information. Some of these magazines include *3D Artist, Computer Graphics World, AV/Video, Computer Artist,* and *Computer Pictures.* These magazines can be found in larger magazine stores and some libraries.

The manuals for your other software packages are also good resources for information. For example, image editing applications often include information on producing hardcopy output of true color bitmap files that not only applies to the specific application, but also to 3D Studio and other applications.

Using the CD-ROM

Included in the back of this book is a CD-ROM that contains all of the project files, maps, and meshes to create all of the special effects in this book. There is also a completed FLIC animation for the animated effects. Several of the effects also have still renderings on the CD-ROM. Each effect's files are in a separate directory on the CD-ROM. The project files are not only useful for creating the specific special effects, but, when analyzed, provide clues beyond the steps in the text about how the effects are created.

You do not need to install the project files from the SF/X CD-ROM onto your hard drive. You can load the project files directly into 3D Studio. 3D Studio will automatically add the CD-ROM directory to the Map Paths list.

Also on the SF/X CD-ROM is a bonus collection of original still and animated maps that you can use in your own animations. You may not resell or otherwise distribute them. This book's appendix includes instructions and tips on how to use these maps. All of the maps are shown in the gallery after the appendix.

Using CompuServe

The Autodesk Software Forum (GO ASOFT) on CompuServe is the best source for information about and help with 3D Studio. In fact, being a part of the forum is just as important as any

software application or piece of hardware for the 3D Studio user. All of the authors in this book are members of the Autodesk Software Forum, as are many other talented 3D Studio animators. If you need help with creating your own special effect, this is the place to go. In addition to other 3D Studio animators, the programmers of 3D Studio also hang out on the forum to answer your deepest and darkest technical questions.

Other Books from New Riders Publishing

In addition to *Inside 3D Studio,* here are some other titles from New Riders Publishing that are useful for 3D Studio users:

Inside CompuServe

Inside Adobe PhotoShop

Adobe PhotoShop Now!

Inside AutoCAD

Inside AutoLISP

Inside CorelDRAW!

CorelDRAW! Special Effects

New Riders Publishing

The staff of New Riders Publishing is committed to bringing you the very best in computer reference material. Each New Riders book is the result of months of work by authors and staff who research and refine the information contained within its covers.

As part of this commitment to you, the NRP reader, New Riders invites your input. Please let us know if you enjoy this book, if you have trouble with the information and examples presented, or if you have a suggestion for the next edition.

Please note, though: New Riders staff cannot serve as a technical resource for 3D Studio or for related questions about software- or hardware-related problems. Please refer to the documentation that accompanies 3D Studio or to the applications' Help systems.

If you have a question or comment about any New Riders book, there are several ways to contact New Riders Publishing. We will respond to as many readers as we can. Your name, address, or phone number will never become part of a mailing list or be used for any purpose other than to help us continue to bring you the best books possible. You can write us at the following address:

New Riders Publishing
Attn: Associate Publisher
201 W. 103rd Street
Indianapolis, IN 46290

If you prefer, you can fax New Riders Publishing at (317) 581-4670.

You can send electronic mail to New Riders from a variety of sources. NRP maintains several mailboxes organized by topic area. Mail in these mailboxes will be forwarded to the staff member who is best able to address your concerns. Substitute the appropriate mailbox name from the list below when addressing your e-mail. The mailboxes are as follows:

ADMIN	Comments and complaints for NRP's Publisher
APPS	Word, Excel, WordPerfect, other office applications
ACQ	Book proposals and inquiries by potential authors
CAD	AutoCAD, 3D Studio, AutoSketch and CAD products
DATABASE	Access, dBASE, Paradox and other database products
GRAPHICS	CorelDRAW!, Photoshop, and other graphics products
INTERNET	Internet
NETWORK	NetWare, LANtastic, and other network-related topics
OS	MS-DOS, OS/2, all OS except Unix and Windows
UNIX	UNIX
WINDOWS	Microsoft Windows (all versions)
OTHER	Anything that doesn't fit the above categories

If you use an MHS e-mail system that routes through CompuServe, send your messages to:

mailbox @ NEWRIDER

To send NRP mail from CompuServe, use the following address:

MHS: *mailbox* @ NEWRIDER

To send mail from the Internet, use the following address format:

mailbox@newrider.mhs.compuserve.com

NRP is an imprint of Macmillan Computer Publishing. To obtain a catalog or information, or to purchase any Macmillan Computer Publishing book, call (800) 428-5331.

Thank you for selecting *3D Studio Special Effects*!

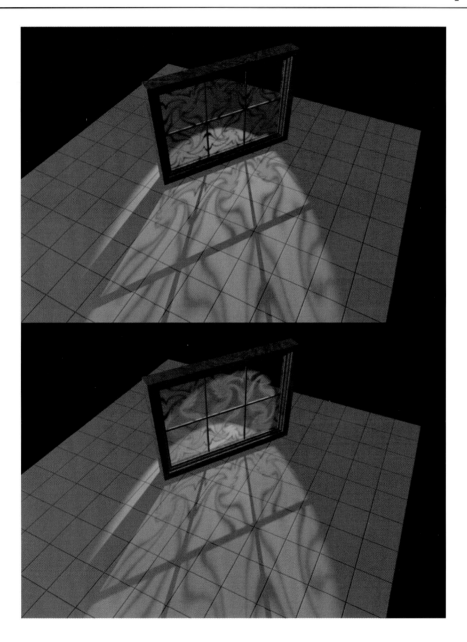

by Tim Forcade

Lawrence, Kansas

Equipment and Software Used

LANtastic networked
IBM PC compatibles

3D Studio Release 3.0

Adobe Photoshop or
HiRes QFX

Artist Biography

Building on an education in traditional fine arts that stressed drawing, painting, sculpture, and graphic design, Tim Forcade's artwork has advanced through optical, kinetic, and digital electronic media. This has resulted in numerous works utilizing photography, electronics, and video as well as the invention of electronic image-processing systems of his own design.

Concurrent with his artwork, Tim (see above left "self portrait: flames, wind, & fire") has over two decades of practice as a commercial artist, designer, and photographer. In 1978 Tim formed Forcade & Associates as a graphics resource to the commercial and professional communities. His project experience extends from illustration and publication design through photography and 3D visualization to computer animation and multimedia.

Tim's work has been exhibited in the U.S., Canada, Europe, and Japan. He has written and presented extensively on the subjects of applied 2D and 3D computer graphics and animation. He is a contributing editor to Computer Graphics World *and* Computer Artist *magazines. He can be reached via CompuServe at* 72007,2742 *or via Internet at* tforcade@falcon.cc.ukans.edu

Working with Tim at Forcade & Associates is Terry Gilbert, who provided invaluable assistance to Tim in creating and documenting this effect.

Effect Overview

Many animations and still images require that transparent and semi-transparent colored objects cast colored shadows. Although 3D Studio's ray-traced shadows represent shadow density accurately, casting shadows of transparent objects and convincingly representing the color of those objects has always been out of reach. The reason is that 3D Studio does not use a ray tracing renderer. Ray-tracing renderings can accurately depict properties such as shadow color based on the paths of light rays in the scene.

This chapter describes a method for simulating and animating high-quality, full-color shadows from transparent objects at a quality level comparable to 3D Studio's shadow-mapped shadows. Aside from generating convincing color shadows, the procedure can offer a considerable speed advantage as well as increased flexibility over 3D Studio's ray-traced shadows.

Look at the images on the opening page of this chapter. The scene depicts a stained glass window sitting on a tiled plane. The window is back lighted, producing a shadow of its pattern on the tiled plane.

The upper image was rendered using 3D Studio's ray-traced shadows. In this image, the opaque objects (the wooden frame and lead leadcame) cast gray shadows that equal the ambient light level. Also note that the transparent areas of the stained glass cast shadows that appear as various shades of gray. This is not how the real world works.

Now look at the lower image. The shadows are of the same quality—well defined and convincing—but now the shadow accurately represents the color as well as the varying densities of the stained glass. Interestingly, neither of 3D Studio's shadow types (shadow-mapped or ray-traced) were used in the image.

The key to this effect lies in the use of three lights that combine to do the work of one. The most essential of these is a projector spotlight that projects a shadow image on the objects in the scene, exactly as a slide projector would. A second light is aligned exactly with the first. The second light is used to light areas that are masked by the projector spot. A third light is used to create the illusion of a cone of light, intersecting the window panes.

The shadow image was rendered from the projector light's viewpoint and saved to disk prior to the final rendering from the camera view. Then, at render time, this shadow image was projected on the scene to produce the shadow effect.

This effect's procedure is the manual equivalent of 3D Studio's built-in shadow mapping and is useful any time a shadow is needed. Because this process enables you to precisely adjust your shadows for properties such as softness, transparency, and color saturation, it offers increased flexibility over either of 3D Studio's shadow types.

Procedure

Table 1.1 lists all the files necessary to produce the colored shadow effect for this chapter. The project files contain all cameras, lighting, and materials. Also included is SHADCOLR.FLI, an example animation. The files are located on the CD-ROM in the /SHADCOLR directory.

Table 1.1
The Mesh, Project, and Bitmap Files for the Color Shadow Example

File Name	Description
SHADRAY.PRJ	Example of 3D Studio ray-traced shadows
SHADMAP.PRJ	For rendering transparent color shadow map
SHADCOLR.PRJ	Final colored shadows project with animation
SHADBOOL.3DS	Incident spotlight alignment template
SHADCONE.3DS	Litecone object for creating alignment template
CSHADOW.MLI	Project materials library
TWIRLBLU.TIF	Custom bitmap for glass texture and opacity
TWIRLYEL.TIF	Custom bitmap for glass texture and opacity
TILE1.GIF	Custom bitmap for Tile_plane bump
TILE2.GIF	Custom bitmap for Tile_plane texture
LTWOOD1.CEL	Standard bitmap for frame texture and bump
CSHADOW.TIF	Custom bitmap for Shadlite shadow map
SHADCOLR.FLI	Animated example of color shadows

1. Load the SHADRAY.PRJ file and examine the objects and materials. The scene, shown in figure 1.1, consists of a stained glass window and a tiled plane (named Tile_plane). The window is composed of the objects Frame, Leadcame, and Glass. The glass alternates between two materials that use TWIRLBLU.TIF and TWIRLYEL.TIF for its texture and opacity maps. This produces a stained glass pattern that provides a mix of color and transparency. The scene consists of a shadow-casting spotlight (named Shadlite) and a fill light (Sidefill). Shadlite has the Cast Shadows button selected and Ray Trace chosen from the Local Shadow Control dialog box. This file was used to produce the upper image on the facing page. Render the Camera_1 view to the screen and notice the colorless ray-traced shadow. The image is rendered using 3D Studio's ray-traced shadows and contains two lights—a back light and a fill light.

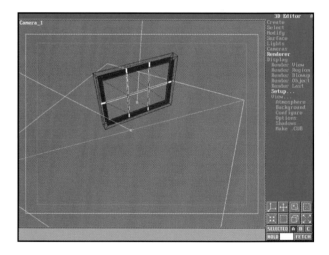

Figure 1.1
The scene used to create the upper image.

Next, you start the process of manually creating the colored shadow maps. Turn off the spotlight's ray-traced shadows and create a rendered image (a shadow map) from its viewport. The result is used with a projector light to create the color shadow effect.

This effect requires two scene setups—one to create the shadow map and one that uses the map in a final rendered image or animation. To create the color shadow map, you need to make several changes to the scene to prepare it for producing the shadow map.

2. Save a project file to store the project's current settings. This speeds the process by making it easier to restore the scene for creating the final image or animation.

 In situations where you plan to do a lot of shadow tweaking, it is very useful to save separate project files for multiple scene setups.

To create a color shadow map, begin by hiding any objects that will receive shadows.

3. Hide the object Tile_plane. Then choose **Lights/Ambient** and set the ambient light level to **0**. This assures that the color shadow map density will match the scene's ambient level. Set the background to white **255,255,255**. This gives the color shadow map a full brightness range. Finally, choose **Lights/Spot/Adjust** and turn off both spotlights in the scene. All scene lights should be turned off to prevent non-transparent colored objects from producing colored shadows.

4. Make the lower left viewport current, press **$**, and select Shadlite from the Spotlight Selector dialog box. This changes the viewport to the Shadlite spotlight view (see fig. 1.2).

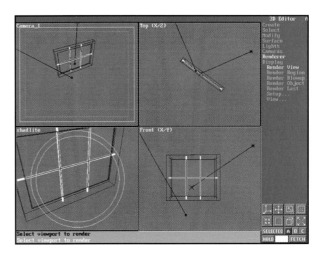

Figure 1.2
SHADMAP.PRJ ready to render the color shadow map.

5. Choose **Renderer/Render View** and select the spotlight's viewport. (SHADMAP.PRJ on the CD-ROM is set up and ready to render the color shadow map). Set the output file's resolution to 1024×1024 and the file type to compressed color TIFF. Be sure that Anti-aliasing, Filter Maps, and Mapping are set to **On**. Turn on No Display to speed rendering. Name the output file CSHADOW.TIF.

The color shadow map resolution is a function of the project output requirements. For the image on the opening page of this chapter, the file was rendered for reproduction at 1536×1024. The aspect ratio of the map file should be equal to that of the light you intend to use. Because this project uses a circular spotlight, the color shadow map will be rendered with a square aspect ratio.

6. When rendering is complete, choose **Renderer/View/Image** to view the image. Select Resize from the dialog box that appears if your display is smaller than the image file's resolution. The image should look like figure 1.3—the opaque objects appear solid black, the background is solid white, and the glass is multicolored.

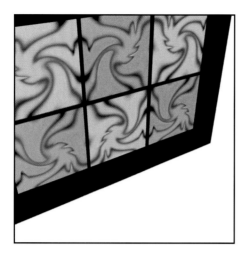

Figure 1.3
The rendered color shadow map, CSHADOW.TIF.

7. Restore the project file you previously saved or re-load SHADRAY.PRJ.

8. Choose **Lights/Spot/Adjust** and select Shadlite. In the Spotlight Definition dialog box, turn off the **Cast Shadows** button, turn on **Projector**, and click on the blank button directly below Projector button. In the File Selector dialog box, select CSHADOW.TIF, the color shadow map you created in a previous step. Exclude all scene objects except Tile_plane using the Exclude Objects dialog box. Choose **OK**, render the scene from the Camera_1 viewport, and view the result.

Figure 1.4 shows the rendered image with the colored shadow. Although the procedure creates a convincing color shadow, the light around the window frame and leadcame is dull and unrealistic; the shadow pattern from the stained glass should fall on both objects. The shadows are missing because the shadow map used to create the color shadow cancels the light that reaches these objects.

Figure 1.4
The rendered image with the color shadow map projected by the Shadlite spotlight.

This problem can be dealt with in two ways. The first, and technically the most precise, is to create two shadow maps: one used for all opaque objects and another for all transparent objects. You could use these with their own respective projector spots to produce the most realistic look and the most flexibility. Further, splitting opaque objects along an axis and separating front-lighted and back-lighted geometry provides even more flexibility. However, these steps also make animating the lights more complex and often may not be necessary.

A simpler method, and one that produces an acceptable result, is to use another spotlight as a back fill light for the frame and leadcame only.

9. Choose **Lights/Spot/Dolly** and, while holding down the shift key, select Shadlite and clone a new spotlight in exactly the same position. Name this spotlight **Backlite**.

10. Choose **Lights/Spot/Adjust**, press **H**, and select the Backlite light. In the Spotlight Definition dialog box, turn off Projector and exclude all scene objects except Frame and Leadcame.

The scene now contains three spotlights. The Shadlite spotlight projects the color shadow map and only lights Tile_plane. The Backlite spot lights Frame and Leadcame only. The Sidefill spot provides fill on the side of the window frame (Frame).

11. Choose **OK**, render the scene from Camera 1, and view it.

The scene in figure 1.5 looks much more realistic with the highlighting added by the Backlite spot. However, another problem remains. Few if any objects in the real world are absolutely transparent. Therefore, if the window were real, an elliptical pattern created by the projector's cone of light would be visible where the light intersects the glass.

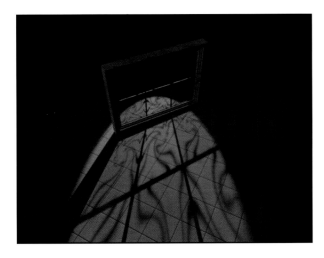

Figure 1.5
The Backlite spotlight produces a more realistic look.

The solution is to use a light that is incident to the projector light and lights the front of the glass only. Creating a new spotlight for this purpose is easy enough, but how can it be exactly positioned, incident to the projector light? A simple way is to use 3D Studio's Boolean functions to create an alignment template.

Because using the Boolean functions destroys the original objects, the next few steps show you how to set up the Boolean operation and provide a completed template. You do not have to create the template yourself.

12. Choose **File/Merge**, make sure that only the **Mesh Objects** button is highlighted, click on **OK**, and select SHADCONE.3DS. From the object list, choose Litecone. This loads a cone at the same position, size, and angle as the Shadlite and Backlite spotlights. This object was used with **Create/Object/Boolean** and the window's Glass object to create the intersection template.

13. Once again, choose **File/Merge**, click on **Mesh Objects**, and select the object Boolean from the SHADBOOL.3DS file. This loads the result of the Boolean intersection. Press **$** and change the lower left viewport to Shadlite and the lower right viewport to Backlite. Hide the object Litecone. The elliptical template on the window is perfectly aligned with both of the spotlights. This will act as a template to position the Incident spotlight that you create in the next step.

14. In the top view, zoom in on the Tile_plane object and create a clone of the Backlite spot using **Lights/Spot/Move**. Using an imaginary centerline with the window top as a guide, place the incident spot at an angle that mirrors the angle created by the Shadlite spot and the window frame. Name this light **Incident** (see fig. 1.6).

Use 3D Studio's Tape feature to help position the Incident light.

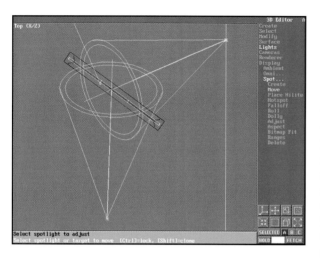

Figure 1.6
The cloned Incident spotlight in position.

15. Make the upper right viewport current, press **$**, and select the Incident light from the list. This changes the view to that of the Incident light. Notice that all three spotlights—Shadlite, Backlite, and Incident—align with the template (see fig. 1.7). Align the spotlight with the cyan template that you merged in earlier. Make sure the Incident light has Projector turned off and that all objects are excluded except for Glass.

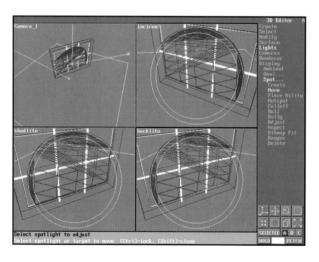

Figure 1.7
The alignment template for positioning the Incident spotlight.

16. When you are done positioning the light, hide the template object and render the scene from the Camera_1 viewport. The result should look like the lower image on the opening page of this chapter.

With all the lights created, producing an animation is a simple matter of using the Keyframer's Hierarchy commands and two dummy objects. The main difference between applying an animated color shadow map and a still one is that you must first render the entire animation from the Shadlite viewport instead of just a single frame. The animation is saved as series of frames or an FLI file, which is assigned to the projector spotlight in the same way as a single frame.

17. Begin the process of creating an animated color shadow map by switching to the Keyframer. Choose **Display/Const/Show** to display the construction plane. Next, choose **Display/Const/Place** and use the Top and Front viewports (see fig. 1.8) to position the construction lines where the spotlight target points intersect the window. This will be the center point for each dummy object.

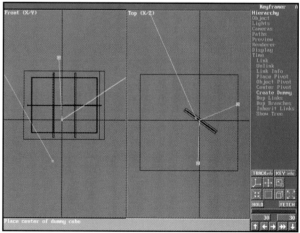

Figure 1.8
The intersection of the construction planes at the spotlight target.

18. Now create two dummy objects in the Front viewport using **Hierarchy/Create Dummy**. Place the center for each dummy object at the intersection of the construction lines and name them **ShadDummy** and **IncidDummy**.

19. Choose **Hierarchy/Link**, press **H**, select Shadlite and Backlite, and make them child objects of ShadDummy. Similarly, link the Incident spotlight to make it the child of IncidDummy.

20. Set up the lights for rendering the shadow map similarly to the way they were set up for rendering the still image.

Now you only need to rotate the dummy objects, which in turn rotate their linked children, thus setting the desired keyframes. To preserve the relationship between Shadlite (Backlite) and Incident, any rotation of the one object must be mirrored exactly by the other (see fig. 1.9). For instance, when ShadDummy rotates in the positive direction, IncidDummy must rotate in the negative direction.

21. Move to frame 30, turn on Angle Snap, and rotate ShadDummy to 90 degrees. Also from frame 30, rotate ShadDummy to –90 degrees. Play back the animation in the top view and observe how the spotlights rotate symmetrically around the centerline of the window.

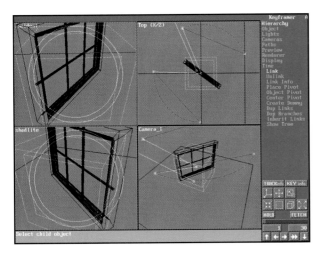

Figure 1.9
The mirrored motion paths for the spotlights.

22. Render the animation from the Shadlite viewport and save the frames to SMAP.TIF. Alternatively, you can render the animation to an FLI file. However, you would lose the ability to soften or otherwise image-process the shadow map frames.

Rendering animations from a spotlight viewport requires 3D Studio Release 4.0 or later.

To use a sequence of animated frames as a map, you need to make an IFL file that lists all the frames comprising the animation—the color shadow map animation in this chapter. It is easy to create an IFL file from DOS.

23. When the shadow map animation is done rendering, press F10 to move to the DOS shell and change to the subdirectory that contains the SMAP????.TIF frames. At the DOS prompt, type **DIR SMAP*.TIF /-P /ON /B > SMAP.IFL** and press Enter. This creates a sequential listing of all the frames from SMAP0000.TIF to SMAP0030.TIF (in this case) and places it in the file SMAP.IFL.

24. Choose **Lights/Spot/Adjust**, press **H**, and select Shadlite. Replace the CSHADOW.TIF projector map with SMAP.IFL. Also, remember to restore the scene lighting to its original state before final rendering.

25. Render the file from the Camera_1 view or playback SHADCOLR.FLI to see the result.

Conclusion

Remember, the shadows produced using this process are subject to the same problems to which all shadow maps are occasionally prone. The most important of these is the aliased or jaggy look that can occur in some areas of the shadow. This aliasing becomes more apparent as the shadow spotlight's angle decreases with respect to the objects onto which the shadow is cast. To put it another way, the more perpendicular the spotlight is to a given shadowed object, the better.

In instances where a spotlight must obliquely skim a surface, and you begin to notice aliasing problems, one solution is to increase the resolution of the color shadow map. Another solution is to soften your shadow maps using a paint program such as Adobe Photoshop, HiRes QFX from Ron Scott, or an IPAS application such HBLUR.IXP from The Pyros Partnership, Inc.

For the additional work involved, the manual shadow-mapping process offers a great deal of flexibility and increased control over shadow color, saturation, transparency, and edge softness. The rotoscoping possibilities alone are fantastic. This chapter has merely scratched the surface of potential effects that you can create using manual shadow mapping.

For instance, you can add complexity and richness to your shadows by applying reflection maps to transparent objects when you are rendering your shadow maps. This generates some fascinating shadow variations. Although this is far from a literal translation of what happens in the real world, it produces some unique and useful effects.

For those instances where you cannot seem to get the desired lighting effect, this approach enables you to mask an object with an alpha channel and paint any pattern you want directly on the object. You can then apply the shadow map as a projector light with the background matted out. Additional effects possibilities include simulated radiosity, density masking, and rotoscoping. Experiment and enjoy!

by Steven D. Elliott

Rockford, Illinois

Equipment and Software Used
IBM-compatible 486/25 with 16 MB of RAM

3D Studio Release 3.0

Artist Biography

Steven D. Elliott is president of Visual Language Systems, Inc., specializing in computer graphics consulting, training, and production. He is co-author of the acclaimed book Inside 3D Studio *and is a regular contributor to CADENCE magazine. Steven has provided consulting and teaching services to Autodesk in support of both AutoCAD and 3D Studio, and he teaches both CAD and multi-media applications at Moraine Valley Community College in Palos Hills, Illinois. He is a registered architect and holds advanced degrees in architecture and computer science.*

Effect Overview

This special effect shows how to use the Copy Tracks and Slide Keys features of 3D Studio to cause a number of objects to follow each other along an animation path.

The effect is commonly used for commercials and the opening titles of television shows, in which text and other objects move through a scene with each object following the other as if they were all on a single track. Many 3D Studio users assume that this technique relies on hierarchical linking. In fact, this effect is accomplished through animating a single object and then copying its motions to all of the other following objects.

Assume that you have been given the task of animating the opening sequence for a television commercial for a travel agency. The name of the agency is Global Travel. You are to animate the name to fly through space as it approaches the Earth. As the text approaches, it performs a barrel roll and then orbits the Earth twice before stopping where the viewer can read the company name.

The key to this effect is in controlling the relationships between the size of each letter, the length of the path, and the number of frames in the Keyframer.

Procedure

Before you dive in, examine the storyboard in figure 2.1 to familiarize yourself with the animation that you are about to produce.

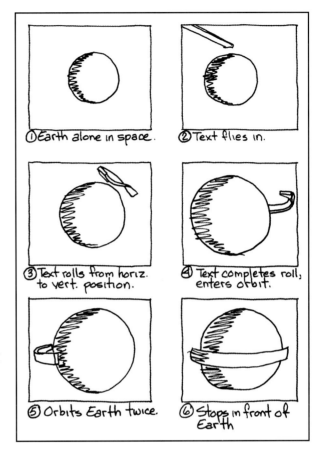

Figure 2.1
The storyboard for the Follow Letters effect.

1. Start 3D Studio and choose **File/Load Project** and load the FLW-LTR.PRJ file from the CD-ROM. The file is located in the \FLW-LTR subdirectory.

This project file, as seen in figure 2.2, contains the text for the animation as well as the background planet with sky. Successfully creating this effect requires that every letter be a separate object. Different people have different preferences for separating the letters. You can either loft each letter individually or loft all of the text at once and then use **Create/Element/Detach** to break the letters apart.

NOTE When creating this type of effect you should be careful about using Create/Element/Detach to break apart the letters. The Element/Detach technique leaves the transformation matrix of each letter equal to the transformation matrix of the original word. This can result in unexpected side effects when you try to animate the letters.

You should use Modify/Object/Reset Xform to redefine the transformation matrix for each letter after it has been detached from the original word.

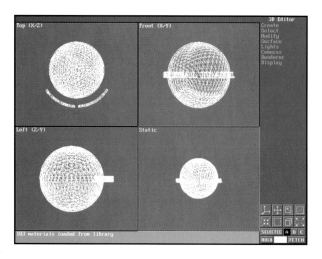

Figure 2.2
The project file FLW-LTR.PRJ in the 3D Editor.

The project file already has materials and lights applied and is ready for you to create the effect. Table 2.1 lists the objects and the materials applied to them. Note that all of the materials use the standard map files that ship with 3D Studio Release 3.

NOTE The EARTH material uses the file EARTHMAP.TGA from the World Creating Toolkit CD-ROM. You should either copy the file from the CD-ROM into your \3DS3\MAPS directory or add the appropriate path on the CD-ROM to your MAP-PATHS. For example, if your CD-ROM is drive E:, add E:\MAPS\MESHMAP2 to your MAP-PATHS in the Configure dialog box.

2. Choose **Renderer/Render View** and select the Camera viewport named Static. The static view that is displayed shows where you want the letters to stop on the final frame of the animation.

The next step is to design the path that you want the letters to follow. In this case, you will create the path in reverse, starting at the final position and proceeding to the start position. The most important scene of the animation is when the letters reach their final position. You will find it easier to control the motion if you start with the letters in the final position and animate them moving off of the screen. When you render the animation, you will instruct 3D Studio to render the sequence backwards.

3. Choose **Program** and then **3D Lofter**. Click in the Top viewport to make it active and click on the Full-screen icon.

4. Choose **3D Display/On**, choose **3D Display/Choose**, click on the **All** button in the View 3D Objects dialog box, and then click on **OK**. Zoom and Pan your view as needed until you see the entire model in the viewport.

The model of the Earth has a diameter of 120 units and the letters are placed along a radius of ~~160~~ 80 units. The storyboard calls for the letters to fly in at an angle and orbit the Earth twice. One possible path that satisfies this requirement is a helix path of two turns for the orbits, with extra vertices added at the end for the straight portion of the flight. Remember that you are animating the sequence backwards, so the orbits now come first.

5. Choose **Paths/Helix** and enter the information in the Helix Path Definition dialog box according to the values in Table 2.2. After entering all of the values, click on the **CW** button for a clockwise path, and then click on **Create**.

Table 2.1
Objects and Materials in FLW-LTR

Object	Material	Description
Earth	EARTH	Texture map with EARTHMAP.TGA
Sky	SKY	Opacity map with REFMAP.GIF
G1	GOLD (LIGHT)	Standard 3D Studio material
L2	GOLD (LIGHT)	Standard 3D Studio material
O3	GOLD (LIGHT)	Standard 3D Studio material
B4	GOLD (LIGHT)	Standard 3D Studio material
A5	GOLD (LIGHT)	Standard 3D Studio material
L6	GOLD (LIGHT)	Standard 3D Studio material
T7	GOLD (LIGHT)	Standard 3D Studio material
R8	GOLD (LIGHT)	Standard 3D Studio material
A9	GOLD (LIGHT)	Standard 3D Studio material
V10	GOLD (LIGHT)	Standard 3D Studio material
E11	GOLD (LIGHT)	Standard 3D Studio material
L12	GOLD (LIGHT)	Standard 3D Studio material

Table 2.2
Values for the Helix Path Definition Dialog Box

Field	Value
Start Diameter:	160
End Diameter:	200
Height:	0
Turns:	2
Degrees:	0.0
Vertices:	17

6. Choose **Path/Rotate** and rotate the helix –22.5 degrees. This rotates the path so that the first vertex will be near the point where you want the letters to be placed.

7. Choose **Path/Move Path** and center the helix on the Earth. Because the path is a helix and not a true circle, it will not match up exactly with the location of the letters. That is OK. Your screen should now look like figure 2.3.

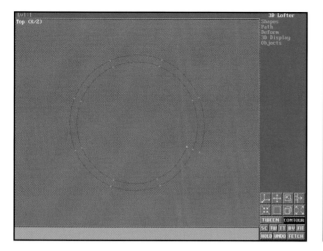

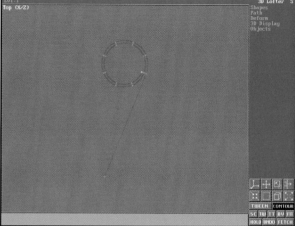

Figure 2.3
The helix path in the 3D Lofter.

You now need to insert a vertex at the end of this path to represent the straight motion as the letters fly into view.

8. Choose **Path/Insert Vertex** and then click on the last vertex on the path. This will be the outer cyan-colored vertex at about the four o'clock position. Move your cursor to the location X: –110.00, Y:0.00, Z: –460.00 and click on it to place a vertex there. Right click to complete the command.

9. Click on the Zoom Extents icon to see the entire path. Your screen now should look like figure 2.4.

Figure 2.4
The helix path after inserting a vertex at the end.

The path that you have created is perfectly flat. The storyboard calls for the letters to fly in from the upper left corner of the screen and move down into orbit. You must move the end vertex of the path up and then adjust a couple of the vertices of the helix to provide a smooth motion down into orbit.

10. Press R to convert the viewport into a Right view.

11. Choose **Path/Move Vertex** and press Tab until the cursor can only move vertically. Select the vertex that you just added to the path (the last vertex) and move it up 130 units.

Continue with the **Move Vertex** command to move the next vertex on the path up 30 units and move the vertex following that up 10 units.

You may find it difficult to select the correct vertices. Turning off 3D Display and zooming in on the helix portion of the path will help make the vertices easier to see. If you select the wrong vertex, right click to release it and try again.

12. With the **Move Vertex** command still active, adjust the spline curves for the two vertices that you just moved to smooth out the curve of the path. To adjust the spline curves, select the vertex and then press and hold the pick button. The spline arrows will appear, and an up and down motion of the mouse will adjust the angle of the arrows.

Your path should now be about 1600 units long and your screen should look like figure 2.5. If you wish, you can load a completed path from the CD-ROM called LTR-PATH.LFT

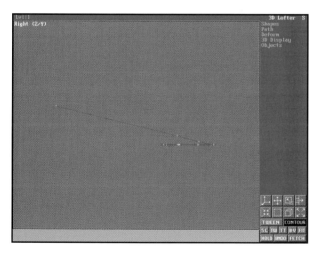

Figure 2.5
The completed path.

You are now ready to enter the Keyframer and begin setting up the animation. You will animate the first letter by making it follow the path that you just created and then manually add the barrel roll. Next, use the **Copy Tracks** command to force all of the other letters to perform the same actions. Then slide their keys in the Track Info dialog box so that they follow each other in sequence. This effect relies on properly controlling the relationship between object width, path length, and the number of frames in the Keyframer.

If all of the objects are the same size, you can divide the path length by the distance from the leading edge of one object to the leading edge of the following object. The resulting number is the minimum number of frames required. Each frame represents motion along the path equal to the length of one object. Making the objects follow each other is then a matter of sliding an object's keys one frame behind its leading object.

Because your letters are not all of a uniform length, however, you must take a different approach. In this case, the number of frames in the Keyframer will equal the length of the path. One frame now represents movement along the path equal to one unit. Making the objects follow each other requires sliding an object's keys a number of frames equal to the width of the leading object.

13. Choose **Program/Keyframer**.

14. The first thing that you need to know is the distance between each of the letters. Click in the Top viewport to make it active and then choose **Display/Tape/Find**.

15. Choose **Display/Tape/Move** and use the tape to measure the distance from the left edge of the first letter to the left edge of the second letter. You can determine the number of frames to slide any letter's keys by adding the widths of all of the letters that precede it. Table 2.3 provides you with the width of each letter and the number of frames to slide the letters.

Table 2.3
Object Widths

Object Name	Measured Width	Frames to Slide
G1	14	0
L2	11	14
O3	14	25
B4	13	39
A5	16	52
L6	18	68
T7	13	86
R8	15	99
A9	16	114
V10	14	130
E11	12	144
L12	11	156

16. Choose **Time/Total Frames** and type **1600** in the Set Number of Frames dialog box. Then click on **OK**. This sets the number of frames equal to the length of the path.

17. Choose **Paths/Get/Lofter** and then press **H** to display the Click on Object by Name dialog box. Select object G1 and click on **OK**.

   When the Get Path dialog box appears, click on the following buttons:

   Relocate object to path start? **Yes**

   Reverse path direction? **No**

   Adjust keys for constant speed? **Yes**

   Then click on **OK**.

Notice that when object G1 is relocated to the beginning of the path, it is no longer parallel with the surface of the Earth. You must rotate object G1 to make it parallel with the Earth again.

18. Make sure that you are on frame 0, choose **Object/Rotate**, and select object G1 in the Top viewport. Press the Tab key until rotation is about the Y axis, and then specify a rotation of –120 degrees. This makes object G1 parallel with the Earth.

19. Choose **Paths/Follow** and select object G1.

   When the Follow Path dialog box appears, click on **No** for Bank: and then click on **OK**.

20. Press and hold the mouse button over the frame slider at the bottom of the screen and drag it from left to right and back again. This lets you check the motion visually. The letter should orbit the planet twice and then head toward the upper left corner of the camera viewport.

Dragging the frame slider back and forth reveals that the letter completes the curving part of the orbit at key frame 1134. This frame is a good choice for one end of the barrel roll because it contains a rotation key. Another rotation key occurs at frame 1376 and is a good choice for the other end of the barrel roll. The **Follow Path** command inserted rotation keys at all of the key frames and will interfere with manually specifying the barrel roll. You will need to delete the rotation keys after frame 1134 before specifying the barrel roll.

21. Click on the **Track Info** button and select object G1. When the dialog box appears, click on the **Delete** button. Next, in the left side of the dialog box, click on the **Rotate** label.

   When the Rotate: Delete Range of Keys dialog box appears, specify a range from 1135 to 1600, and then click on **OK**.

   Click on **OK** in the Track Info dialog box to complete the command. All of the rotation keys after frame 1134 are now removed; you have a clean slate for specifying the barrel roll.

22. Advance to frame 1376 and choose **Object/Rotate**, and then select object G1 in any viewport. The Static camera viewport is probably the most convenient. Press the Tab key until rotation is about the X axis and specify a rotation of 450 degrees. Object G1 now appears to be laying on its side. Figure 2.6 shows a detail of the Static camera viewport after completing the rotation.

You are now ready to begin sliding keys for the letter objects to create the following letters effect. First, drag the frame slider back and forth again and notice the result of the previous step. All of the letters have bunched up in the same place and move together, as seen in figure 2.7. This is why you had to measure the letter spacing earlier even though you did not need that information until now.

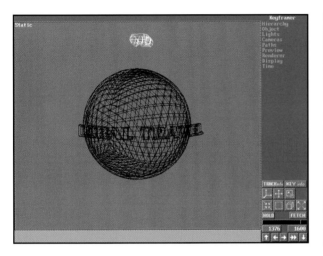

Figure 2.6
The rotated object G1 at frame 1376.

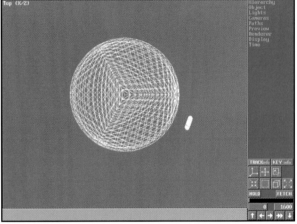

Figure 2.7
A detail view of the result of the Copy Tracks step.

23. Drag the frame slider back and forth to check the motion of the barrel roll.

Now that you have completely set up the motion of the first letter, you are ready to copy that motion to all of the other letters.

24. Choose **Object/Tracks/Copy** and select object G1 as the source object. Press **H** to display the Select Destination Objects dialog box, select the objects L2, O3, B4, A5, L6, T7, R8, A9, V10, E11, and L12, and then click on **OK**.

    When the Copy Tracks dialog box appears, leave all of the Tracks buttons selected, click on the **Absolute** button, and then click on **OK**.

25. Click on the **Track Info** button and press **H** to display the Click on object by name dialog box, and then select object L2. Object L2 is the first object that requires you to slide its keys. Because object G1 is the lead object, leave its keys alone.

    When the Track Info dialog box appears, click on the **Slide** button and select the All Tracks key at frame 0. Slide this key to frame 14. Figure 2.8 displays the resulting key placement in the Track Info dialog box.

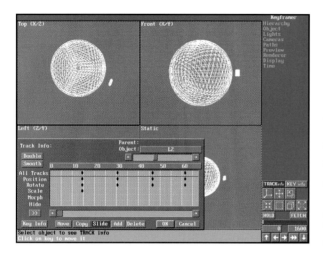

Figure 2.8
The keys for object L2 after sliding 14 frames.

26. Click on the right arrow icon in the upper right corner of the Track Info dialog box to advance to object O3. Select the All Tracks key at frame 0 and slide it to frame 25.

    Repeat this procedure for all the other letters, sliding them by the number of frames specified in table 2.3. After sliding object L12 to frame 156, click on **OK**.

27. Drag the frame slider again and observe the motion of the letters. It takes the first 156 frames for the letters to spread out. Then they correctly follow each other around the orbits and out through the barrel roll.

You may notice that the letters appear to stop short at the end of the animation. That is because the keys that would carry these objects off screen have been pushed beyond the last frame at 1600. You can recover these keys by extending the total number of frames by 156, the maximum amount of slide applied to the last object, L12.

28. Choose **Time/Total Frames** and type **1756** in the Set Number of Frames dialog box. Then click on **OK** to close the Track Info dialog box.

You are now ready to render your animation. Your model comes with materials, lights, and cameras already set up, but you might want to design a more artistic lighting arrangement or add some camera movement. For your convenience, there is a moving camera already defined in the file. Just press C in any viewport and select the Movie-Cam from the dialog box.

Your main concern at rendering time should be what range of frames to render and how to get 3D Studio to render the animation backwards. Dragging the frame slider reveals that the letters are nicely centered on the Earth at frame 172. You want to render frames 172 through 1756 in reverse order.

You can easily specify reverse order rendering by using the Range option in the Render an Animation dialog box. Click on the **Range** button to make it active. Then specify the last frame of your animation in the First field and the first frame of your animation in the Last field. Specifying the range this way causes 3D Studio to begin rendering with the last frame and to count down to the first frame. The following steps show how to do this for the Following Letters animation.

29. Configure your rendering parameters as you desire. If you want to render a 320×200 FLI file, choose **Renderer/Setup/Configure** and then click on the **Flic** button, the **Medium** palette button, and the **320×200** resolution button, and then click on **OK**. Choose **Renderer/Render View** and click in a camera viewport.

    When the Render Animation dialog box appears, click on the **Range** button and specify a range from 1756 to 172. This causes 3D Studio to render backwards from the last frame in the Keyframer to frame 172. You probably do not want to render all the frames, as that would create an extremely slow-motion animation. Specifying **12** in the Every Nth Frame field produces an animation with 132 frames for about 4.5 seconds of animation at a playback speed of 30 FPS.

Be sure to click on the **Disk** button to save your animation to disk.

30. Play your animation or, if you wish, play the animation FLW-LTR.FLC on the CD-ROM.

Conclusion

This effect demonstrates how you can make multiple objects follow each other on the same motion path. Although using **Copy Tracks** to get objects to perform the exact same motions is not too difficult, getting a feel for sliding keys and maintaining the appropriate spacing between objects can take some time. Just remember that the primary concept is matching the number of frames with the length of the path and the width of the objects to get the proper control over object spacing.

by Keith A. Seifert

Castle Rock, Colorado

Equipment and Software Used

IBM-compatible 486/66 with 32 MB of RAM

3D Studio Release 3.0

3D Studio IPAS Toolkit

Metaware High C compiler

PharLap DOS Extender Software Development Kit

Artist Biography

Keith A. Seifert is V.P. of Engineering in charge of program development at Schreiber Instruments, Inc. He has created a series of visual design programs for use with and within 3D Studio and AutoCAD. This series of programs brings true 3D design and modeling to the engineering, architectural, and animation professions. He has an extensive background in engineering problem solving using computer-aided modeling and simulation. He enjoys adding the forces of chaos to mechanical geometries to model the unpredictable 4D geometries of nature. He creates programs that have a functional blend of hard geometry and aesthetics.

Effect Overview

Cattails are a common sight along the edges of quiet water in some parts of the country. Using cattails in your scene adds detail and realism. Modeling cattails by hand is a very complex task. You can make this task much simpler by using an *animated stand-in external process* (AXP) to build cattails. The cattail generator AXP enables you to add cattails blowing in a light breeze exactly where you want in your scene, without any difficult modeling.

Procedure

The cattail generator runs as an AXP inside 3D Studio Release 2.0 or higher. The AXP—a very powerful feature of 3D Studio—enables a programmer to write programs that generate objects at the time rendering is taking place. The process is executed anew for each frame so it can change objects from frame to frame.

The cattail generator takes advantage of this feature of the AXP by moving the cattails slightly from frame to frame. The resulting animated motion simulates the effect of cattails blowing in a light breeze.

To use the cattail generator included on the CD, you must first install it and set up 3D Studio:

1. Add the \CAT-TAIL subdirectory on the CD-ROM to 3D Studio's map paths by editing one of the MAP-PATHn parameters in the 3DS.SET file. If you are using 3D Studio Release 3, this is not necessary, because it automatically adds the project load path at the head of the Map Path queue.

2. Copy the CATAIL_I.AXP file to your 3D Studio process directory. Usually, this is the \3DS3\PROCESS subdirectory.

3. Start 3D Studio as you normally do.

4. Load the CATAILS.PRJ project file from the \CAT-TAIL subdirectory on the CD-ROM. Figure 3.1 shows the 3D Editor with this file loaded.

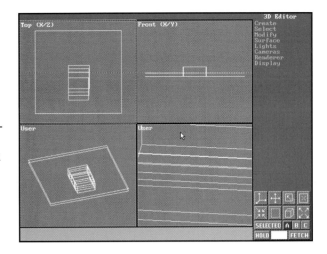

Figure 3.1
The CATAILS.PRJ project file in the 3D Editor.

The cattails are created by attaching the CATAIL_I.AXP to stand-in boxes in the scene. The process uses a stand-in box as the extents of the region to be filled with cattails. The height of the box is used by the cattail generator to determine the maximum height of the cattails. The actual height and placement of any individual cattail will be randomly determined. By using a different seed number for each stand-in box the cattail generator will create different stands of cattails. The stand-in boxes will not appear in the final rendered scene, they will be replaced by the cattails. The stand-in boxes represent the number of various cattail stands to be generated. The following steps are used to attach and configure the cattail generator.

1. Choose **Modify/Object/Attributes** and then select one of the stand-in box objects in the scene. Figure 3.2 shows the Attributes dialog box for one of the cattail stand-in objects. The CATAIL AXP process appears in the External Process Name edit box in the Object Attributes dialog box.

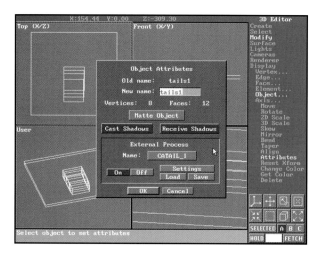

Figure 3.2
The Object Attributes dialog box.

2. Click on the External Process **Settings** button to bring up the Settings dialog box for the CATAIL process (see fig. 3.3).

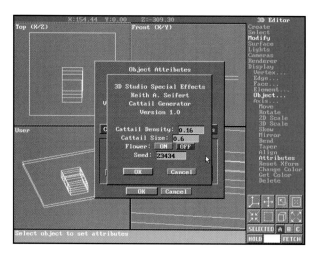

Figure 3.3
The cattail generator settings dialog box.

The settings dialog box for the CATAIL process has several options for controlling the creation of the cattails. The Density control determines the number of cattails generated in a stand-in box. You can change the density setting to change the number of cattails in the scene. Increasing the density setting creates more cattails. The density can range from 0.01 to 1.0. A good setting is about 0.2, which will create about 100 cattails.

The Size control determines how large the cattails will be. The AXP process does not have real scene coordinates, so it does not know the actual size of the stand-in box. A size control is provided to allow the cattails to be sized in relation to the stand-in box itself. You can change the size of the cattails to be created by changing the Size setting.

The Flower control enables you to create flowering cattails. If the Flower control is set to On, all of the cattails created within a stand-in box will have flowers. Two of the stand-in boxes used to create the cattails in this chapter's example scene have the Flower control turned on.

The Seed control sets a random number generator that controls the placement and location of the cattails within the stand-in box. If the Seed number is set to zero, the random number seed is taken from the current time, and a different set of cattails is created in every frame. Usually, you will not want this to happen. Specifying a constant seed for the random number generator ensures that every frame of the animation has the cattails in the same position.

 You can change the whole scene by changing the random number seed. One way you can show the passage of time is to create two segments of your animation with different random number seeds, and then fade from one segment to the other in Video Post.

3. When you have finished with the CATAIL AXP Settings dialog box, choose **OK** to return to the Object Attributes dialog box.

You can save the settings in the Object Attributes dialog box, enabling you to transfer the settings of the current CATAIL AXP to another object that uses the CATAIL process. To save the settings, click on Save and enter a file name for the CATTAIL settings. To load previously saved settings, click on Load and choose the file with the settings you want to use.

To test the lighting, camera angle, and background, you can do test renderings of your scene without using the CATAIL process to generate cattails by turning it off in the Object Attributes dialog box. The current settings of the CATAIL process are retained even though the process is off. If you turn the CATAIL process on again, it uses the same settings as when it was turned off.

4. When you finish with the Object Attributes dialog box, choose **OK**.

Now that you understand how to set up the cattails, you are ready to add cattails to a scene—a very easy process. To add cattails to the supplied example scene or load your own, follow these steps:

5. If you are not in the 3D Editor, switch to it by pressing F3 or by choosing 3D Editor from the Program pull-down menu.

6. Create a new stand-in box object for the cattails. Choose **Create/Box** and draw the new stand-in box in the Top viewport. Make the box about 130 units in length.

7. Name the new box object **CATTAILS** and then click on **Create**. If you create the stand-in object in a viewport different from other stand-in boxes, the cattails will not be created properly.

The Top viewport should always be used for creating stand-in objects for use with an AXP. An AXP program processes a stand-in object's vertex coordinates based on the orientation of the object's local axis; an AXP process does not know how the stand-in object relates to the rest of the scene. Because an AXP program processes vertices relative to an object's local axis, you must be careful when creating stand-in objects in different viewports. The local axis for an object is based on the orientation of the viewport in which the object was created.

Now that you have created a new stand-in box object, you need to apply a material to the object. The CATAIL process applies the material from the stand-in object to the cattail objects that it creates.

8. Choose **Surface/Material/Acquire** and select one of the existing stand-in box objects. The Material Selector dialog box appears, showing the materials currently applied to the selected object. Figure 3.4 shows the Material Selector dialog box for one of the stand-ins.

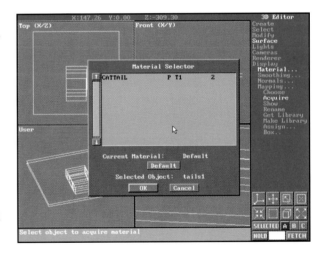

Figure 3.4
The Material Selector dialog box.

9. Select the CATTAIL material, and then choose **OK** to close the dialog box. This makes the CATTAIL material the current material. Select **Surface/Material/Assign/Object** and then select the newly created stand-in box object. Choose **OK** to apply the CATTAIL material to the stand-in object.

The CATAIL process uses mapping coordinates to apply the correct colors to the different parts of a cattail. For the cattails to render correctly, mapping coordinates must be applied to the stand-in box object.

10. Choose **Surface/Mapping/Apply Obj** and select the newly created stand-in box object. Choose **OK** to apply the current mapping coordinates to the object. Note that it does not matter which type of mapping coordinates are applied or what their spacial relationship is to the stand-in object.

If an AXP requires mapping coordinates, all stand-in objects in the scene that use the AXP must have mapping coordinates applied to them. The type and scale of the mapping coordinates determine how a texture map is applied to an object. If the AXP only uses a stand-in object as a bounding box and creates new vertices, the value of the stand-in's mapping coordinates does not matter.

Next, apply the CATAIL external process to the newly created stand-in box.

11. Choose **Modify/Object/Attributes** and select the new stand-in object. Click on the External Process Name box to display the AXP Selector dialog box. Select the CATAIL process from the list, and then click on **OK** to return to the Object Attributes dialog box. You can change the CATAIL settings by clicking on the External Process Settings button.

12. Click on **OK** when finished with the CAT TAIL settings. Choose **OK** again when you are finished with the Object Attributes dialog box.

You are now ready to render your scene with the newly created cattails.

13. Change to the Keyframer by pressing F4 or by selecting the Keyframer from the Program pull-down menu.

14. Choose **Renderer/Render View** and then select User viewport.

15. Specify the rendering options you want to use. At a resolution of 640×480 each frame could take several minutes to render. Start with a resolution of 320×200 to accelerate the rendering time.

16. When the rendering has finished, choose **Renderer/View/Flic** and select CATAILS.FLI from the file selector dialog box to see the animation.

The animation shows cattails in calm water blowing slightly in a light breeze. Figure 3.5 shows a single frame of the rendered animation.

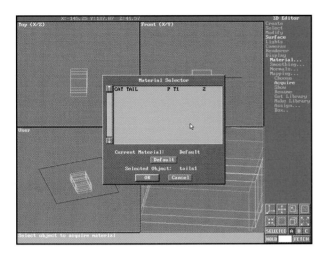

Figure 3.5
A scene from the CATAILS animation.

Try rendering the animation at a higher resolution to see more detail. The cattails create a lot of detail with very little work. Try rendering a high-resolution still image. The AXP adds power and flexibility to your animation toolkit.

On the CD-ROM with this book is a file with the source code for the Cat Tail Generator along with some helpful information for creating your own IPAS routines. The file is named CATSRCE.TXT in the \CATAIL subdirectory.

by Martin Foster

Laguna Hills, California

Equipment and Software Used

LANtastic network of three IBM PC-compatibles: 486/66, 486/50, and 486/33, each with 16 MB of RAM

Sony Beta SP frame-accurate video tape recorder

Sony Laserdisk video recorder

3D Studio 3.0

Animator Pro 1.3

Photostyler 2.0

Artist Biography

Martin Foster is a 3D artist and owner of Animatrix in Laguna Hills, California. He works predominantly with 3D Studio to create all kinds of animation and graphics for a broad client base. Martin worked on the award-winning architectural animation project "Port de Plaisance" for the Pyros Partnership; the previsualization of stunts and special effects for the feature films "My Life" and "Wolf" for Sony Pictures; and the award-winning, CD-ROM–based game "Rebel Assault" for LucasArts. Other samples of his work can be found on the 3D Studio Siggraph 1993 tape and on the 3D Studio World Creating Tool Kit CD-ROM. He is currently working on 3D game development for a next generation video game platform.

Effect Overview

The Mountain Water effect shows how to use 3D Studio's Video Post features to realistically combine computer-generated animations with real life scenes, simulating shadows and reflections. This chapter demonstrates how to achieve movie- and TV-style composition of foreground objects with background scenes such as live video or photographs. The effect is known as *chromakeying* in film and TV, and it involves shooting actors or objects in front of specially lighted blue or green backgrounds. The blue or green background is removed (or made transparent) and replaced by live video or a still image. Any shadows cast on the blue screen are preserved because they are black and appear to be cast onto the background image.

In 3D Studio's Video Post module, you can achieve similar effects and go even further by having unlimited layers of images for which each layer has multiple masking or transparency options. These allow subsequent layers to be visible in a controlled way.

Imagine that you are asked to create a TV commercial that shows a bottle of mountain water in a surrealistic, abstract, animated commercial. The storyboard calls for a computer-generated model of the bottle flying from behind some mountains, over a mirror-like lake and into full-screen view. The image of the mountain lake appears to be a framed photograph hung on the wall, and the bottle flies completely out of the photograph at the end to complete the illusion. This trick is fairly common, but achieving it requires careful planning and several steps.

Procedure

First, start 3D Studio and examine the items necessary for the effect.

Choose **File**, **Load Project** and load the MTN-WATR.PRJ project file from the CD-ROM included with this book. The project file is located in the \3DS-SFX subdirectory on the CD-ROM. You do not need to add the path because 3D Studio Release 3 automatically adds the project or scene source directory at the top of the map paths list.

Table 4.1 is a list of objects and assigned materials for this project.

Table 4.1
Objects and Materials in MTN-WATR

Object	Vertices	Faces	Material
Frame shad	8	12	MATTE WHITE
Frame uppr	96	184	WOOD - ASH
Frame lowr	96	184	WOOD - ASH
Bottle	2580	5028	BOTTLE-GREEN LOW BOTTLE-GREEN UPR BOTTLE-CAP GOLD BOTTLE-CAP GREEN BOTTLE-LABEL1 BOTTLE-LABEL2
Ground	4	2	MATTE WHITE
Wall	16	32	WALL OFF-WHITE
Black-box	8	12	BLACK ABSOLUTE

If you need to access these materials at any time, just choose Surface/Material/Get Library and then select the MTN-WATR.MLI file.

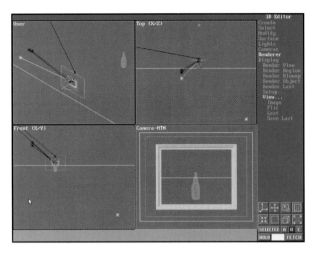

Figure 4.1
The MTN-WATR.PRJ file loaded in 3D Studio.

Familiarize yourself with the project and the effect you are going to achieve.

1. Choose **Renderer/Setup/Background**, turn on the Bitmap option to use PHOTO.TGA as a background, and then choose **Views/See Background**. After a moment, you should see a proxy image of PHOTO.TGA appear in the Camera viewport. Use this mountain lake photograph for your simulated fly-over effect. For a better look at the image, choose Renderer, View, Image and select the PHOTO.TGA file.

You could simply render the bottle over this background image with the frame and wall visible, but to make the illusion more impressive, you need to simulate appropriate shadows and reflections in the correct perspective. These shadows do not need to be absolutely accurate, but the suggestion of them convinces most people they are real and adds that extra dimension to your animation.

To produce the final effect, render several layers of animated sequences for later composition: a fully detailed rendering of the flying bottle; a simulated reflection of the bottle on the lake surface; and a layer of simulated shadows cast on the lake, grassy bank, photo frame, and the wall upon which everything is hung. You also need to mask various areas of the photograph to make the bottle appear to come from behind the mountains and the long grasses in the foreground.

Masks, or cutouts, are grayscale images in which the white portion masks an image and the black portion does not. Luminance values in between have a proportionate effect on the transparency. For this effect, they were created in Animator Pro 1.3, but any paint package should work fine.

The Ground object is positioned to approximate the perspective of the lake, and it is this object that catches the reflections and shadows. To accomplish this, different lighting situations are necessary for each sequence.

2. To render the frame on the wall as a still image, choose **Display/Hide/All**, and then **Display/Unhide/By name**. Unhide Frame lowr, Frame uppr, and Wall. Next, choose **Renderer/Setup** and set Background Method to None.

These objects are rendered to create an image that will be the picture frame on the wall that "contains" the animation. There are several lights in this scene that you turn on and off according to which stage you are rendering.

The frame rendering requires a spotlight and an omni light. These are already set up because placement is critical, although you should check them and examine their settings to get a better understanding of their use.

Light placement and settings are very important throughout this chapter. Generally, you should choose the direction of the main light source and then stay consistent for each layer. The main light source is usually a spot light and casts a shadow.

The shadow's placement is important mainly for artistic reasons. This is usually achieved by trial-and-error. You place a spotlight in the general area you want lit, do a test render, adjust the spotlight's color and position if necessary. The last two steps are repeated until you are satisfied with the result. Omni lights are useful as extra lights to control contrast, to add interesting glows, and to simulate radiosity or bounced light. They are often placed opposite the main light to fill the dark side of the scene.

3. Adjust the spotlights to check the settings by choosing **Lights/Spot/Adjust** and press the H key for a list of lights. Spot-detl, Spot-fram2, Spot-fram3, and Spot-grnd should all be off and appear black in the 3D Editor when in this state. Spot-fram1 should be on; shadows should be on and set to Ray-Trace (see fig. 4.2). Spot-fram1 illuminates the frame and casts a downward and diagonal shadow from the picture frame to the wall.

4. Choose **Lights/Omni/Adjust** and select the Omni-fram light. Make sure it is on and matches the settings in figure 4.3. Omni-fram provides a fill-in light for the picture frame to add warmth and prevent excessive contrast caused by the much brighter spotlight.

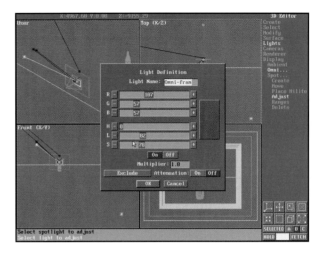

Figure 4.3
Omni light settings for picture frame rendering.

5. Choose **Lights/Ambient** and set to pure black (RGB 0,0,0). You are now ready to render this still image.

6. Choose **Renderer/Render View** and then select the Camera-MTN viewport. Make sure the settings match those in figures 4.4 and 4.5. Save the file as FRAME.TGA.

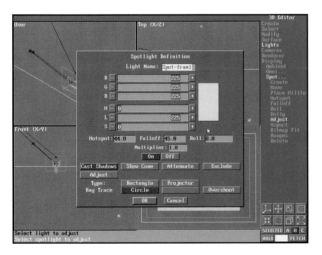

Figure 4.2
Spotlight settings for picture frame rendering.

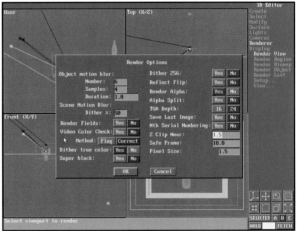

Figure 4.4
Renderer options settings for picture frame rendering.

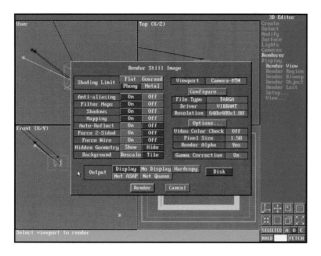

Figure 4.5
Renderer settings for picture frame rendering.

7. Examine the results; you should have a nice-looking, wooden picture frame on a slightly bumpy wall with a square, black hole in the center. Compare it to the image in figure 4.6 (and FRAME.TGA on the CD-ROM).

Figure 4.6
Picture frame sample output.

Next, prepare to render the fully detailed bottle flying over a black background. The images will be saved as a sequence of 32-bit TGA files with their Alpha channel included. This means that every pixel is given a transparency value and allows perfect composition of images over any background. Because the bottle is a somewhat-transparent glass material, it would help the illusion to be able to see the background through the bottle.

8. In the Keyframer module, choose **Display/Hide/All**, then choose **Display/Unhide/By name**, and unhide Dummy-BOTL and Bottle.

9. Choose **Object/Attributes** and then select the bottle. Make sure Cast Shadows and Receive Shadows are on and Matte Object is off.

10. Choose **Render/Setup/Background** and make sure Background Method is set to None.

11. Choose **Lights/Spot/Adjust** and then press the H key for a list of lights. Turn Spot-fram1, Spot-fram2, Spot-fram3, and Spot-grnd off. They appear black in this state. Spot-detl should be on with Cast Shadows off. Spot-detl provides main lighting for the bottle as it flies and spins. The positioning of the spotlight causes interesting glints and highlights on the bottle and its metal cap.

12. Choose **Lights/Omni/Adjust** and ensure that Omni-fram is On and set with the same parameters as the previous rendering. (Refer to figure 4.3, if necessary.) Omni-fram provides a fill-in light for the bottle to add a little warmth instead of ambient light.

13. Choose **Lights/Ambient** and set to pure black (RGB 0,0,0).

You are now ready to render the fully detailed bottle animation. Compare your scene to figure 4.7 to ensure you have all the items in place.

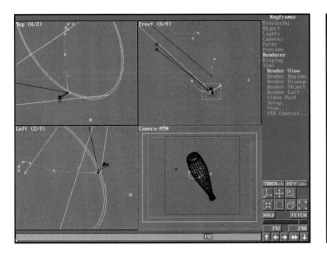

Figure 4.7
Fully detailed bottle scene.

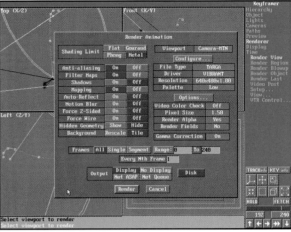

Figure 4.8
Render Animation settings for the fully detailed bottle scene.

14. Choose **Renderer/Render View** and select the Camera-MTN viewport. Make sure the Render Animation settings match figure 4.8 and the render Options settings match figure 4.9. Try a few single images at first to make sure that you have a green bottle against a pure black background. Compare your sample image to BOTTLE.TGA on the CD-ROM.

15. When you are satisfied that everything is set up correctly, render all the frames and save the sequence as FULL.TGA.

 When rendering with Metal shading, Render Alpha on, and Anti-aliasing on, turning off Shadows is crucial.

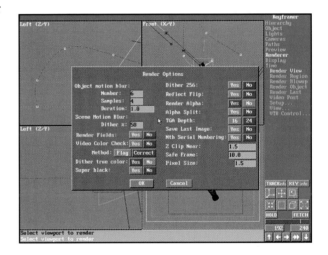

Figure 4.9
Render Options for the fully detailed bottle scene.

The next stage is to render a sequence of images that simulates the reflection of the bottle on the lake. The object Ground is positioned to match the perspective of the lake and has a flat-mirror reflection material assigned to it. Also, an object called Black-box masks the camera's view of the actual bottle, leaving just the reflection against a black background. The box surrounds the entire bottle and is excluded from the effects of the shadow-producing light. When you combine all the layers, the background will be treated as transparent, leaving the reflection visible.

16. In the Keyframer module, choose **Display/Hide/All**, then choose **Display/Unhide/By name**, and unhide Dummy-BOTL, Bottle, Ground, and Black-box.

17. Choose **Object/Attributes** and then check the attribute settings of each of the objects listed in table 4.2.

18. The lighting is the same as for the previous rendering: Omni-fram and Spot-detl are on, and all other lights are off.

You are now ready to render the reflection sequence. Compare your scene to figure 4.10.

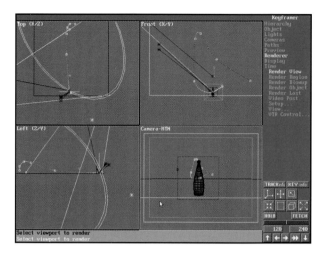

Figure 4.10
Bottle reflection scene.

19. Choose **Renderer/Render View** and select the Camera-MTN viewport. Make sure the settings match those in figures 4.11 and 4.12. Try only a few sample images at first to make sure you have an inverted, reflected green bottle against a pure black background. Compare your sample image to REFLECT.TGA on the CD-ROM.

20. When you are satisfied that everything is set up correctly, render frames 0 to 125 and save this sequence as **REFL.TGA**.

Table 4.2
Object Attributes for Reflection Rendering

Object Name	Cast Shadows	Receive Shadows	Matte Object
Bottle	On	Off	Off
Ground	Off	On	Off
Black-box	Off	Off	On

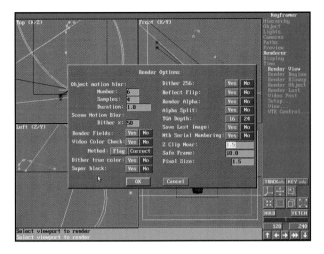

Figure 4.11
Render options for the bottle reflection scene.

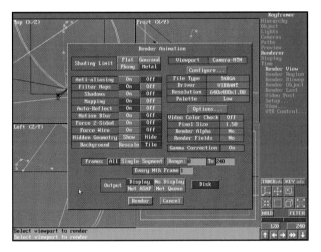

Figure 4.12
Render settings for the bottle reflection scene.

When rendering with Dither True Color set to No and the shading limit set to Metal, it is crucial that Anti-aliasing and Shadows are Off and Auto-Reflect is On.

Shadows should be Off because they will be created separately in the next stage. Anti-aliasing needs to be Off because the edges will be softened during the Video Post stage. Auto-Reflect needs to be On so the reflection that this rendering requires will be created. Dither True Color needs to be set to No so that 3D Studio does not dither the black areas—those need to be pure black throughout.

Next, prepare to render a sequence of images that simulates a shadow of the bottle cast on the lake, the lake shore, picture frame, and wall. The object Ground is used to catch shadows, only this time it needs a different material that will show the shadows and allow them to be separated out during the composition process. You cannot use a black-colored ground to simulate shadows because the shadows themselves are black and would be indistinct. Instead, use a white matte material and very intense lights to create a two-color scene—black-and-white. When you compose this layer, the white will be treated as transparent, leaving the black shadow visible.

21. In the Keyframer module, on frame zero, choose **Display/Hide/All** and **Display/Unhide/By name** Dummy-BOTL, Bottle, Ground, Frame lowr, Frame uppr, and Wall.

22. Choose **Object/Attributes** and check the attribute settings of each of the objects listed in table 4.3.

Table 4.3
Object Attributes for Shadow Rendering

Object Name	Cast Shadows	Receive Shadows	Matte Object
Bottle	On	Off	On
Ground	Off	On	Off
Frame lowr	Off	On	Off
Frame uppr	Off	Off	On
Wall	Off	On	Off

23. Choose **Render/Setup/Background** and set Background Method to Solid Color with pure white (RGB 255,255,255). The lighting is quite different for this rendering because lights that cast ray-traced shadows are used to produce accurate, sharp-edged shadows. Ray-traced shadows look more realistic.

24. Turn off all lights except Spot-grnd and Spot-fram3. Set these two lights to pure white (RGB 255,255,255) with a multiplier of 5.0, Turn on Overshoot, turn on Cast Shadows, and set the shadow type to Ray-Trace. Set the ambient light to pure black (RGB 0,0,0).

25. In the 3D Editor, choose **Display/Unhide/All**, then choose **Surface/Material/Choose**, and select WHITE MATTE. Then choose **Surface/Material/Assign/By name** and assign WHITE MATTE to Ground, Frame lowr, and Wall.

Next, render the animated shadow sequence. Remember, it is always a good idea to do a few pre-view frames. Compare your scene to figure 4.13 to ensure everything is in place.

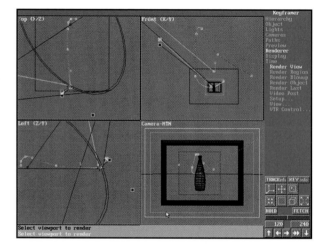

Figure 4.13
The bottle shadows scene.

26. In the Keyframer module, choose **Renderer/Render View** and then select the Camera-MTN viewport. Make sure the rendering settings match those in figures 4.14 and 4.15. Try a few sample images and look for a black shadow against a pure white background. The shadow will probably not be visible until frame 40 or so when the bottle comes closer into view. Compare your sample images to SHADOW.TGA on the CD-ROM.

27. When you are satisfied that everything is set up correctly, render all the frames and save this sequence as **SHAD.TGA**.

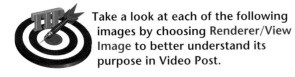

For this rendering, the critical settings are to have Dither True Color set to No, Anti-aliasing set to Off, and Shadows set to On. Dither True Color needs to be set to No because this would add dithering or intermediate colors, but the scene needs to be only two colors. The same is true for Anti-aliasing, which adds extra colors at the edges. Those edges will be blurred during the Video Post stage. Shadows need to be On to generate the shadows needed for this effect.

The final task is to put all these images together in a seamless composition. This takes quite a bit of trial and error, but the rewards can be incredible.

28. In the Keyframer module, choose **Renderer/Video Post** and select the Camera-MTN viewport. Load the file MTN-WATR.VP from the CD-ROM. The MTN-WATR.VP file contains multiple layers, and each one, except the first, has an entry in the Alpha column that determines how transparency is dealt with for that image or set of images. You can even have an entry for a transition that allows additional transparency control for the purposes of fade-ins, fade-outs, masks, and so on. In this example, use it to give additional transparency to your shadows and reflections to make them blend into their surroundings.

Take a look at each of the following images by choosing Renderer/View Image to better understand its purpose in Video Post.

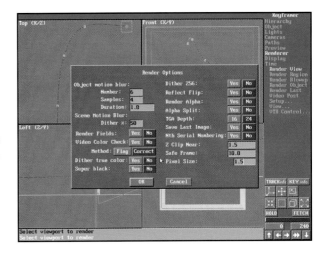

Figure 4.14
Render options for the bottle shadow scene.

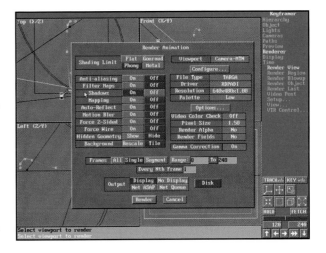

Figure 4.15
Render settings for the bottle shadow scene.

The first Video Post layer in this example uses PHOTO.TGA. It is the background mountain lake image. Because nothing appears behind it, there is no point in having any alpha information assigned to it. The red, single-range bar denotes the number of frames in which the layer is active. This layer is active on all frames, 0 to 240.

The next layer uses REFL0*.TGA. This layer uses the sequence of reflections you previously rendered. Even though the whole animation is 240 frames long, the reflection is obscured after 125 frames, so you only need to have the red, single-range bar extend from 0 to 125. If you click on the Alpha slot for this entry, you will see that Queue RGB, key color (black), and Blur Edges are on. This causes pure black (RGB 0,0,0) in the Queue image to be transparent, enabling the layer behind (PHOTO.TGA) to show through. Also, the edges will be blurred.

Because the reflection of the bottle is too strong, it needs to be blended slightly with the lake surface behind it. An image in the Trans column is used to control the amount of reflection. The REFL-MSK.GIF file used for this purpose is a grayscale bitmap gradient created in Animator Pro 1.3. The image progresses from white at the top to black at the bottom. The amount of reflection increases as the reflection moves toward the bottom.

The next layer uses PHOTO.TGA again. This time, however, a mask (GRASSMSK.GIF) in the alpha column makes only the grass on the lake shore opaque. This is used so the bottle, its shadow, and reflection appear to be in front of the grass after frame 125.

The first 181 frames of the SHAD0*.TGA sequence of frames are on the next layer. These use an RGB key color of pure white (RGB 255,255,255), leaving the black shadow visible and the white background invisible. In the Trans column, the image GRAY185.GIF uses the luminance value of 185 to give about 28 percent transparency to the shadow. This makes the shadows appear more realistic—it would look unnatural if the shadows completely blocked out images underneath them.

The fifth layer serves a similar purpose to layer three—except that this layer is intended to ensure that the bottle, its shadow, and the bottle's reflection appear to be behind the grass on frames 0 to 125.

The next two layers use the first four frames of FULL0*.TGA and the PHOTO.TGA image with HILL-MSK.GIF as a mask to show the fully detailed bottle emerge from behind the mountains. After frame four, the bottle appears in front of the hills.

The next layer demonstrates a nifty little illusion by using a bitmap painted in Animator Pro (FRAMSHAD.TGA) to represent a shadow cast from the picture frame onto the surface of the photo. This shadow also is given about 28 percent transparency using GRAY185.GIF in the Trans column. Using a bitmap to fake a real shadow saves the time it would take to set up lighting and do the tests necessary to create a shadow that is the same throughout the animation. It often saves time to use a paint package for static two-dimensional effects.

The ninth layer uses FRAME.TGA. This is the highly detailed image of the frame hanging on the wall that was rendered earlier as a 32-bit TGA file so that the center would be transparent.

The next layer uses frames 182 to 240 of the SHAD0*.TGA images. In these frames, the shadow appears in front of the picture frame, as if the bottle has left the confines of the photograph. The shadow outside the frame has about 50 percent transparency, controlled by GRAY128.GIF in the Trans column, representing different indoor-type lighting.

Finally, the fully detailed bottle, contained in images FULL0*.TGA, is used on frames 5 to 240. These frames are on the last layer, so they appear in front of everything else—after earlier appearing from behind the mountains on frames 0 to 4 in layer 5.

29. When you have examined all the Video Post entries and files and understand their use, render the whole sequence. You can render it to an FLC file, using the custom palette MTN-WATR.COL from the CD-ROM, for computer playback. You can also render it as a sequence of TGA files for video output. The final output should look like MTN-WATR.FLC on the CD-ROM.

Conclusion

Experiment with different variations of this effect. You could redo the animation with the bottle flying up, down, and around the mountains before it appears over the lake.

Substitute a completely different object of your own choosing for the bottle—possibly a spaceship that casts colored lights onto the lake.

Try a completely different scene—for example, a street with vehicles—and add a computer-generated vehicle to it with appropriate shadows and reflections.

The ultimate effect would be to have a live-action scene and to get your 3D Studio renderings to blend convincingly into the action. A video camera mounted on a tripod could be used to tape a live scene. You could then capture or rotoscope this footage into your computer for use with your animation and appropriate shadows, reflections, and masks.

by Tim Forcade

Lawrence, Kansas

Equipment and Software Used

LANtastic networked
IBM PC compatibles

3D Studio Release 3.0

Adobe Photoshop or
HiRes QFX

Yost Group's DISPLACE
IPAS routine

Artist Biography

Building on an education in traditional fine arts that stressed drawing, painting, sculpture, and graphic design, Tim Forcade's artwork has advanced through optical, kinetic, and digital electronic media. This has resulted in numerous works utilizing photography, electronics, and video as well as the invention of electronic image-processing systems of his own design.

Concurrent with his artwork, Tim (see above left, "self portait: bioluminescent") has over two decades of practice as a commercial artist, designer, and photographer. In 1978 Tim formed Forcade & Associates as a graphic resource to the commercial and professional communities. His project experience extends from illustration and publication design through photography and 3D visualization to computer animation and multimedia.

Tim's work has been exhibited in the U.S., Canada, Europe, and Japan. He has written and presented extensively on the subjects of applied 2D and 3D computer graphics and animation. He is a contributing editor to Computer Graphics World *and* Computer Artist *magazines. He can be reached via CompuServe at* 72007,2742 *or via Internet at* tforcade@falcon.cc.ukans.edu

Working with Tim at Forcade & Associates are Terry Gilbert and Mark Anderson, who provided invaluable assistance to Tim in creating and documenting this effect.

Effect Overview

Ray tracing is considered by most to be the ultimate in rendering quality, particularly because of its capability to convincingly represent optical properties such as refraction.

In spite of all the physical and optical phenomena accessible via 3D Studio's renderer, refraction remains distant. However, consider the fact that when asked to describe what a glass of water or crystal ball (with refraction) actually looks like, most people would be unable to accurately describe them. This is no surprise given the intricacies of light bouncing around multiple levels of transparent material, each with a different refractive index, not to mention the numerous surface reflections involved.

Refraction phenomena is so laden with complex visual variables that few people know exactly what refraction should or should not look like. This fortunate circumstance allows for enormous latitude in producing objects that suggest refraction in 3D Studio, in spite of the fact that it does not support ray tracing.

Look at the image on the opening page of this chapter. It consists of a glass of ice water with a lime and a pink transparent straw sitting on a slate coaster. A pale green marble sits on the sand in front of the glass and an alternating pattern of gold and cyan stripes forms the scene's backdrop. Four spotlights light the scene: a projector light and a main light from above right, a backlight spotlight, and a front-left fill spotlight.

Notice the water in the glass. The ice cubes and straw appear magnified, slightly stretched, and offset, suggesting refraction caused by the water. The water has a meniscus and its transparent surface permits you to see the ice and straw as well as the opposite side of the glass.

The marble shows multiple specular highlights and displays an inverted spherical image of the scene. Both objects cast shadows that suggest the translucent nature of the water, glass, ice, straw and marble. Finally, there is a suggestion in the shadows of light refracting through the ice cubes.

The animation (see REFRACT.FLI) consists of a 90-degree camera rotation around the glass. As the camera rotates, both refractions move, thus enhancing the refraction effect.

This animation was not produced with a ray-trace renderer. It was produced using 3D Studio and the following refraction mapping procedure.

Procedure

Table 5.1 lists all the files necessary to reproduce the refraction special effect. These files contain all cameras, lighting, and materials and are located on the CD-ROM in the /REFRACT directory.

> **NOTE:** This effect assumes that you are familiar with the process used in Effect 1 of this book, "Animated Shadows with Color and Tranparency."

1. Load REFRACT.PRJ. When loaded, the scene should appear similar to figure 5.1.

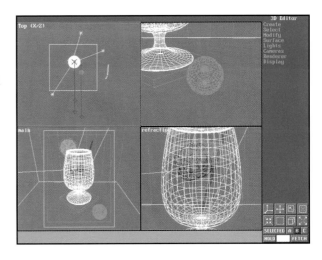

Figure 5.1
The scene used to render the finished effect.

Table 5.1
Files Needed for the Refraction Effect

File Name	Description
REFRACT.PRJ	Refraction map still image project
REFANIM.PRJ	Refraction map animation
REFSHAD.PRJ	For creating transparent shadows
REFMAPS.PRJ	For creating all refraction maps
REFRACT.MLI	Refraction materials library
CAMOFLAG.CEL	Standard 3D Studio bitmap for Beach bump
GRAYSPEK.GIF	Standard 3D Studio bitmap for Beach mask
LEAD2.TGA	Custom bitmap for Coaster bump
REFMARB.TGA	Refraction map for Marble
REFFRONT.TGA	Refraction map for Liquid_frt
REFBACK.TGA	Refraction map for Liquid_bak
REFSHAD.TGA	Shadow map for projector spotlight
REFSHAD2.TGA	Shadow map for projector spot animation
ICE.CUB	Cubic envrionment map for the ice cubes
ICEBK.TGA	Custom bitmap for the ice cubes
ICEDN.TGA	Custom bitmap for the ice cubes
ICEFT.TGA	Custom bitmap for the ice cubes
ICELF.TGA	Custom bitmap for the ice cubes
ICERT.TGA	Custom bitmap for the ice cubes
ICEUP.TGA	Custom bitmap for the ice cubes
REFFRONT.FLC	Animated refraction map for Liquid_frt
REFBACK.FLC	Animated refraction map for Liquid_bak
REFMARB.FLC	Animated refraction map for Marble_ref
REFRACT.FLI	Animated refraction example

This file contains everything used to create the shadow map and refraction maps, as well as render the image on the opening page. Some special modeling techniques are needed to create objects for this effect. The following list describes the objects and how they were created:

- The water glass was lofted in a single step using a SurfRev and broken into two objects, Glass and Glass_base. This enables you to assign separate materials to each piece. The reason for this is discussed in step 20 of this chapter. The object is named Glass.

- The water was similarly lofted and broken into four objects: Liquid_frt (the liquid faces with normals toward camera), Liquid_bak (the liquid faces with normals away from camera), Liquid_top (the faces comprising the flat surface of the liquid), and Liquid_rim (the water's meniscus).

- The marble is made from three concentric spheres: Marble, Marble_in, and Marble_ref. As with the water glass, multiple objects, along with multiple materials, make it possible to convincingly render the marble's reflecton. The materials for the marble objects are discussed in step 19 later in this chapter.

- The two ice cubes are created from a single tessellated cube that was processed using DISPLACE.PXP from Yost Group, Inc. This was copied and both were rotated and positioned inside the liquid object. The ice cubes are named Icecube01 and Icecube02.

- The lime pulp (Lime_pulp) is created from a single wedge, which was also tessellated and processed using DISPLACE. A few manual vertex moves were used to increase the faceted look. The result was arrayed to create the six lime sections. The lime skin (Lime_skin) is also created using **SurfRev**.

- The coaster (Coaster) is created from a cube. The remainder of the scene objects (the stripes, beach, etc.) are quads created in the 2D Shaper.

- The scene is lit by four spotlights. The principal lighting comes from the combination of the Projector and Keylite spotlights. Neither of 3D Studio's shadow types are used in this scene. Instead, the projector light uses a manual shadow map. Using the projector light's exclusion list, only the Beach and Coaster objects receive the projected shadow map.

- The second part of the principal light, Keylite, lights all but the Beach and Coaster, providing the main light for the scene. Icelight1 and 2 provide highlights for the ice cubes, straw, lime pulp, and the glass base, and were positioned using **Lights/Spot/Place Hilite**. The two reflector objects at scene right use white, self-illuminated materials to provide additional highlights for Glass.

- There are three cameras in the scene. The Main camera is the point of view used for the final rendered image. The Refraction camera is used to create the refraction map for the liquid and the Marblecam is used to create the refraction map for the marble.

Because the refracted images seen in the water and marble are composed from essentially everything in the scene, all scene lighting, shadows, and materials assignments must be created and assigned before the refraction maps can be made. Some 25 materials are used in the image and animation for this example and are available in REFRACT.MLI. Along with those used on the scene objects themselves, several materials were created specifically for use during the shadow-map–making process. This was essential to maintain the desired shadow density and color for the liquid, marble, straw, and ice cubes.

The scene's only shadow was produced using the procedure described in Effect 1, "Animated Shadows with Color and Transparency." The process consists of rendering a view from a shadow-casting spotlight of all the objects that will cast a shadow. Then the resulting bitmap is projected on the scene from the same light, thus producing a shadow.

Rendering animations from a spotlight viewport requires 3D Studio Release 4.0 or later.

2. Before creating the shadow map, save the project with an alternate file name so you can easily return to the final rendering setup after you create the maps.

The simplest solution to restoring settings often is to save a separate version of the project file for each map type.

3. The process of creating the shadow map for this example begins by hiding all objects that do not cast shadows. Hide everything except the glass, ice cubes, water, straw, lime, and marble.

4. Assign the shadow materials to Marble_ref (MARBLE_SHADOW), Liquid_frt and Liquid_bak (LIQUID_SHADOW), the two ice cubes (ICE_SHADOW), and the straw (STRAW_SHADOW). These alternative materials provide the desired level of transparency and color to the shadow map elements. In addition, the ICE_SHADOW material uses an automatic spherical reflection map to break up the shadow pattern and suggest light refracting through the ice cubes. These materials are only used to render the shadow map.

Normally, all scene lights should be turned off, ambient light should be 0, and the background set to white. This insures that only transparent objects appear colored and that the spotlight cone, as projected by the projector spotlight, will appear white. However, here it is important to produce a shadow with variations created by the spherical reflection maps on the ice cubes. The solution is to exclude the Lime_skin object from all the lights in the scene.

5. Choose **Lights/Spot/Adjust** and exclude Lime_skin from each spotlight, including the Ambient light.

6. In the Projector spotlight view, render a 640×640 image and save it to disk as **REFSHAD.TGA**. The image is rendered to match the aspect ratio of the spotlight, which in this case is circular. REFSHAD.PRJ from the CD-ROM is already set up to produce the shadow map (see fig. 5.2). REFSHAD.TGA is used in the Projector spotlight to project the shadow map on the scene.

Animating the color shadow map requires 3D Studio Release 3.5 or later to render. Still shadow maps can be rendered with Release 3.0 or later.

7. Restore your original materials, spotlight exclusions, and the ambient level, or load the original project file if you saved it earlier.

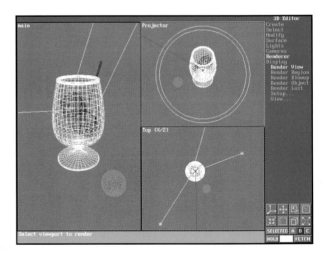

Figure 5.2
The ready-to-render scene for the shadow map.

With all modeling, scene lighting, and materials assignment complete, the refraction mapping process begins by producing the two maps for the liquid. Remember that the liquid was separated into two objects—one facing toward camera(Liquid_frt) and the other (Liquid_bak) away from camera.

8. Clone another camera from the Main camera using **Cameras/Perspective**. Drag the mouse to minimize the new camera's perspective. Name the camera **Refraction**. Dolly in to the view shown in the refraction viewport in figure 5.3. This camera position simulates the effect of the magnification and distortion by the liquid inside the glass.

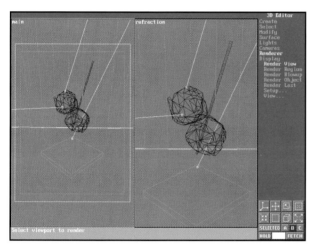

Figure 5.3
The view needed to create the refraction maps.

9. Hide all objects except Icecube01, Icecube02, Straw, Stripes_1, Stripes_2, Coaster, and Beach. Although technically Glass should be visible too, it would muddy the reflections, so leave it hidden.

10. Increase the ambient light level from L:25 to L:75.

11. Render the refraction map for Liquid_frt from the Refraction viewport at 512×512 and save it to disk as **REFRONT.TGA**.

12. Hide the straw and ice cubes, and then render the refraction map for Liquid_bak to disk as **REFBACK.TGA** from the same camera view. The two finished maps are shown in figure 5.4.

Figure 5.4
The two refraction maps used for the water: the map on the left for liquid front, the other for liquid back.

13. Get the materials LIQUID_FRONT and LIQUID_BACK and assign them to two sample windows. These materials use their respective maps as 100% texture maps. No reflection map of any kind is used in these materials. LIQUID_FRONT uses 50% self-illumination to lighten the texture slightly, particularly in the ambient areas.

14. Load the refraction maps you just created into their respective material's texture map.

15. Apply these materials to Liquid_frt and Liquid_bak respectively using a planar map type. Align the planar mapping icon to the camera view by first creating a User view from the main camera view. Then choose **Surface/Mapping/Adjust/View Align** and select the User view. Next, choose **Mapping/Adjust/Scale**, hold down the Alt key, and click on the Liquid_frt object to scale the icon to the object.

16. Use the the same planar mapping and icon scaling technique for the Liquid_bak object. The liquid's meniscus (Liquid_rim) uses a

spherical reflection map. The top surface of the liquid (Liquid_top) uses a semi-transparent material with a planar reflection map.

17. Create the marble's refraction map in the same way. Clone the Refraction camera and position it as shown in figure 5.3. Name the camera **Marblecam**.

18. Hide the three marble components (Marble, Marble_in, and Marble_ref).

19. Render the marble's refraction map the same way as the previous refraction map. Save the image as **REFMARB.TGA** and use it in the MARBLE_REFRACT material as 100% texture with 50% self-illumination.

    The marble consists of three centered, progressively scaled spheres. The middle sphere, Marble_ref, uses the single-sided material MARBLE_REFRACT as an opaque texture map. This sphere's normals are flipped, causing it to render as a concave hemisphere. This enables the innermost sphere, Marble_in, to be used to create the specular highlights that are not visible because of Marble_ref's opaque refraction map. The largest sphere, Marble, used a spherical reflection map to reflect the environment.

20. Assign the mapped material to the Marble_ref object in the same way you did for the liquid refraction components.

The glass is divided into multiple objects, so separate materials can be applied to Glass and Glas_base. Separate materials are needed because using a two-sided spherical reflection map on the upper part of the Glass produces an irregular reflection pattern where the liquid and Glass overlap. However, a two-sided material is essential to get the desired look from the Glass_base.

With the components in place to produce the still image, creating an animation of the camera view is a relatively simple matter.

21. Load REFRACT.PRJ—the still image project—and go to the Keyframer. Create two dummy objects. The first (Dummy01) should be centered on the Glass object and the second (Dummy02) centered on the Marble object.

22. Link the Main camera, Main.target, Refraction camera, Refraction.target, Liquid_frt, Liquid_bak, and the two reflectors to Dummy01. Similarly, link Marble_ref, Marblecam, and Marblecam.target to Dummy02.

23. Go to frame 0, rotate Dummy01 around the y axis 45 degrees counterclockwise. Also at frame 0, rotate Dummy02 around the y axis 50 degrees.

24. At frame 30, rotate Dummy01 clockwise –90 degrees and Dummy02 –110 degrees.

25. Play back the animation and notice how the keyframed objects rotate synchronously about their respective dummy objects (see fig. 5.5).

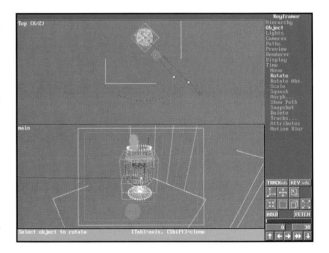

Figure 5.5
Two dummy objects and their links used to maintain alignment between the Marblecam, the Main camera, and the refraction-mapped objects.

The idea here is to maintain alignment between all refraction-mapped objects and the main camera view. This is essential to assure that the planar mapping assigned earlier to the refraction-mapped liquid and marble remains perpendicular to the camera throughout the animation. Because they are linked, the Main camera, the Refraction cameras, and the objects `Liquid_frt` and `Liquid_bak` maintain perfect alignment.

The Marble camera, target, and refraction-mapped object are a different issue. The Marble camera axis must converge to the same point of view as the Main camera.

26. In the Top view, align `Dummy02` to the Main camera using the camera axis as a guide. This axis should converge on an imaginary point that coincides with both cameras (Main and Marble). Although somewhat imprecise, this approach is adequate.

All that remains is to produce three FLC files: two from the Refraction camera (one each for `Liquid_frt` and `Liquid_bak`), and one from the Marblecam. These animations replace the TGA images used to create the still picture. The finished animation setup is on the CD-ROM and is named REFANIM.PRJ.

Conclusion

This refraction mapping procedure is based on a combination of numerous experiments and aesthetic judgments. However, consider that applied ray tracing is not absolute either, and it is subject to a lot of variation from program to program. If the same scene was set up the same in several ray tracing programs, the differences would very likely outnumber the similarities.

Determining whether or not this chapter's special effect will work for you almost certainly calls for a lot of experimentation and will be heavily dependent the project/client mix for any given animation. And there is plenty of room for experimentation and improvement. For instance, you could

enhance this process by creating multiple reflection maps for each object and then using alpha composition to combine them in a second step. This would help resolve refractions that call for both mirrored and non-mirrored elements to share the same map.

Using video effects programs such as AfterEffects can be very useful for animating warps and various distortions that could be used to simulate moving optical patterns.

Nonetheless, given the high level of subjectivity involved in understanding refraction phenomena—not to mention the variation in ray-tracing programs—this process is capable of producing some surprising and often useful results.

by Greg Phillips

Indianapolis, Indiana

Equipment and Software Used

IBM-compatible 486/66
with 64 MB of RAM

3D Studio Release 3.0

Cannon CLC500

Artist Biography

Greg Phillips is Director of the Visual Communication Group at Diversified Graphics in Indianapolis, Indiana. He works extensively on 3D Studio and has used this software in all aspects of his design and graphics work. Greg won First Prize in the design category of Computer Pictures *magizine's Art & Design contest. Many of Greg's designs can also be found on book covers for AutoCAD and other design publications.*

Effect Overview

This Wind Tunnel special effect uses examples of lighting, materials, morphing, and motion blur effects. All objects for this example were created in 3D Studio Release 3 using the Shaper, Lofter, and 3D Editor. This 3D model consists of 17 objects, 21,748 vertices, 43,224 faces, two lights, and one camera. I hope these effects will help you understand the multiple effects that you can create inside 3D Studio.

Through this chapter you will work with lighting, morphing, motion blur, and animation. Start 3D Studio and get ready to create special effects.

1. Choose **File/Load Project** and load WIND1.PRJ from the \WIND\PROJ directory on the CD-ROM included with this book (see fig. 6.1).

2. Go to your program configuration menu and add \WIND\MAPS on the CD-ROM to the Maps Path. You will need to access these materials for this rendering exercise.

3. From the 3D Editor, choose **Display/Hide/By Name** and hide everything except blades, fan ring, floor, wall2, wall left and wall prop.

4. Choose **Surface/Material/Get Library** and select WIND.MLI from the \WIND\MATLIBS directory on the CD-ROM. This is the material library for this project.

Table 6.1 lists the materials provided on the CD-ROM and to which objects they are assigned.

Lighting can create great effects. Proper lighting will give you highlights, shadows, and reflections, bringing your materials and renderings alive.

5. First, choose **Lights/Omni/Create**. Then in the Top viewport, create an Omni light in the lower right corner of the view. Set the Omni light color to R:23, G:50, B:57 and choose **Create**.

6. Choose **Light/Omni/Move** and move the light above the wall in the right view (see fig. 6.2).

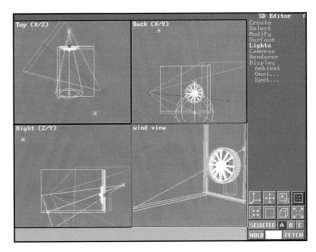

Figure 6.1
The WIND1.PRJ project file.

Figure 6.2
The Lighting creation and setup.

Table 6.1
Wind Tunnel Material Assignments

Material	Object
BRUSHED METAL tiled texture map	wall 2 wall left wall prop
METAL BUMP texture map	floor
CHROME BLUE SKY reflection map	blades sphere fan ring
SILVER reflection map	Outside of fan ring prop motor motor ring
CHROME VALLEY reflection map	base stand
GREY PLASTIC	prop base
RAYS SMOKE 2 transparency texture map	dust
CHROME COLOR W	sphere2

7. Choose **Lights/Spot/Create** and create a spotlight outside of the blades to create the effect of outside light coming through the porthole. Name the spotlight **Sun** and set the spotlight to R:145, G:215, B:255, Hotspot:24, and Falloff:32. Turn on Cast Shadows, Show Cone, and Circle, and choose **Create**.

8. Use **Light/Spot/Move** to adjust the spotlight to match figure 6.2.

9. Choose **Camera/Create** and create a camera looking from left to right in the Top view. Name the camera **Wind View**, use the default lens type and settings, turn on Show Cone, and choose **Create**.

10. Use **Camera/Move** and **Camera/FOV** to adjust the location and field of view to match figure 6.2.

 You may want to change the Snap Angle to 1.0.

Once you have the lighting and camera direction set up for the scene, you need to render and preview your lighting and material effects.

11. Choose **Renderer/Render View**, select your camera viewport, and render to display only. Check the effects of lighting and material selection. (See the image on the opening page of this chapter for reference.)

12. Choose **Display/Unhide/By Name** in the 3D Editor and unhide all of the objects except dust (see fig. 6.3).

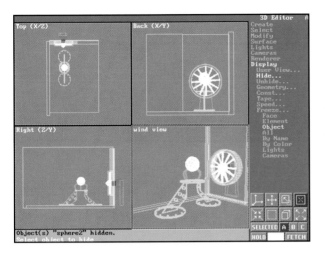

Figure 6.3
Object dust is not displayed.

13. Choose **Renderer/Render View** and render the camera viewport with the addition of the other objects.

14. Choose **Display/Unhide/All** to unhide the object dust. This object has the material RAYS SMOKE 2 assigned to it. It has transparency properties and a sky texture map to give it a random look of dust from an outside light source.

15. Switch to the Material Editor and choose **Materials/Get Material From Scene**. Select RAYS SMOKE 2 and try changing the amount of texture map and transparency.

16. Return to the 3D Editor, choose **Renderer/Render View**, and render the camera viewport to see the effects from the object dust.

You should now have the sun beaming through the porthole, creating the dust effect.

Try different materials, like animated texture maps, to give it a spinning or swirling look, as if the wind is being forced in.

In the next steps, you will create an object for morphing the sphere.

17. In the 3D Editor, choose **Modify/Object/Move** and hold down the Shift key on the keyboard to copy the object sphere. Copy the new sphere above the old sphere and call it **sphere2** (see fig. 6.4).

18. Choose **Surface/Material/Choose** and select the material CHROME COLOR W. Choose **Surface/Material/Assign/Object** and select the new object sphere2. The new material on sphere2 will be used for texture map morphing from CHROME BLUE SKY to CHROME COLOR W, creating the effect of the texture changing from the force of the wind.

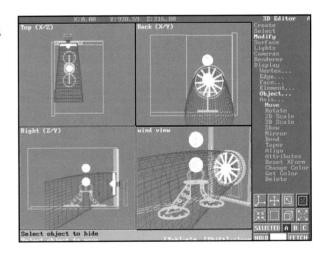

Figure 6.4
Creating a clone object.

19. Choose **Modify/Vertex/Move** and move single random vertices from the new cloned ball called sphere2. Pull the vertices away from the wind tunnel blades and from the top and sides of sphere2 (see fig. 6.5).

22. Choose **Object/Rotate Abs.** and select the blades. Press the Tab key until you reach the Z axis, and then rotate the blade object –360 degrees (see fig. 6.6).

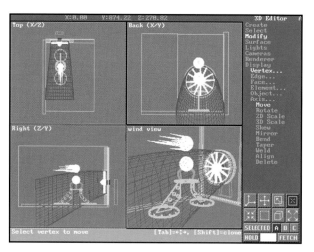

Figure 6.5
Modifying sphere2 for morphing.

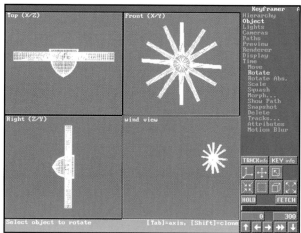

Figure 6.6
Creating blade rotation.

With the creation of the modified sphere2 and the new material, the current object sphere will have a morphing effect. The texture will appear to evaporate and be forced off the sphere from the wind off the blades.

The next steps deal with the Keyframer. You will create an animation of rotating blades using motion blur and morphing the sphere objects to create the animation effect of the wind tunnel blowing off the sphere texture.

20. Switch to the Keyframer, choose **Display/Hide/By Name**, and hide all objects except blades.

21. Set the number of frames to **300** and go to frame 300.

23. Choose **Object/Motion Blur**, select the blades, and turn on Object Motion Blur. This will make the blades blur in motion during the animation effect of rotation.

24. Choose **Display/Unhide/All** to view all of the objects. Choose **Object/Morph/Assign**, select the object sphere to morph, then select sphere2 as the object to morph to, and click on **OK**.

25. Choose **Object/Morph/Options** and select the sphere. Turn on Morph Materials and click on **OK**.

26. Choose **Display/Hide/By Name** and hide sphere2 from the scene.

27. Choose **Track Info** and select the sphere. Move All Tracks to frame 60. The sphere will start morphing after the fan starts turning, creating the effect of force from the wind tunnel (see fig. 6.7).

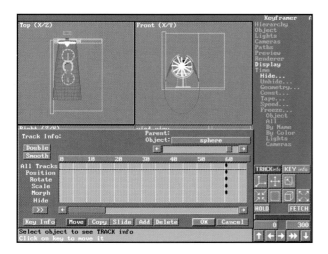

Figure 6.7
Keyframe edits.

Now you are ready to start your animation. A completed animation called WIND.FLC is located in the \WIND\FLC directory on the CD-ROM included with this book.

Conclusion

Now you are ready to start your animation. A completed animation called WIND.FLC is located in the \WIND\FLC directory on the CD-ROM included with this book.

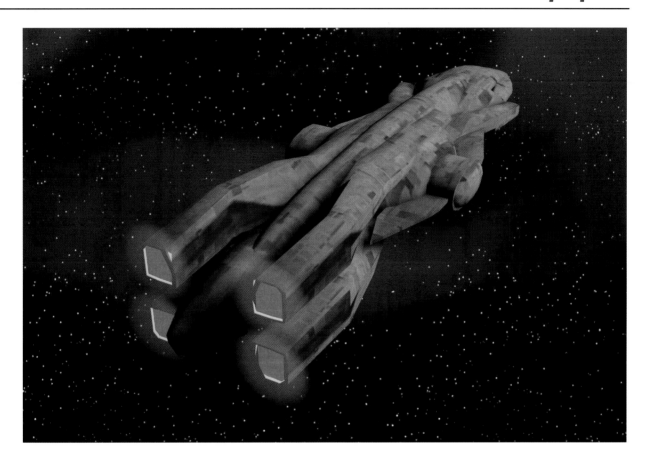

by Jon A. Bell

San Francisco,
California

Equipment and Software Used

IBM-compatible 486/33
with 32 MB of RAM

Diamond Speedstar 24x
video card

Toshiba 877M hard
drive

NEC Multisync 3D
monitor

Sharp JX-450 color
flatbed scanner

3D Studio Release 3.0

Animator Pro 1.0

Yost Group IPAS
routines

Adobe Photoshop for
Windows 2.5

Artist Biography

Jon A. Bell is a 3D computer graphics artist and writer living in San Francisco, California. After working for 10 years as an editor and writer in the computer magazine publishing industry, Jon changed careers to concentrate full-time on 3D computer graphics and animation for the film industry, computer games/multimedia, and for print. He has provided computer graphics for the films "Exorcist III: Legion," "Terminator 2: Judgment Day," "Honey, I Blew Up The Kid," and several Autodesk promotional videotapes, including the 1991 Siggraph reel and the 1994 NAB (National Association of Broadcasters) reel. His game industry work includes model designs and animation for LucasArts Entertainment's "X-Wing" and "Rebel Assault," and Sega of America's "Jurassic Park" CD-ROM game. Currently, Jon works as a 3D artist for Sega, and continues to do 3D contract work under his company name Virtu.

Effect Overview

The techniques described in this chapter show the 3D Studio user how to create exciting outer space special effects, similar to those seen in popular science fiction TV shows. This chapter describes how to create colorful, "realistic" spaceships and deep-space vistas using special texture mapping and painting techniques to produce complex spacecraft surface details quickly. (To produce these effects, you'll need a 2D paint program, such as Autodesk Animator Professional, or for better results, a program that handles 24-bit images, such as Adobe Photoshop.) In addition, this chapter explores how to use combinations of lights and unseen geometry to create striking nebula and engine-glow effects.

Procedure

Load the first 3D Studio file. Choose **File** and then load the XCRUISER.3DS file from the CD-ROM included with this book. The file is located in the /3DS-SFX subdirectory on the CD-ROM.

Add the path on the CD-ROM that contains the maps for this project to your Map-Paths. The maps are in the same sub-directory as the project file. If you are using 3D Studio Release 3, this step is not necessary, because Release 3 adds the project load directory to the map paths automatically.

Take a look at the 3DS file as shown in figure 7.1.

As figure 7.1 shows, in the center of each of your 3D Editor screens should be various views of the XCRUISER, the spaceship model with which you'll be working. If parts of it look somewhat familiar, it's because the model is actually a heavily modified version of the X-29 jet aircraft model that comes on the 3D Studio release disks.

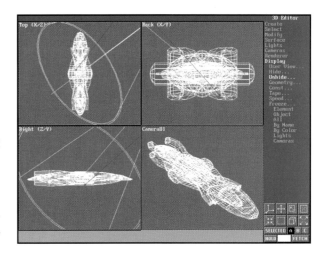

Figure 7.1
The XCRUISER spacecraft.

To build this simple demonstration ship, I took the X-29 model and removed various pieces that were too recognizably jet-like, such as the wings, tail fin, and canards. Then I squashed and stretched the fuselage, using the 2D Scale function, until its conventional origins weren't readily apparent. (This technique can be applied to many different vehicles, enabling you to create a futuristic hovercraft from, say, a racecar model.) After that, I used the Mirror and Copy functions to duplicate the front half of the ship, flipped it around, and created the back half of the vessel. Modified jet intakes formed the engines, and with the addition of miscellaneous cylinders and ovoid shapes (stretched LSphere primitives), the basic ship was complete.

As you can see, the spacecraft has a vague Star Wars appearance, looking like a cross between the Rebel Blockade Runner and one of the "pickle" ships from "Return of the Jedi." Now, take a look at building an interesting texture for it quickly.

1. Select **Surface/Material** and then select **Get Library**. As the dialog box appears, choose the Materials Library file XCRUISER.MLI, load it, and press the F5 key to switch to the Materials Editor.

2. From the Material menu, choose **Get Material** and then select ALUMINUM 3. The material will load, and you will see a sample of it in the first sample box. This material uses a Targa image texture map called ALUMINM3.TGA, without any Bump or Shininess maps to accent it.

   Take a look at this texture. The quickest way to see an image used as a map is to drag its name onto the **View Image** button. (You can also see details about the file by dragging its name onto the **File Info** button.) Position the cursor over the Texture 1 Map filename button, press and hold the left mouse button, and then drag the filename to the **View Image** button. The image, as shown in figure 7.2, is a collection of largely monochromatic squares, from white to dark gray, with bits of subtle colors here and there.

Amazingly enough, this image began life as a 3×5-inch color photo of the bottom of a refrigerator's aluminum drip pan! I came across this item discarded near a trash bin at an industrial park when I was out with my camera collecting interesting-looking textures. You can see the original scanned photo in figure 7.3 (and included on the CD-ROM as ALUM_ORG.TGA).

After developing this photo, I scanned it at 300 dpi on a Sharp JX-450 color flatbed scanner and loaded it into Windows Photoshop 2.5. With the Marquee tool, I began cutting and pasting tiny squares and rectangles, rearranging textures within the photo until I produced the results in figure 7.2, and then saved the Targa texture at a resolution of 640×480.

Regardless of its humble origins, this single scanned image has proven itself incredibly versatile as an all-around generic spaceship texture—slap it on a collection of odd shapes, and you've got the beginnings of a respectable spaceship.

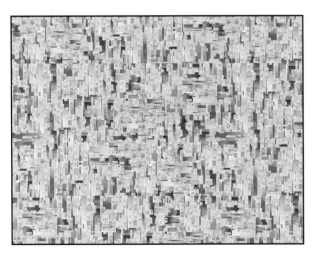

Figure 7.2
The preliminary XCRUISER texture map.

Figure 7.3
A "found" texture—a discarded refrigerator drip pan. The photo was taken outdoors in bright sunlight.

3. Return to the 3D Editor by pressing the F3 key or by clicking on the arrow in the upper-right corner of the screen.

4. Click in the Top viewport to select it, and then click on the Full Screen Toggle icon to enlarge this viewport.

5. Select **Surface/Mapping/Adjust/View Align**. Click in the Top viewport and the Planar mapping icon appears over the ship, as shown in figure 7.4.

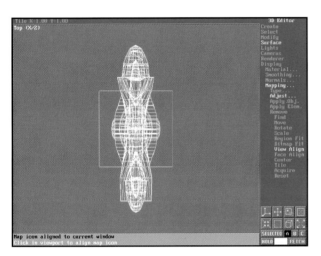

Figure 7.4
Mapping the ship pieces.

6. Select **Mapping/Apply Obj** and click on the XCRUISER model to apply the mapping coordinates to it. When the dialog box appears, press the Enter key or click on the **OK** button.

You'll notice that the mapping icon does not cover the entire spaceship. This is OK because we want the simulated panel lines that a non-tiling repeated material provides.

7. Now you'll want to apply the material. Click on **Material/Choose**, select ALUMINUM 3, choose **Apply/Object**, click on the XCRUISER model, and then press Enter in response to the dialog box. Select **Render/Render View**, make sure the Camera view is active, and left-click in the Camera window to render and view the ship. After a few minutes, the image will appear.

As you can see in figure 7.5, what you have is the decent beginnings of a Star Wars-style cruiser. The complex texture helps the simple geometry considerably, and suffices for most of the ship fuselage.

Some areas, such as the vertical sides of the engines and the oval pods amidships, show smearing due to the planar mapping. You can correct this by selecting and separating the offending faces and mapping them with cylindrical and/or planar maps.

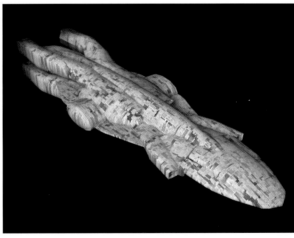

Figure 7.5
A highly detailed texture map provides the illusion of greater object complexity.

Now you're ready to enhance the texture of the main body of the ship.

8. Return to the 3D Editor screen and select **Lights/Cameras** to display these items if they are not already visible. As the various views indicate, the spotlight illuminating the ship is pointing down at roughly a 45-degree angle as seen from both the Top and the Left viewports.

9. Using **Lights/Spot/Move**, move the spotlight down so that it projects directly from the side in the Top view, as shown in figure 7.6.

10. Select **Display/Hide/Lights** and hide the cameras. Then select the Top viewport and click on the Full Screen Toggle icon.

11. Click on the Zoom Extents icon to center the ship in the screen.

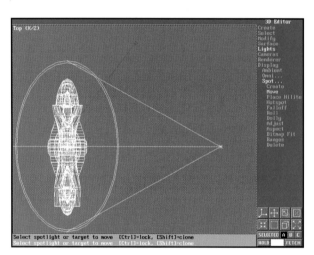

Figure 7.6
Adjust the spotlight so that it shines on the ship from an acute side angle.

12. The next step is to render an orthographic top view of the ship with severe lighting to delineate the gross geometric shapes comprising the ship. Click on **Render/Render View** and save this image as **SHIP_TOP.TGA** for 24-bit paint programs such as Photoshop, or **SHIP_TOP.GIF** if you will be working with an

8-bit program such as Animator Pro. Your render resolution is up to you, of course; for best results, your minimum rendered resolution should be 640×480. The SHIP_TOP image should look like figure 7.7.

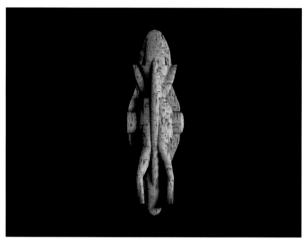

Figure 7.7
An orthographic top view of the XCRUISER.

For the next part, you'll want to quit (or shell out of) 3D Studio so you can load your paint program. Don't worry about saving the current settings of 3D Studio; you can set this up again easily.

Manipulating the Texture

Regardless of whether you're working in Animator Pro or Photoshop, the basic principle demonstrated here is the same. What you want to do is load the paint program, load the SHIP_TOP image you just rendered, copy it, mirror it along the vertical axis, and paste it back down on top of the original using a translucent ink. Here's how to do it.

1. In Animator Pro, set your screen resolution to the same resolution in which you rendered the SHIP_TOP.GIF image. Load the image from the \IMAGES directory in 3D Studio.

2. Press the Tab key to clip the ship image as a cel.

3. From the **Cel** menu, select **Anim Cel**. On the Anim Cel screen, you should see the clipped image of the XCRUISER with a bounding box denoting the edges of the ship image area.

4. From the **Position** menu, select **Mirror**, and then select **Vertical Axis** to flip the image from side to side.

5. From the **Cel** menu, select **Quit Anim Cel** to return to the main screen.

6. In the Inks panel, right-click on **Glass**. Glass Ink should be set at 50 percent, with Dither activated. Right-click again to return to the main screen.

7. Select **Paste** from the **Cel** menu or press the accent mark/tilde key to paste the clipped, mirrored image on top of the original rendering. When the box appears, right-click to set its location without moving the cursor.

As you can see, when you paste the mirrored cel on top of the original image using 50% Glass Ink, the shadows from one side of the model darken the highlights on the other side; the highlights from the other side brighten the shadowed side. The effect is twofold: the highlights and shadows help to accentuate and outline the edges of the existing geometry, and the texture map has become bilaterally symmetrical, with increased pixel detail now identical on both sides.

8. Now, press the Tab key to clip this image as a cel, select **Files** from the **Cel** menu, and save this cel in your 3DS \MAPS directory as **SHIP_TOP.CEL**. When you're finished, quit Animator Pro and return to 3D Studio. This cel will now form the basis of a new 8-bit texture map for the XCRUISER.

If you have Photoshop 2.5 for Windows, you can also use this technique to create a 24-bit texture map.

1. From Windows, load Photoshop, select **Open** from the **File** menu, and load the SHIP_TOP.TGA image from your 3DS \IMAGES directory.

2. From the Toolbar, select the Marquee tool, move the crosshair to the furthest upper-left corner of the SHIP_TOP window, left-click, hold and drag the cursor down diagonally to the right-most bottom of the window, and then release the mouse button.

3. Select **Copy** from the **Edit** menu, and then select **Paste**.

4. From the **Image** menu, select **Flip**, then **Horizontal**. The clipped, floating image will then be mirrored about the vertical axis.

5. Select **Composite Controls** from the **Edit** menu, set Opacity to 50%, and set Mode to Normal. Click on **OK**, and then left-click to paste the floating image.

When you paste the mirrored image on top of the original image using 50% transparency, the shadows from one side of the model darken the highlights on the other side; the highlights from the other side brighten the shadowed side. The effect is twofold: the highlights and shadows help to accentuate and outline the edges of the existing geometry, and the texture map has become bilaterally symmetrical, with increased pixel detail now identical on both sides.

6. For the next step, you may have to enlarge the image window; you can do this by pressing the Ctrl and + keys.

7. Select the Cropping tool from the Toolbar and carefully click and drag the cursor over the spaceship image, again diagonally from the upper left to the lower right. The edges of the Cropping box should just barely touch the nose and tail of the ship's top and bottom and the edges of the side pods on the left and right. When you're confident that you have

the Cropping tool positioned correctly, right-click within the tool borders to crop the image. (You may have to undo this and try several times to get the image cropped perfectly.)

8. When you're satisfied that you have a closely-cropped bounding box containing the ship, save this image as **SHIP_TO2.TGA** in your 3DS \MAPS directory and quit Photoshop.

Now you're ready to re-texture and re-map the ship.

1. Restart 3D Studio and load the XCRUISER.3DS file from the CD-ROM.

2. Click in the Top viewport to make it active. Click on the Zoom Extents icon to enlarge the viewport to full-screen.

3. Select **Display/Geometry/Box** to change the mesh display to box mode. This makes using the Region Fit tool easy.

4. Now, select **Surface/Mapping/Adjust** and click on **Region Fit**. Bring the crosshairs to the upper left corner of the ship box image, left-click, and then drag the crosshairs diagonally to the lower right corner of the box. Left-click to set the crosshairs. The Region Fit mapping icon should appear to cover the box outlines, as shown in figure 7.8.

5. To apply these new mapping coordinates, select **Surface/Mapping/Apply Obj** and click on the cruiser. In the confirming dialog box, click on **OK**.

6. Select **Surface/Material**, and then select **Get Library** to load the XCRUISER materials library once again. As the dialog box appears, choose the Materials Library file XCRUISER.MLI, load it, and then press the F5 key to switch to the Materials Editor.

7. In the Materials Editor, select **Materials/Get** and then select the ALUMINUM 3 material. Click in the Texture 1 Map slot, which displays ALUMINM3.TGA.

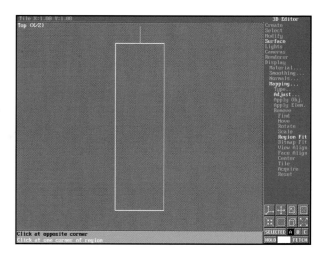

Figure 7.8
Region Fitted mapping coordinates applied to the XCRUISER boxed image.

8. From the \MAPS directory, select either SHIP_TOP.CEL or SHIP_TO2.TGA, depending on which one you created, and load it in the Texture 1 slot.

9. Select **Material/Put To Scene** and press Enter to send the modified material to the scene in the 3D Editor.

10. Press F3 to return to the 3D Editor and select **Render View** to render the scene, as shown in figure 7.9.

Examine this image. As you can see, the new texture map helps to accentuate the geometry of the ship and provides the illusion of greater surface detail without having to build extremely complex geometry.

This mapping technique—applying a preliminary texture on some 3D geometry, rendering it, retouching the image, and then re-applying this image to the model—is extremely useful. By working with an image of the actual geometry, you can see exactly where certain physical details are, and in effect paint directly on the model. If you want to add additional shading, panel lines, or decals to a particular model piece, you can simply add them

CRITICAL —
DO THIS
CHAPTER

...and those
...tly where you
...process as
...-increasing

...mapping
... few under-
...ture smear-
...ding model
...r detach
...priate map-
...r, I find this
...led models
... time to put
...his case, that

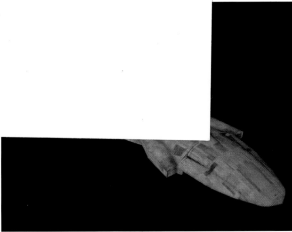

Figure 7.9
The rendered ship with an enhanced texture map.

Engine Glows

After you've created a spaceship to your liking, you'll probably want to see it cruising among the stars and nebulae, its engines firing.

1. Load the XCRUISE2.3DS file from the CD-ROM. This section will examine the various effects elements in the scene and discuss how to produce them. (Make sure that **Display/Geometry/Full Detail** is on instead of Box view.) As you can see in figure 7.10, the XCRUISER is surrounded by various lights, with four spotlights pointing at a 2D shape sitting just behind the four engines. These four spotlights form the basis for the engine glow effect.

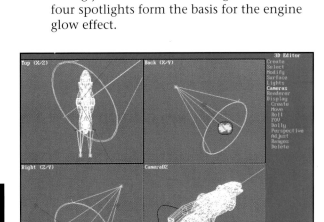

Figure 7.10
The XCRUISER model with glow geometry and spotlights.

2. Select the Camera view and render the image. The XCRUISER should now have red and orange engines, with a glow or halo radiating out from each engine.

3. To create the illuminated engine plates, select the faces you want to isolate (detaching if necessary) and map them with the correct materials. Notice that the 2D plane, called EngineGLOW, isn't visible. You'll see why in a moment.

Although you can produce this effect by using the Yost Group Glow IPAS routine within Video Post, not every 3D Studio user has these routines. Also, even if you do, it's sometimes more convenient to create similar effects *in camera* instead of rendering multiple passes in Video Post and creating a composite with the glow effects later.

Here's how it's done. I drew the EngineGLOW shape in the 2D Shaper and then brought into the 3D Editor using **Create/Object/Get Shape**. After positioning it directly behind the engines, I selected **Modify/Object/Attributes** and toggled Cast Shadows and Receive Shadows to Off.

> **NOTE** For these optical effects, this step is very important. Otherwise, as you move the lights around, the invisible shape may cast an undesired shadow on the ship.

I created the four spotlights, adjusted their color, hotspot, and falloff size, and set them to exclude everything in the scene save for the EngineGLOW shape. Then I assigned a shiny but completely transparent material to the EngineGLOW object.

4. Press F5 to go to the Materials Editor, select **Material/Get Material**, and load SHINY GLOW 1SIDE. The material isn't double-sided; this is important for the engine glow effect, because you want to see the effect only from the back of the ship. If you linked the spotlights to the EngineGLOW shape and this shape to the ship, and then rendered a fly-by animation sequence, the glow effect would become apparent only when the back of the ship—not the front—becomes visible. (As proof, you can return to the 3D Editor, right-click in the Camera view, select Camera01, and render the scene again.)

Again, creating the effect this way can eliminate the need to do Video Post optical processing, saving you one or more rendering steps. Shininess and Shininess Strength are set at 20 and 40, respectively, creating a soft glow. Transparency and Transparency Falloff are set at 100%, with Additive

toggled On. When assigned to an object with Shadow Casting and Receiving attributes turned off, this material will render as invisible except for soft highlights as lights bounce off it. By playing with the Shininess values, you can adjust the intensity of the glow effect; you can also adjust the spotlight settings.

In addition, there are many ways to vary this effect. For instance, you can create separate shapes for each light or engine, Tesselate the shapes to enlarge their face count, apply the SHINY GLOW material, and then use the RIPPLE.PXP or WAVE.PXP to distort them into multiple morph objects. If you morph the objects properly in the Keyframer and render an animation, the glow effect will appear to pulsate. You could also show only one morph object per engine and rotate that object quickly about its Z axis, providing a spinning glow effect. (Just remember to link the respective lights and objects together in the Keyframer before you move the spaceship model, or your ship will leave the glow behind.)

Out in the Void: Creating Nebulae

It's time to enhance this scene further. If you're still in the Materials Editor, press F3 to return to the 3D Editor and select **Display/Unhide/All**. A giant mesh object should fill your viewports; right-click on the Zoom Extents icon to zoom the Top, Back, and Front viewports to see the entire object, as shown in figure 7.11.

This object, called NEBULA, enables you to dress up your ordinary starfield background with colorful gaseous nebulae without having to create custom texture maps or go through extensive optical processing. Select the Camera02 view and render the scene.

Now you should see the ship, engines glowing, against a backdrop of stars and soft purple gas clouds. Again, you can create this effect very simply, using geometry, shiny transparent materials and carefully placed colored lights.

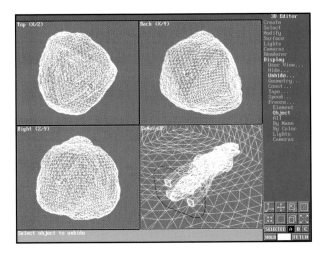

Figure 7.11
A Fractalized GSphere forms the NEBULA *object.*

Following are several different ways to create your own nebula object. (If you want to simply examine the current effect, skim over the next three steps now and follow their instruction when you're ready to create your own.)

1. Create a smoothed, 16-segment (or more) LSphere or GSphere, large enough to encompass your entire scene universe, and call it SPACE.

2. Select **Modify/Vertex/Move**, push and pull vertices (subtly) in each of the orthographic views and/or in a User view. You merely want to distort the surface—not create a Christmas tree ornament.

3. When you're finished distorting the SPACE object, select **Create/Object/Tessellate**, click on the SPACE object, and press Enter. In the resulting dialog box, select **Edge** and set Face Tension to 25. Press Enter.

> **NOTE** As you render the SPACE object and experiment with this effect, you may want to repeat the Tessellation to smooth the object further.

4. If you have the Fractalize IPAS routine, you could also create a 16-segment GSphere called SPACE, select **Program/PXP Loader** from the drop down menus, and then select FRACT.

5. Leave the default settings as they are, press Enter, and then press Enter again. The PXP will fractalize the SPACE object, leaving the original geometry, which you can either hide or, preferably, discard.

6. When you've created your own SPACE object, turn its Shadow Casting and Receiving Attributes to Off using **Modify/Object/Attributes**.

7. Assign the material SHINY GLOW 2SIDE to the SPACE object. This material is identical to the material used for the engine glows discussed earlier, although it's two-sided, because you're going to be inside the object. (If you used the one-sided material, you would have to perform a **Surface/Normals/Object Flip** to reverse the normals of the object. Otherwise, the effect wouldn't be visible.) Now, the only thing missing is the light source.

As you can see from examining the current 3D scene, there is an Omnilight floating away from the ship's nose, down and to the left. If you select **Lights/Omni/Adjust** and click on the Omnilight, you'll see that it's set to a dark purple. In addition, the Exclude button is activated, with every object in the scene except for the NEBULA excluded from the light's effects. (If you want, you could adjust your Ambient lighting to match the color of the nebula light, providing a moody fill light.) The shiny material of the NEBULA object picks up soft highlights from the Omnilight, much as the EngineGLOW object described previously provides circular glow effects.

Once you've created your own nebula effects and seen the results, you can begin to experiment. You can try different levels of geometry distortion and see how they affect the highlights the Omnilights produce. You can set Ranges and Attenuation in the Omnilights to provide soft washes of color in specific places and create multiple lights with differing colors, allowing them to blend. You could animate the lights or the NEBULA object itself during a rendered sequence. You could even apply the RIPPLE.PXP or WAVE.PXP and morph the NEBULA object during an animation, making the clouds appear to ebb and flow.

Finally, one of the best advantages in creating nebula effects this way is that the object and its effects are part of the in-camera 3D universe. For example, if you have the camera tracking a spaceship flying by, left to right, completely within the NEBULA object, the swirls of color will track right by in the background. Also, because the NEBULA object is completely transparent, you can place the STARS.IXP above the Keyframe scene in the Video Post queue, and the gas clouds will pivot and turn properly with the motion control stars.

Conclusion

As anyone who has seen recent science fiction TV shows can attest, realistic computer graphics from desktop systems have come into their own. No longer are Star Trek or Star Wars-style effects limited only to those people who can afford the services of professional special effects companies. With an investment of less than $10,000, you can produce your wildest flights of fancy on your own personal computer.

The techniques described in this chapter aren't the final word in creating far-flung vistas, of course; they're merely the spark to ignite your imagination. Luckily, as a 3D Studio user, you now have the tools at your fingertips to create and visit whatever fantastic worlds you can envision.

by Richard Sher

Los Angeles, California

Equipment and Software Used

Sicilicon Graphics Workstations

IBM-compatible 486/66 and Pentium 90 with 64 MB of RAM

Alias Research Power Animator

Autodesk 3D Studio

Yost Group IPAS Routines

Autodesk Animator Pro

Altamira Composer

Fractal Design Painter

Artist Biography

Richard Sher started as an artist creating abstract paintings with water color and acrylic media. Upon entering college, photography became his medium of choice. After discovering the television studio, he began working with analog video processing.

Richard began creating computer animations with 3D Studio in 1991. His first job using 3D Studio was creating animations for a children's TV show called "Chip and Pepper's Cartoon Madness." This first job paid for the equipment to run 3D Studio. He later went on to do the opening for a Lucas Film pilot called "Defenders of Dynatron City." In 1993, Richard's company 3SPACE was able to purchase a Beta SP video tape recorder, three Silicon Graphics computers, Alias, Prisms, Wavefront Composer, and Pandemonium. With a group of five very dedicated employees and his partner, Alberto Menache, he has created animations for a number of CD-ROM projects including 3D Body Adventure, Windows Animation Festival, and Mathimagics. Having sold his interest in 3SPACE, Richard is now working with Metrolite Studios producing interactive media.

Effect Overview

The special effect described in this chapter animates a glint highlight on an object, while enabling you to maintain much control over the placement of the highlight in time. The DYNAMIC.FLI animation in the \DYNAMIC directory on the CD-ROM shows one application of this special effect. The highlight travels from left to right along the front of the text object. What makes this effect so neat is that the highlight travel can be timed and placed precisely. In this chapter's example, the glint starts and stops exactly at the start and end of the animation. It is possible, however, to have the traveling highlight start and end at any point in your animation.

The effect goes together in four stages. First, you build and animate your scene exactly as you want it to appear—except for the glint. Next, you create and animate the highlight. Third, you apply any special filters and image processing to the animated highlight. Finally, you combine the highlight and the rendered scene.

This chapter uses Animator Pro, 3D Studio, and the Yost Group HILITE image-processing routine. You can use the same procedure to animate streaks and glows. For example, you can substitute the Yost Group GLOW in place of HILITE to get an animated glow that travels across the text. You could even use the two IPAS routines together to get even more interesting effects. Experiment to see what combinations of effects look good to you.

Procedure

The first step is to create your main scene and render it. You can make your own scene or use the MAIN.PRJ project file on the CD-ROM in the \DYNAMIC directory.

1. Start 3D Studio and load the MAIN project file from the CD-ROM. Your screen should resemble figure 8.1. This project consists of

some lofted text, a spotlight, and an omni-directional light and a camera. If you are creating your own scene, keep it simple while you experiment—you will save lots of time when you do test renderings.

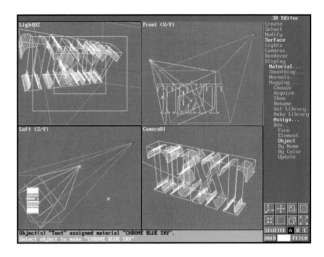

Figure 8.1
The MAIN.PRJ file loaded in the 3D Editor.

2. Apply a material to the text object. Normally, the material should be shiny. Feel free to experiment and create your own material. The DYNAMIC.FLI animation uses the CHROME BLUE SKY material from 3D Studio's standard materials.

3. Go to the Keyframer and set up a simple animation. Set the number of frames in the animation to 30. Limit the animation to two or three key frames—just a little text rotation and a gentle camera move is all that is needed. Keep the text centered and large in the camera view (you want to see the subtleties in the highlighting).

4. Next, choose **Renderer/Render View** and select the Camera01 viewport. Make sure the Render Animation settings match those in figure 8.2. Save the frames to MAIN.TGA.

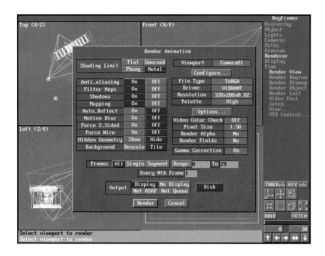

Figure 8.2
The Render Animation settings for the MAIN animation.

5. When the MAIN animation is done (see fig. 8.3), save the project as MAIN.PRJ. You will return to this file to render the highlight.

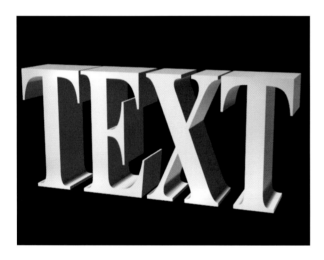

Figure 8.3
A rendered frame from the MAIN animation.

The next step is to create the highlight. The highlight is created using an animated texture-map material applied to the object. The animated

texture map is a vertical white line that moves horizontally across the screen. Use Animator Pro to create the animated texture map.

6. Start Animator Pro.

7. Set the number of frames in the animation to 30. This is the same as the number of frames in the MAIN animation you created previously in 3D Studio. Thirty frames are used so that the highlight travels from one end of the object to the other over the entire animation. If you want the highlight to travel across the object in a shorter period of time, use fewer frames.

8. Set the brush size to 4 pixels and set the current color to white.

9. Draw a vertical line with the Line tool on the left-hand edge of the screen. The line should extend the entire screen height. You can experiment with multiple lines and lines of various colors.

10. Choose **Cell/Clip** to make a cell out of the white line.

11. Press **O** to go to the Optics panel.

12. Choose **Element/Cell** to use the cell for the optics move.

13. Click on the **Move** button, and then set the horizontal slider to 320 pixels. This sets the cell to move 320 pixels over the course of the animation. Click on the **View** button to verify the cell movement.

14. Click on the **Use** button to go to the Time Select panel.

15. Click on **Render** to create the line movement animation.

16. When the rendering is done, go to the Home panel and save the animation as **LINE.FLC** in the \3DS3\MAPS directory.

Next, re-render the animation in MAIN.PRJ using the LINE.FLC as an animated texture map. This creates frames that will be used in Video Post to create the highlight.

17. Start 3D Studio and load the MAIN.PRJ file you saved before creating LINE.FLC.

18. Go to the Materials Editor and make a material that uses the animated line as the Texture 1 Map. You may need to experiment with various levels of self-illumination to get a sufficiently bright highlight. The material used to create the highlight in the DYNAMIC.FLI animation used a 100% self-illuminated material. A 100% setting produces a very bold highlight.

19. Set the ambient and specular colors to H:0 L:0 S:0. You can experiment with the specular color values to get a slightly over-amplified (different yet useful) effect.

20. Choose **Material/Put** and name this material **MOVE_LINE**.

21. Go to the 3D Editor and choose **Surface/Mapping/Apply Obj** and apply planar mapping coordinates to the text object in the Front viewport. Map the text across the front of the letters.

22. Next, choose **Surface/Mapping/Adjust/Scale**, press and hold down the Alt key, and then select the text object. This scales the mapping icon to the extents of the text object.

23. Enlarge the mapping icon so that it is slightly bigger than the text object.

24. Choose **Surface/Material/Choose** and select the MOVE_LINE material.

25. Choose **Surface/Material/Assign/Object** and then select the text object. This assigns the animated texture map material to the object.

26. Go to the Keyframer and choose **Renderer/Render View** and select the Camera01 viewport. Make sure the Render Animation settings match those shown in figure 8.4.

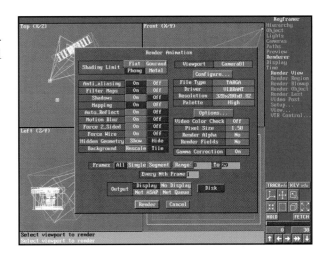

Figure 8.4
The Render Animation dialog box settings for rendering the LINE animation.

27. Render the animation frames to LINE.TGA.

If you play back the frames you just rendered, you will see a white line that appears to move across the text. You never actually see the entire text, however. The parts of the text that are made visible by the mapped white line will be used as key points by the HILITE IPAS filter that makes these white areas appear to glint as they move across the text.

28. Save the project as **LINE.PRJ** in case you need to return to it at a later time.

The next step in the dynamic highlight process is to process the images in the LINE frames. This project only uses the HILITE image processing filter from Yost Group, Inc., but you can use any number of processing techniques. You could even import the frames into a third-party image processing program such as Adobe PhotoShop or Aldus PhotoStyler. However, programs like PhotoShop will not batch a sequence of pictures like Video Post will.

The HILITE IPAS filter places a star cross highlight on key pixels of an image. The number of points, size of the points, and various key methods, as well as other parameters, can be controlled by HILITE.

29. Start a new project and go to the Keyframer. Choose **Renderer/Video Post** and select any viewport.

30. Add two lines to the Video Post Queue. Both Queue entries are set to KF Scene by default.

31. Click on the **Edit** button and then select the first Queue entry.

32. In the Queue Entry dialog box, change the entry type from KF Scene to Bitmap, and then click on the blank Bitmap filename button. In the File dialog box, enter **LINE*.TGA** in the Filename box.

33. Click on **OK** to return to the Video Post dialog box and select the second Queue entry.

34. In the Queue Entry dialog box, change the entry type from KF Scene to Process, and then click on the blank Process name button.

35. Select the HILITE IPAS routine in the IXP Selector dialog box and choose **OK**.

36. Click on the **Process Setup** button and set the Hilite Filter dialog box settings similar to figure 8.5. You might need to experiment with the various HILITE settings to get the exact look you want. Render single test frames to the display only to check the effect of the filter before rendering the entire animation.

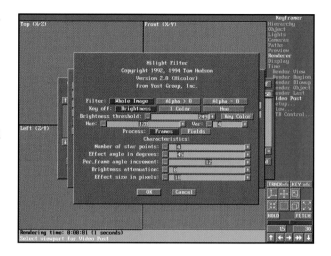

Figure 8.5
The Hilite Filter settings used for the DYNAMIC animation on the CD-ROM.

37. When you are satisfied with your settings, choose **OK** to accept the changes and return to the Video Post dialog box.

38. Click on the **Render** button and set up the Render Video Post Animation dialog box as shown in figure 8.6. Be sure Render Alpha is set to Yes.

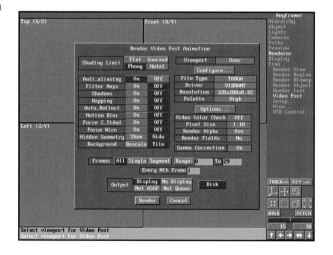

Figure 8.6
The Render Video Post Animation dialog box settings for rendering the highlight.

39. Click on the **Render** button and name the frames **HILT.TGA**.

40. After the rendering is complete, save the project as **HILT** so you can reprocess the highlight if you decide to change the look of the highlight at a later time.

Now all that is left to do is to combine the highlight on top of the MAIN animation. The process for building the composite image is very similar to the highlight process and is performed entirely in Video Post.

41. Start a new project and go to the Keyframer, choose **Renderer/Video Post**, and then select any viewport.

42. Add two lines to the Video Post Queue. Both Queue entries are set to KF Scene by default.

43. Click on the **Edit** button and then select the first Queue entry.

44. In the Queue Entry dialog box, change the entry type from KF Scene to Bitmap, and then click on the blank Bitmap filename button. In the File dialog box, enter **MAIN*.TGA** in the Filename box.

45. Click on **OK** to return to the Video Post dialog box and select the second Queue entry.

46. In the Queue Entry dialog box, change the entry type from KF Scene to Bitmap, and then click on the blank Bitmap filename button. In the File dialog box enter **HILT*.TGA** in the Filename box.

47. Click on **OK** to return to the Video Post dialog box.

48. Click on the Alpha entry next to the HILT*.TGA queue entry to display the Alpha dialog box.

49. Set up the Alpha dialog box as shown in figure 8.6, and then choose **OK** to return to the Video Post dialog box.

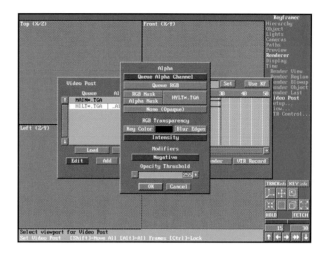

Figure 8.7
The Alpha dialog box settings for the composite image.

50. Choose **Render** and save the animation as **DYNAMIC.FLI**.

51. Click on the **Render** button and set up the Render Video Post Animation dialog box as shown in figure 8.7.

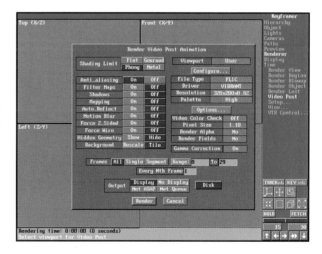

Figure 8.8
The Render Video Post Animation settings for the composite animation.

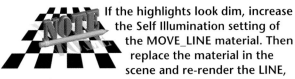 **If the highlights look dim, increase the Self Illumination setting of the MOVE_LINE material. Then replace the material in the scene and re-render the LINE, HILT, and DYNAMIC animations.**

52. When the animation is done rendering, save the project as **FINAL** in case you want to experiment or need to make changes to the animation in the future.

That is it. When you play back the animation, you will see what appears to be a row of highlights twinkling across the text as it moves in space.

Conclusion

Experiment with this effect. The applications of the technique extend beyond this simple example.

The \DYNAMIC directory on the CD-ROM also contains an animation and project file with the mapped glint only applied to the faces on the front of the text object. The text object has the MOVE_LINE material assigned to the faces and a matte black material assigned to the rest of the object. The project file is named FACEMAP.PRJ and the animation is named FACEMAP.FLI.

Try using lines of different colors and creating several highlight passes. Add them to the FINAL project's Video Post queue. Also, try using an animated map of small, different-colored circles that fly around the screen instead of the white vertical line. Your only limit is your imagination!

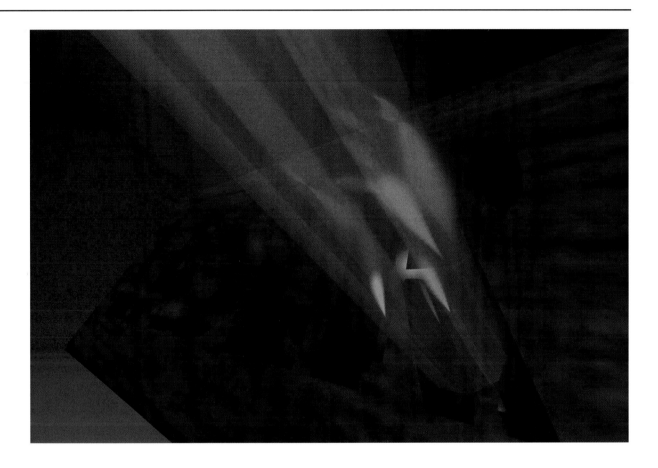

by Martin Foster

Laguna Hills, California

Equipment and Software Used

LANtastic network of three IBM PC-compatibles: Pentium 60, 486/66, and 486/33, each with 32 MB of RAM

Video output to a DPS personal animation recorder and a 1 GB dedicated hard drive with the TBCIV option for video capture

3D Studio Release 3.0

Animator Pro 1.3

Photostyler 2

All output can be to SVGA FLC file format. For better results, however, the output can be TGA files sent frame-by-frame to video tape or to motion JPEG animation recorders for real-time playback.

Artist Biography

Martin Foster is a 3D artist and owner of Animatrix in Laguna Hills, California. He works predominantly with 3D Studio to create all kinds of animation and graphics for a broad client base. Martin worked on the award-winning architectural animation project "Port de Plaisance" for the Pyros Partnership; the pre-visualization of stunts and special effects for the feature films "My Life" and "Wolf" for Sony Pictures; and the award-winning, CD-ROM–based game "Rebel Assault" for LucasArts. Other samples of his work can be found on the 3D Studio Siggraph 1993 tape and on the 3D Studio World Creating Tool Kit CD-ROM. He is currently working on 3D game development for a next generation video game platform.

Effect Overview

Using the new IPAS3 add-on effects *vapor* and *flame*, this chapter demonstrates how to achieve the much requested logo burn-in effect. This is a popular logo treatment that clients ask for because it involves a lot of dynamic, attention-grabbing special effects with the suggestion of permanence, especially if the effect is carved out of solid rock or wood. Until recently, this effect would have been hard to create with 3D Studio due to the lack of realistic flame and smoke routines. These effects are now available as third-party additions to 3D Studio, called IPAS routines, and can substantially contribute to stunning sequences.

Imagine a client asks you to animate a logo treatment that shows a text logo being burned into a highly polished block of wood. It should be exceptionally dynamic with a powerful looking laser-beam, producing a fast-burning flame with lots of smoke. As the smoke clears, it reveals the smoldering logo. The appearance of the text in the wood should be perfectly synchronized in time with the advance of the laser-beam.

Ownership of the Yost Group's IPAS3, Disk #6 is required for this effect.

Procedure

To start 3D Studio and choose **File,Load Project** and select LASR-BRN.PRJ from the \LASER directory of the CD-ROM included with this book. Then choose **Info/Configure**, click on **Map Paths** in the program configuration menu, and add the CD-ROM directory \LASER to access the images and maps necessary for this exercise.

Table 9.1 lists the objects and assigned materials for this project.

Table 9.1
Objects and Materials Summary

Object	Vertices	Faces	Material
Wood-text	712	1196	WOOD-ROSEWD
			WOOD-ROSEWD BURN
			WOOD-ROSEWD MIRO
Wood-opac	232	226	WOOD-ROSEWD OPAC
Laser-int	50	64	LASER INT OP
Laser-ext	34	64	LASER EXT OP
Vapor-L	36	12	VAPOR SPECIAL
Vapor-A	43	12	VAPOR SPECIAL
Vapor-S	94	12	VAPOR SPECIAL
Vapor-E	31	12	VAPOR SPECIAL
Vapor-R	68	12	VAPOR SPECIAL
Flame	12	14	FLAME SPECIAL

Wood-text

To create the carved wooden logo in its final state, you use the 2D Shaper and 3D Lofter.

1. Choose 2D Shaper from the Program menu (or press F1), and examine the shapes that are used to create the wooden logo. The large and small rectangles are used to create the beveled edge on the block of wood. There are also large and small letters that are used to create the carved look of the letters in the wood. The last shape is a path you will use later in the Keyframer.

2. Choose **Shape/Assign** and select the small rectangle and the large letters L, A, S, E, and R. Don't forget to select the small inside pieces of the letters A and R. Choose **Shape/Hook/Center** to position the hook in the center of the rectangle.

3. Choose 3D Lofter from the **Program** menu (or press F2), and press the Page Up or Page Down keys to go to the top vertex of the path. Place the shape on the vertex by choosing **Shape/Get/Shaper**.

4. Return to the 2D Shaper and choose **Shape/Assign**. Deselect the small rectangle and select the large rectangle. This will create the beveled edge on the block of wood.

5. Return to the 3D Lofter and select the second vertex on the path by pressing Page Up. Choose **Shape/Get/Shaper** to place the shape on the path.

6. Go back to the 2D Shaper and choose **Shape/None** to clear the current shape.

Choose **Shape/Assign**, and this time select the large rectangle and small letters L, A, S, E, and R (don't forget the larger inside pieces on the letters A and R). These will create the carved look of the letters after they are lofted.

7. Return to the 3D Lofter and move to the bottom vertex of the path. Choose **Shape/Get/Shaper** to place the bottom shape on the path. Choose **Object/Preview** to see how the logo will be lofted (see fig. 9.1).

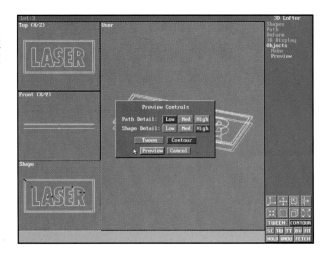

Figure 9.1
Preview of the lofted logo.

8. Choose **Object/Make**, name the object **Wood-text**, and press **Create**. Choose 3D Editor from the Program menu (or press F3) to return to the 3D Editor.

Examine the object you just created. Notice that Wood-text will need a back piece attached to it so you cannot see through it. You can easily create this by modifying the path in the 3D Lofter and using the existing shapes in the 2D Shaper.

9. Return to the 2D Shaper and choose **Shape/None** to clear the current shapes. Choose **Shape/Assign** and select the large outer rectangle.

10. Switch to the 3D Lofter and choose **Shape/Delete** to delete the current shapes from the path. Repeat this for each of the vertices on the path.

11. Choose **Path/Delete Vertex** and delete the top vertex on the path. Choose **Path/Move Vertex** and, in the Front view, select the new top vertex. Press Tab until you are constrained to vertical movement. Then move the top vertex until it is slightly below the bottom vertex.

12. Choose **Shape/Get/Shaper** to place the rectangle shape on the path. Then choose **Object/Make**, name the object `Wood-back`, and choose **Create**.

13. Return to the 3D Editor to examine the logo. To make it easier to work with, attach the `Wood-back` object to `Wood-text`. Choose **Create/Object/Attach** and choose `Wood-back` (or use the H key and pick from the scrolling dialog box). Then choose `Wood-text` to attach the back (see fig. 9.2).

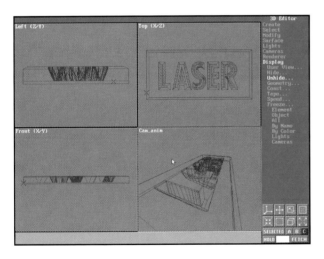

Figure 9.2
The completed `Wood-text` *logo.*

14. Choose **Surface/Mapping**. You should be able to see the yellow and green mapping icon from the Top viewport. Notice that it totally covers the object to avoid seams in the texture map. Choose **Surface/Mapping/Assign/Object** and click on `Wood-text`.

15. Choose **Surface/Materials/Get Library** and select the library LASR-BRN.MLI from the CD-ROM.

16. Go to the materials editor and take a look at the materials that `Wood-text` uses. Choose **Materials** from the **Program** menu (or press F5).

 If at any time you lose track of any materials, use the command Get From Library from the Materials menu.

In the first sample box you should see the material WOOD-ROSEWD that is used for the beveled edges. The sides and back of the object uses a rich wood texture map called ROSEWOOD.JPG.

In the next sample box is WOOD-ROSEWD BURN, which is used on the inside surface of the logo characters and is meant to represent the look of burnt wood. This is accomplished by using a low setting of 15% on the texture slider, allowing the dark diffuse color of the material to be more prominent. Also, the specular color is much darker, and shininess and shininess strength are much lower as befits a burnt look.

WOOD-ROSEWD MIRO is similar to WOOD-ROSEWD, with the addition of a 25% flat-mirror reflection map that is applied to the front faces of the `Wood-text` object. This gives the wood a rich, highly polished appearance.

17. Return to the 3D Editor. Assign the material WOOD-ROSEWD BURN to the inside surfaces of the logo characters. Assign the material WOOD-ROSEWD MIRO to the front faces of

Wood-text. Finally, assign WOOD-ROSEWD to the beveled edges, sides, and back of Wood-text.

 You can use Select/Faces/Quad to select the appropriate face in either the front or right view port. Then use Surface/Material/Assign/Faces and choose Selected to assign the material.

Wood-opac

The Wood-opac object is used to cover up the holes in the Wood-text object and, by using an animated opacity map, reveals the burnt-in letters as the laser passes by.

1. Switch to the 2D Shaper and choose **Shape/Assign/None** to clear the existing shapes. Then choose **Shape/Assign** and click on each of the polygons that make up the word LASER. Choose **Shape/Hook/Home** to return the hook to its home position.

2. Return to the 3D Editor and choose **Create/Object/Get Shape**. Call the object **Wood-opac**, choose **Modify/Object/Move**, and place the object on the face of Wood-text.

3. Choose **Surface/Mapping/Assign** and use the same mapping coordinates as Wood-text to ensure a perfect match for the wood texture map that both use.

4. Switch to the Materials Editor to take a look at the material WOOD-ROSEWD OPAC, which is crucial to this effect.

WOOD-ROSEWD OPAC should appear in the fourth sample box from the left. It is identical to the WOOD-ROSEWD MIRO material in most ways, but it has some important additions. It uses an animated map called TEXT-OP.FLC—which was hand painted in animator pro—to control opacity and shininess. Take a look at this map to see how it works.

5. Using the left mouse button, click and drag the word TEXT-OP.FLC that appears in the opacity slider slot and drop it onto the **View Image** button on the right side of the screen. Alternatively, you can click on the **View Image** button and find TEXT-OP.FLC in the \LASER directory on the CD-ROM. The former method is a quick way of examining your maps.

You should see a white-on-black animation with the characters L A S E R being painted over with black one after the other. It may look a little messy, because there needs to be some overlap of the map to make sure no gaps appear between the Wood-text and the Wood-opac objects during the animation. However, it is an opacity map and there's no need for it to be pretty. The same map is used to control the shininess of Wood-opac object—as the logo disappears, the shininess of the object also needs to disappear in a synchronized fashion.

6. Return to the 3D Editor and assign the material WOOD-ROSEWD OPAC to Wood-opac. Choose **Rendering/Render View** and render the Cam-still viewport. You should see a solid block of wood with Wood-opac exactly covering the carved letters as shown in figure 9.3.

Figure 9.3
The rendered block with the object Wood-opac *covering* Wood-text.

Lasers

Laser-int and Laser-ext are the inner and outer pieces of the laser-beam. They were made in the 3D Editor from primitive cylinders of different diameters. Laser-Int represents the core of the laser and Laser-Ext represents the soft falloff edge.

1. In the 3D Editor, choose **Create/Cylinder** and create a cylinder called **Laser-int** in the Top view. It should be centered at the top of the letter L. The diameter should match the width of the letters. Make the cylinder tall enough so it extends off screen in the Camera view. Choose **Modify/Object/Move** and position the cylinder so that it sits just inside the letter L.

2. Repeat the process and create a slightly larger cylinder called **Laser-ext**. Position it around Laser-int so the bottom of the cylinder just touches the face of the block as shown in figure 9.4

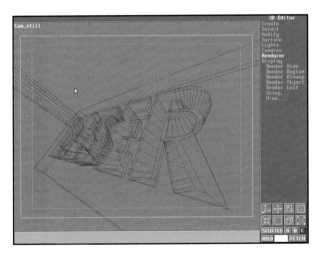

Figure 9.4
Laser-int *and* Laser-ext.

3. In the Materials editor, look at the materials in the fifth and sixth sample slots. LASER INT OP uses transparency falloff at the outer edges, combined with an animated opacity map created from animated clouds, to give some motion. This is planar mapped with a 90-degree rotation down the core of the laser beam in the Front viewport of the 3D Editor. LASER EXT OP also uses outside transparency falloff and an opacity map painted in Animator Pro using the radial gradient tool.

4. Switch to the 3D Editor and choose **Surface/Mapping/Adjust/Region Fit** and place a planar mapping region along the length of Laser-int in the front view port. Position the mapping coordinates along the core of the cylinder with **Surface/Mapping/Adjust/Move**. Apply the surface mapping coordinates to Laser-int.

5. Choose **Surface/Mapping/Adjust/Region Fit** and place a planar mapping region around Laser-ext in the Top view. Apply these surface mapping coordinates to Laser-ext.

6. Apply the material LASER INT OP to Laser-int and the material LASER EXT OP to Laser-ext.

Vapors

Vapor-L, Vapor-A, Vapor-S, Vapor-E, and Vapor-R are the objects that create the vapor/smoke effect as the laser passes by the letters. The reason for having one for each character is that this is the only way to offset the timing of the smoke release for each. If there was only one vapor object for the entire logo, all the vapor would start at the same time—not particularly realistic.

1. Switch to the 2D Shaper and choose **Shape/Assign/None** to clear the existing shapes. Then choose **Shape/Assign** and select the inside letter L.

2. Return to the 3D Editor, from the Top view choose **Create/Object/Get Shape**, and name the object **L**. Repeat this process for all of the letters in the 2D Shaper until you have a separate object for each of the small letters (see fig. 9.5).

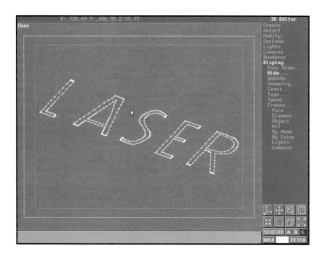

Figure 9.5
The small letters used to create smoke.

The actual vapor objects are created with the AXP-BOX utility provided with the IPAS Vapor routine.

3. Choose **PXP Loader** from the Program menu (or press F12) and select AXPBOX.

4. Choose **Custom** and enter a relative emitter size of **0.50**. This will determine the size of the emitter box relative to the size of the object you choose. Choose **Emitter Location Base** and click on **OK**. Select the object L (or use the H key and pick from the scrolling dialog box) to use as the emitter. This creates the emitter box that will create the vapor/smoke effect.

5. Repeat the process for each of the other letters.

The AXPBOX routine creates copies of the original objects L, A, S, E, and R and makes them part of the emitter boxes. Because the original letters are no longer needed, you can delete them.

6. Choose **Modify/Object/Delete** and delete the objects L, A, S, E, and R.

7. Choose **Surface/Mapping/Adjust/Region Fit** and create a planar mapping region in the Left view that completely covers the emitter

boxes. Assign these mapping coordinates to each of the emitter boxes.

8. Choose **Surface/Material/Choose** and select VAPOR SPECIAL from the list of materials. Apply this material to each of the emitter boxes.

The material VAPOR SPECIAL is a material included in a library with Disk #6 of the Yost Group's IPAS routines. If you like, load the library DISK6.MLI (not included on the CD-ROM) and try some different vapor materials from this library.

9. Choose **Modify/Object/Attributes** and select the letter L emitter box. Change the name to **Vapor-L**, and then choose **External Process** and select VAPOR from the list of IPAS routines. Repeat this for each of the letters.

10. Switch to the Keyframer (or press F4) and choose **Object/Attributes**, press the H key, select Vapor-L, and click on the External Process **Settings** button.

Figure 9.6 shows the setting for the smoke effect (for a full explanation of the settings of VAPOR_I.AXP, refer to the manuals that were included when you purchased the routine).

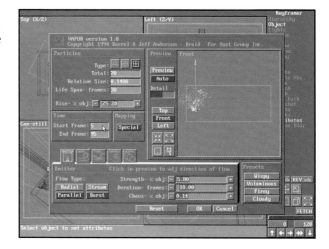

Figure 9.6
Vapor settings.

Timing is especially pertinent to this effect. The starting and ending frames will determine the timing of the smoke effect. You don't want the smoke to appear before the laser hits. Table 9.2 lists each of the vapor objects and their starting and ending frames.

Table 9.2
Vapor Object Timing

Object	Start Frame	End Frame
Vapor-L	5	95
Vapor-A	20	105
Vapor-S	42	110
Vapor-E	60	115
Vapor-R	80	120

Adjust the parameters for each letter. Feel free to try some test renderings in the Keyframer at various frames of the animation—frame 80 is a good choice because all vapor objects will be active and in view. Also try some of the different preset vapor types available that offer some interesting variations.

The vapor routine can cause rendering times to skyrocket. If you find your times are unacceptable, you can try adjusting various parameters. For example, reducing the particles total number and reducing their relative size can help bring rendering times back under control. There is a real trade-off here, however; it comes down to making a choice between a more dramatic effect with longer rendering times or settling for a less dramatic effect in a shorter time.

Flame

The Flame is an AXPBOX that uses FLAME_I.AXP, which is a flame and fire IPAS routine that you can use to create all kinds of fire effects.

1. Choose **PXP Loader** from the Program menu and select AXPBOX from the list. Choose Default and enter **4** for the Number of Emitter Points, **30** for the Box Size, and **.20**

as the Relative Size of Emitters. Choose **Emitter Location Base** and then **OK**. This creates an emitter box for the flame.

2. Move the emitter box so that it is positioned at the center of Laser-ext on the face of Wood-text. You might want to move some of the emitter vertices to adjust the size and shape of the flame. Assign the same mapping coordinates that you used for the vapor objects and apply the material FLAME SPECIAL to the emitter box.

3. Return to the Keyframer and choose **Modify/Object/Attributes**, press the H key, and pick the flame emitter box. Name the object **Flame**, choose **External Process**, and assign the process Flame to the emitter box. Then click on the External Process **Settings** button.

Figure 9.7 shows the settings used for Flame. I chose a fast-burning variation on the candle preset. In particular, note the life span of five frames and the strength of 15%, which result in a short, fast flare-up. Again, feel free to try different types of presets and settings. FLAME SPECIAL is one of the materials supplied with the IPAS set and there are plenty of others you might try.

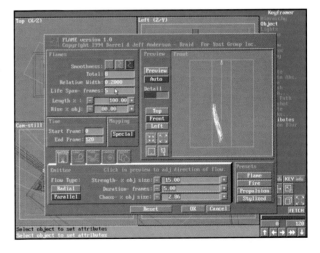

Figure 9.7
The flame settings.

Lighting

The lighting for this scene is very low ambient light of RGB 9,9,9 and four omni lights. Omni-main is for overall scene lighting; Omni-purp casts a low, deep-purple light; Omni-glow is a deep red light to give the effect of glowing, hot wood following the passing of the laser; and Omni-laser moves along with the laser to cast a localized light as if it was coming from the laser itself.

Animation

Next, create a dummy object. The path from the 2D Shaper will be applied to it and Flame, Laser-int, Laser-ext, and Omni-laser will be hierarchically linked to it so they all move as one.

1. Switch to the 2D Shaper and choose **Shape/None**, then **Shape/Assign** and select the path that follows the letters. This path was created in the 2D Shaper with **Create/Line** and then edited vertex by vertex to write out the word LASER using **Modify/Vertex/Move**.

You want the laser to pass over the letters in the first 90 frames and then disappear, leaving the smoking logo in the wood.

2. Return to the Keyframer, select the active segment bar, and set the active segment between frames 0 and 90. Set the current frame to frame 0.

3. Choose **Create/Dummy Box** and call it Dummy-lasr. Place it in the Top view centered at the start of the letter L. Move it so it sits on the face of the block of wood.

4. Choose **Paths/Get/Shaper** and assign it to Dummy-lasr. Choose **No** for Relocate and Reverse Path and choose **Yes** for Adjust Keys.

5. Reset the active segment to frames 0 and 120 and make frame 91 the active frame. In the Top view, choose **Object/Move** and move

Dummy-lasr to the far right. Make sure it does not appear in any of the camera views. This will make it appear that the laser turns off after it completes the path.

6. Make frame 0 active and choose **Hierarchy/Link/Object/By Name**. Choose the objects Flame, Laser-int, Laser-ext, and Omni-laser as the children and Dummy-lasr as the parent. Update the Flame Secondary Motion by choosing **Object/Attributes/Settings**, and then click on **OK**.

You are now ready to render the animation. There are two camera viewport choices. Cam-still is probably preferable for computer playback of FLI or FLC files because the camera is static. This results in a smaller disk file with fewer changes per frame, and therefore faster playback. Cam-anim is an animated camera for a more dramatic effect and can be used where frame rate is not an issue, such as when the output is to video.

7. Choose **Renderer/Render View** and click in the camera viewport of your choice. In the Configure box, choose an appropriate resolution and output file type for your equipment. This could be 320×200×0.82 or 640×480×1.0 flics for computer playback, or 752×480×0.85 and targa files for video output to a personal animation recorder. Try every 30th frame, as a test to make sure everything is in order and rendering times are acceptable. You could turn off Auto-Reflect if rendering is too slow.

8. When you are satisfied that everything is set up correctly, render all the frames and save the sequence with a name of your choice.

If you render an animation, you can compare your output to the sample file LASR-BRN.FLC on the CD-ROM. You can also load a completed project file called LASER.PRJ.

Conclusion

Experiment with different variations of the Vapor and Flame routines. Add to the animation, for example, by having the letters tumble into view in the beginning before the laser action starts. Substitute a granite or marble block for the wood and change the laser to an engraving tool. Try a different logo entirely—one that is not just text— and use a different background.

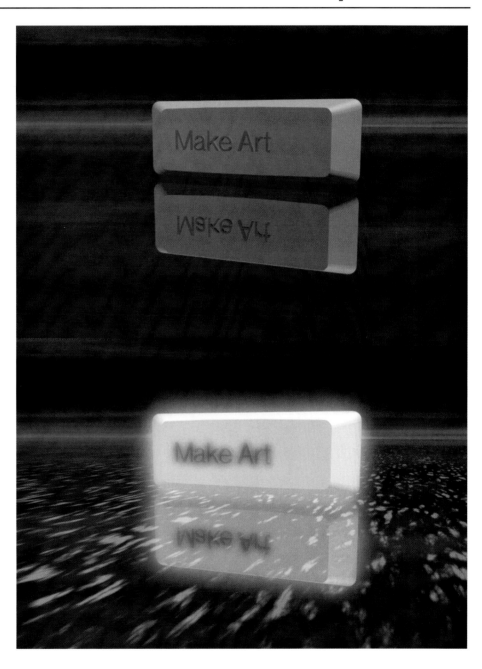

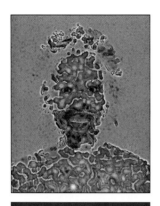

by Tim Forcade

Lawrence, Kansas

Equipment and Software Used

LANtastic networked
IBM PC compatibles

3D Studio Release 3.0

Adobe Photoshop or
HiRes QFX

Artist Biography

Building on an education in traditional fine arts that stressed drawing, painting, sculpture, and graphic design, Tim Forcade's artwork has advanced through optical, kinetic, and digital electronic media. This has resulted in numerous works utilizing photography, electronics, and video as well as the invention of electronic image-processing systems of his own design.

Concurrent with his artwork, Tim (see above left "self portrait: grown in agar") has over two decades of practice as a commercial artist, designer, and photographer. In 1978 Tim formed Forcade & Associates as a graphic resource to the commercial and professional communities. His project experience extends from illustration and publication design through photography and 3D visualization to computer animation and multimedia.

Tim's work has been exhibited in the U.S., Canada, Europe, and Japan. He has written and presented extensively on the subjects of applied 2D and 3D computer graphics and animation. He is a contributing editor to Computer Graphics World *and* Computer Artist *magazines. He can be reached via CompuServe at* 72007,2742 *or via Internet at* tforcade@falcon.cc.ukans.edu

Working with Tim at Forcade & Associates is Terry Gilbert, who provided invaluable assistance to Tim in creating and documenting this effect.

Effect Overview

Most people agree that 3D Studio has a very complete materials editor. In fact, given its eight mapping types and numerous masking options and shading modes, it is rare that you cannot create the exact material you want for a given object. Occasionally, however, either because two effects are mutually exclusive or because there simply is not a specific map type that applies, you must look to other means.

For example, consider a flat mirror reflection that also must appear dusty or mottled. The fact that 3D Studio's flat, automatic reflection maps do not allow Reflection Blur to be used with them precludes a dusty or smeared look. Often, combining textures and reflections on the same objects calls for compromise.

Another example is an object glow that must not only animate—moving with a 3D object as it moves—but must also reflect accurately in a flat mirrored object. Furthermore, reflected glows should clip properly, disappearing where the edges of the mirror surface or object end. Although you can accomplish this effect using Video Post and an IPAS application such as Yost Group's Glow filter, it is very difficult to get the glow to clip properly. Also, options such as animating glow texture to produce a rippling aura are equally difficult.

For instances like these, the best approach is also the simplest—make a copy of the object in question or create a second object to receive a mask effect or texture. Then link the supplemental object to the original for animation.

Look at the upper image on the opening page of this chapter. It depicts the mythical "Make Art" key, which some people believe should be (or perhaps is) located somewhere on the keyboard of every computer on the planet. This scene consists of the lone Make Art key hovering above an infinite mirrored plane at dusk. Notice that the mirror accurately reflects the key and sunset. However, the reflection competes for the viewer's attention with the key itself.

Although one solution would be to "turn down" the reflection by decreasing the mirror's reflection parameter, this would have a generalized effect and reduce not only the key's reflection but that of the subtle tones in the sunset as well. What is called for is a way to break up or dull the reflection while preserving the reflection's other qualities.

Now look at the lower image. Once again, the key reflects in the mirror, but this time the reflection is broken up by a pattern of white, cloud-like streaks. This could just as easily be a dust filter or effect mask. The net effect is that the mirror plane has become more unified while maintaining a mirror reflection of the Make Art key.

Also notice the glow around the Make Art key. It is visible not only around and in front of the key, but is also convincingly reflected in the mirrored plane. Both effects, as well as numerous others, can be accomplished with the following procedure, which combines supplemental geometry and materials to get an exact look.

Procedure

Table 10.1 lists all the files necessary to reproduce these effects. The project files contain all cameras, lighting, and materials. Also included is ARTGLOW.FLI, an example animation. These files are located on the CD-ROM in the /ARTGLOW directory.

Table 10.1
Project Files, Bitmaps, and FLI File for the Make Art Key

File Name	Description
ARTREF.PRJ	Simple mirror reflection
ARTGLOW.PRJ	Masked reflection and projected glow
ARTMAP.PRJ	Project for creating "Make Art" glow matte
ARTDUSK.TGA	Custom bitmap for dusk texture

continues

Table 10.1
Continued

File Name	Description
CLOUDX.TIF	Custom bitmap for mirror plane
CLOUDX4.TIF	Custom bitmap for mirror plane
GLOWKEY.TIF	Custom bitmap for key glow
GLOWKEY2.TIF	Custom bitmap for key glow softened
ARTGLOW.FLI	Example of animated glow

1. Start 3D Studio and load the ARTREF.PRJ project file (see fig. 10.1). This is the scene used to generate the upper image on the facing page. It consists of the objects Refl_plane, (the mirrored surface), Sky (the plane on which the sunset is mapped), Key, and Key_label (which comprise the Make Art key). The scene is lit from above by Toplight. The Orangefill spotlight provides orange light, suggesting fill from the sunset.

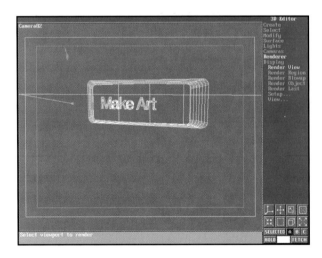

Figure 10.1
The ARTREF project loaded in the 3D Editor.

2. Render the Camera02 view and compare the results to the top image.

The problem with this image is that the mirrored reflection is so prevalent that it competes for your attention with the Make Art key itself.

Using a Reflection Mask

What you need is a method for toning down the reflection while tying the plane together (the area that reflects the sunset appears separate from the area that reflects the key).

1. Change to the Materials Editor. All of the materials used in the scene are preloaded, but you need to render the samples to see them. Render the sample materials for the first four sample windows. Make the REFLECTION material's sample window active (see fig. 10.2) and look at its settings.

   There are two essential variables that have immediate impact on the reflection. These are the Reflection Map settings and the hue, luminance, and saturation settings of the material's Specular attribute. Manipulating these two variables enables you to render the reflection anywhere from invisible to full brightness in any color you wish.

2. Set the Reflection Map slider to 30, and then click on the Specular attribute and change its color to H:27, L:120, and S:255. With the REFLECTION material still current, press **T**, and then choose **OK** to replace the material in the scene with the new one you just created.

3. Now click the **Render Last** button and view the results (see fig. 10.3).

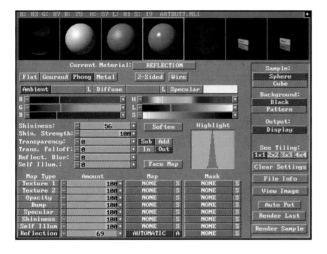

Figure 10.2
The materials used in ARTREF.PRJ; the REFLECTION material uses an automatic flat mirror reflection map.

reflection broken up while maintaining its brightness and detail.

4. Make sure the REFLECTION material is still current and choose **Material/Get Material** and load the REFLECT-MASKED material. This material's attributes are the same as REFLECTION with one exception: the reflection map is masked by CLOUDX.TIF. Click on the **Current Material** button and rename REFLECT-MASKED to **REFLECTION**. Replace the material in the scene by pressing **T**.

5. Go to the 3D Editor and assign planar mapping coordinates to the Refl_plane object.

6. Go back to the Materials Editor, click on **Render Last**, and then view the result (see fig. 10.4).

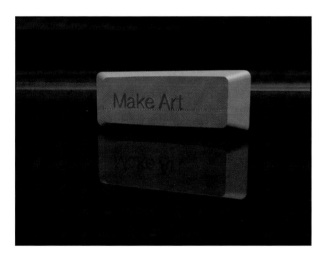

Figure 10.3
A darkened reflection. The subtleties in the sunset are all but lost.

The reflection is darker overall, with an orange cast appearing in the mirrored key. This certainly places more emphasis on the key, but the sunset's reflection is all but lost. It is more desirable to have the

Figure 10.4
The rendered image using CLOUDX.TIF as a reflection mask with the original reflection material.

This time the reflection is broken up by the curvilinear texture of the map. The rest of the mirror, where nothing is reflected, is unaffected. Interestingly, as the contrast of CLOUDX.TIF (the

---

mask) decreases, the contrast of the effect diminishes. You can try this yourself by substituting CLOUDX4.TIF for the material's reflection mask and clicking on **Render Last** again. CLOUDX4.TIF is a brighter version of CLOUDX.TIF.

Although the result is interesting, it still falls short of the desired effect. The solution lies in separating the mask from the reflection. This provides the most flexibility, enabling you to independently adjust the parameters for each.

7. From the 3D Editor, unhide `Refl_mask`. This object is a copy of the original mirrored plane, `Refl_plane`. It is placed above and very close to the original. As its name implies, its function is to enable you to mask the reflection with any texture.

8. In the Materials Editor, get the material REFLECTION from the materials library and replace that material in the scene. This resets REFLECTION's properties to their original state. Click on an empty sample window, choose **Material/Get Material**, and load the REFLECTION MASK material.

    The REFLECTION MASK material uses the same bitmap mask in the previous material. This time, however, the bitmap is used as an opacity map. The map, along with the Self Illumination slider, enables you to continuously vary the mask texture from black to white. Further map adjustments for blur and scaling enable you to vary the mask from wispy to sharp. You can control color by varying the material's diffuse values (see fig. 10.5).

9. Render this scene. The REFLECTION MASK material has already been assigned to the `Refl_mask` object. Experiment by changing various settings of the REFLECTION MASK material. Be sure to put your changed materials into the scene (press T).

Figure 10.5
A rendering of the original reflection applied to `Refl_plane` *and a second material, REFLECTION MASK, applied to a copy of* `Refl_plane`.

Applying Glows

Another instance where supplemental geometry can be useful is when applying glows and other simulated optical effects to 3D objects. Essentially, the process consists of rendering the scene's camera view to a file, processing this in a paint program to blur or otherwise manipulate it, and then mapping the result on a plane that is aligned in front of the camera. The following steps take you through this process.

1. Load the ARTMAP.PRJ file, which appears in figure 10.6.

The first thing to do is create a mask image that can be used to create the glow. This bitmap need only consist of flat matte shapes for the key text and the key itself, and the reflection of the matte shapes.

2. In the Materials Editor, load the materials GLOW and NOGLOW.

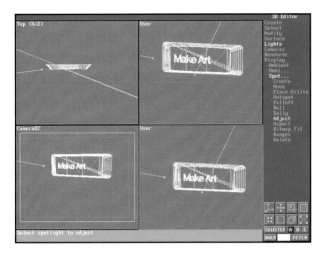

Figure 10.6
The project used to render the matte image that is used to create the glow.

These materials are designed to make it easy to create glow masks. GLOW is a white material with no shininess and 100 percent self-illumination; NOGLOW is matte black. As you might expect, applying GLOW and NOGLOW to a 3D object results in a picture of the object's silhouette. This makes these materials perfect for creating flat masks from 3D geometry. Before rendering the mask, you must hide all objects except those that will appear glowed (Key and Key_label in this chapter) or any objects that reflect the glow (Refl_plane). You must also turn off all lights prior to rendering.

3. In the 3D Editor, use **Surface/Material/Choose** and **Surface/Material/Assign** to apply the GLOW material to the Key object and the NOGLOW material to the Key_label object. If the scene had other objects other than those that glow or reflect the glow, you would hide them at this point before rendering. Make sure all the lights in the scene are off. Don't forget the Ambient light. Everything is now set up to produce the mask image.

4. Render the scene from the Camera02 viewport and save the result to disk as GLOWKEY.TIF. When the rendering is done, view the image. The rendered image consists of a flat white matte of the key with a black matte of the label text "Make Art" and its reflection (see fig. 10.7).

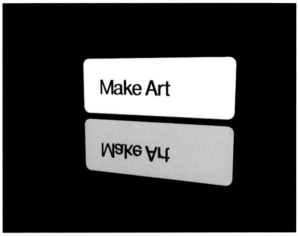

Figure 10.7
The rendered matte image.

5. Next, process the matte image with an application that can apply effect filters to a bitmap image. Load the GLOWKEY.TIF file and apply a blur effect to the entire image. The image should look similar to figure 10.8 when you are done. Use a Gaussian blur in Adobe Photoshop or Aldus PhotoStyler, or a Glow in HiRes QFX. Any number of other single or multiple filter combinations may be applied to simulate numerous optical effects. Save the image as GLOWKEY2.TIF.

Figure 10.8
The result of blurring the GLOWKEY image.

The next step is to create a plane in front of and aligned to the camera view. The GLOWKEY.TIF bitmap is applied to the plane to create the glow. Because aligning the plane is a time consuming and tedious task, the plane has been created and aligned for you in ARTGLOW.PRJ. You can either create and align the plane yourself or load the ARTGLOW project file and follow the description of how the scene was created.

1. Load the ARTGLOW.PRJ file.

The scene in this project file was created in the following way:

- In the Shaper, a quad was created with the same aspect ratio as the final image output. For this example, the output file aspect ratio is that of a 640×480 image. A quad was made to the same dimensions.

- In the 3D Editor, a User view was created from a second camera view. The quad was then imported from the 2D Shaper into this User view with shape detail set to Low. The object was named FXscreen and appears in the scene as a red rectangle aligned to the camera view.

- Some moves were necessary to precisely align FXscreen to the Camera view. 3D Studio camera cones do not always exactly reflect either the aspect ratio or crop of the current output resolution. For this reason, the alignment process was one of working in the Top, Front, and User views and assessing the results in the Camera view. The 3D Editor's viewports were set as in figure 10.9, with the Camera view and a User view made from the second camera view.

- Precise alignment of the FXscreen is critical to assure that the effect is positioned as expected. This was accomplished in ARTGLOW.PRJ by zooming in very close and moving FXscreen to assure an exact match with the camera view. 3D Studio's safe frame feature was used in the camera view to provide an alignment template that reflects the aspect ratio of the output image.

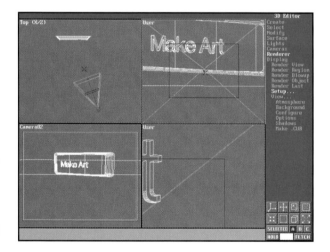

Figure 10.9
Aligning FXscreen to the Camera02 view.

2. In the Materials Editor, get the material SCREEN GLOW. This material uses GLOWKEY2.TIF as an opacity map with 100% Self Illumination. Ambient, Diffuse and Specular are set to the same pale orange.

Varying the Self Illumination and Opacity sliders provides a useful range of transparency and glow brightness. You can change the GLOWKEY2.TIF opacity map to use the image you blurred in an earlier step.

3. Apply the SCREEN GLOW material to the FXscreen object using Planar mapping. Choose **Surface/Mapping/Adjust/Face Align** to align the planar mapping icon to the FXscreen object. Then choose **Surface/ Mapping/Adjust/Scale**, hold down Alt, and click on the FXscreen object. This scales the icon exactly to the object.

4. Render the scene. The result should look like the lower image on the first page. A pale orange glow appears around the Make Art key and in its reflection as well.

Animating the glow is a simple matter of creating an animated version of GLOWKEY2.TIF after you have keyframed the Make Art key's moves. If you intend to animate the camera, be sure to link the camera, camera target, and FXscreen object to a common dummy object. This is essential because the spatial relationship between the camera and FXscreen must remain constant. Load ARTGLOW.PRJ and render the animation or playback ARTGLOW.FLI. Remember that the procedure works most effectively if you think of it as a final step in your animation. It is best applied after all scene elements, lighting, and camera view have been perfected.

Another interesting possibility would be modeling the light pattern around the translucent end of a burning candle or sparkler. Once again, you could use animation to vary the object's translucency or lighting based on the position of a flickering candle flame or pattern of sparks.

The glow procedure is, in part, based on the photographer's matte box, which functions as a combined lens shade, soft edge mask, and optical effects tool. These are used to create vignettes, glows, streaks, smears, and numerous color effects such as gradations. Remember that any number of FXscreens may be stacked to create intricate effects.

Essential here is a reasonable level of facility with your paint program's image processing, brushes, and masking tools. The use of scripting with such programs as Norton's Batch Builder can save a lot of tedium, particularly when processing numerous matte frames.

An interesting alternative to paint programs are any number of video-editing and special-effects programs such as Adobe Premiere, Razor, or Aldus AfterEffects. These are particularly useful for animated mattes or for effects that must vary smoothly or randomly.

Linked together, the camera, camera target, and screen work in very much the same way as the photographer's matte box, but with far greater flexibility.

Conclusion

Using supplemental geometry for masking and effects has uses that extend way beyond the two offered here. For instance, consider its use for modeling hot objects, such as branding irons, coals, or animated embers in a fire. Furthermore, you could animate the glows to produce the effect of distortion due to air convection around a heated object.

by Keith A. Seifert

Castle Rock, Colorado

Equipment and Software Used

IBM-compatible 486/66 with 32 MB of RAM

3D Studio Release 3.0

3D Studio IPAS Toolkit

Metaware High C compiler

PharLap DOS Extender Software Development Kit

Artist Biography

Keith A. Seifert is V.P. of Engineering in charge of program development at Schreiber Instruments, Inc. He has created a series of visual design programs for use with and within 3D Studio and AutoCAD. This series of programs brings true 3D design and modeling to the engineering, architectural, and animation professions. He has an extensive background in engineering problem solving using computer-aided modeling and simulation. He enjoys adding the forces of chaos to mechanical geometries to model the unpredictable 4D geometries of nature. He creates programs that have a functional blend of hard geometry and aesthetics.

Effect Overview

Energy shields are often used in science fiction stories to protect spaceships and space beings. Usually, energy shields are shown as invisible spheres or walls that appear to absorb and dissipate an energy beam. The Energy Shield AXP enables you to easily add this effect to your animations. The use of an *animated stand-in external process* (AXP) to create the energy shield effect enables you to link the shield to another object. With the two objects linked, you can move the shield along with the other object. Animating the appearance of the energy shield linked to a moving ship is a realistic and complex effect.

Procedure

The energy shield effect runs as an AXP in 3D Studio Release 2.0 or higher. This process is a very powerful feature of 3D Studio. It enables you to write a program that generates objects at the time the rendering is being done. The AXP is called for in every frame so it can change the object created from frame to frame.

The energy shield effect takes advantage of the AXP by animating the texture coordinates from frame to frame. These changing coordinates animate the energy shield and create the effect of objects appearing and then disappearing.

Take a look at the sample animation, SHIELD.FLC in the SHIELD directory of the CD-ROM. You can choose **Renderer/View/Flic** in the 3D Editor or Keyframer to play it. The animation shows an attacking beam coming into view from the left side and striking the invisible energy shield protecting the spaceship. The shield begins to absorb the energy and grows, becoming visible over more of its surface. When the beam quits, the shield returns to normal; the ship has been protected. The figure at the beginning of this chapter shows a single frame from the rendered animation. This is the effect you will create with the SHIELD.AXP.

To use the energy shield effect included on the CD, transfer the following files:

1. Add the \SHIELD subdirectory on the CD-ROM to 3D Studio's map paths. If you are using 3D Studio Release 3, this step is not necessary, because Release 3 adds the project load directory to the map paths automatically.

2. Copy the SHIELD_I.AXP file to your 3D Studio process directory. Usually, this is the \3DS3\PROCESS subdirectory.

3. Start 3D Studio as you normally do.

4. Load the project file SHIELD.PRJ from the \SHIELD subdirectory on the CD-ROM. Figure 11.1 shows the 3D Studio 3D Editor with the SHIELD project file loaded.

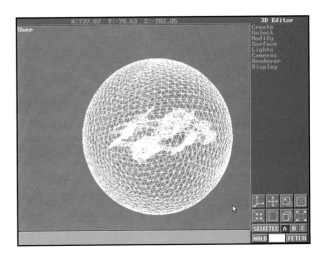

Figure 11.1
The SHIELD.PRJ project file in the 3D Editor.

The energy shield in the scene is made by the AXP during rendering, while the effect itself is created by attaching the SHIELD AXP to the sphere in the scene. In each frame of the animation, the Energy Shield AXP renders all, part, or none of the faces from the sphere. This process could be applied to any object, although any mapping coordinates used by the object would be lost. The more faces the object has, the smoother the effect will look.

1. Choose **Modify/Object/Attributes** and then select the sphere object in the scene. Figure 11.2 shows the Attributes dialog box for the sphere. The SHIELD AXP appears on the External Process Name button.

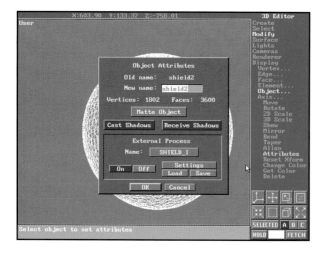

Figure 11.2
The Object Attributes dialog box for the energy shield sphere.

2. Click on the External Process **Settings** button to display the Settings dialog box for the SHIELD process. Figure 11.3 shows the SHIELD AXP Settings dialog box.

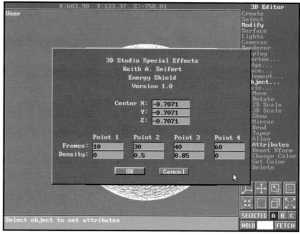

Figure 11.3
The Energy Shield settings dialog box.

The Settings dialog box for the SHIELD process has several options for controlling the creation of the energy shield. These include include setting the starting point for the effect and the density of the effect over time.

The Center X,Y, and Z options enable you to control the location of the starting point or "hot spot" for the energy shield effect. The Center X, Y, and Z coordinates specify a point relative to the local axis origin (0,0,0). If you were to draw a line from the object's origin, through the specified center point, and then to the edge of object, the point where the line intersects the object's edge is the starting point or "hot spot" for the effect. The beam absorbed by the energy shield should travel from it's emitting point along this same line.

The SHIELD AXP has four density animation control points. For each control point, you specify the frame where the control point is located and the density of the effect at that frame. The density value controls the number of faces rendered as a percentage of the total number of faces. Valid values for density are from 0 to 1 (0 = 0% of the faces, 1 = 100% of the faces).

The density value ramps evenly between the density control points. The SHIELD AXP uses the density value of Point 1 in frames prior to its location and the density value of Point 4 in all frames after its location. The density value for Point 1 is usually 0. Point 1 should be set to the frame where the energy beam strikes the shield.

3. When you have finished with the energy shield settings, choose **OK**.

You can save the SHIELD AXP settings in the Object Attributes dialog box. Saving the settings enables you to transfer the settings of the current SHIELD AXP to another object that uses the SHIELD process. To save the settings, choose **Save**, and then enter a file name for the SHIELD settings. To load previously saved settings, click on **Load**, and then select the file with the settings you want to use.

You can do test renderings of your scene without the SHIELD process by turning off the process in the External Process section. The **OFF** selection causes the stand-in box object to render in the scene without creating any energy shields. The current settings of the SHIELD process are retained even though the process is off; turned back on, the SHIELD process uses the same settings as when it was turned off.

> **Try turning off the SHIELD process and rendering one frame of the animation. You'll be surprised by the result. Next, go to the Materials Editor and use Get From Scene on the Material menu to examine the Blue Shield material. You will see that it uses an opacity map named BLK-WHT.TGA that has a resolution of 256×10 and a file size under 8 KB. This small, skinny map is wrapped completely around the sphere when the strength is sufficient, and the gradation in the map provides the shield fading at the opposite point from where the energy beam strikes the sphere.**

4. When you have finished with the Object Attributes dialog box, choose **OK**.

Now that you understand how to set up the energy shield process, you are ready to render the effect.

5. Change to the Keyframer by pressing F4, or by selecting the Keyframer from the Program pull-down menu. Figure 11.4 shows the SHIELD project in the Keyframer.

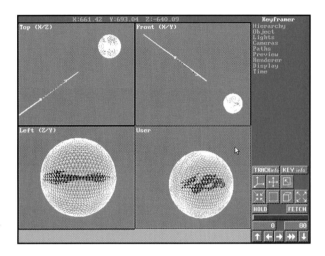

Figure 11.4
The SHIELD.PRJ file in the Keyframer.

6. Choose **Renderer/Render View**, and then select the User viewport.

7. Specify the rendering options you want to use.

8. When the rendering has finished, choose **Renderer/View/Flic** and then select SHIELD.FLC from the file dialog box to see the animation.

The animation shows an attacking beam coming into view and then striking the invisible energy shield. The shield begins to absorb the energy and grows. When the beam quits, the shield returns to normal—the ship has been protected. Figure 11.5 shows a single frame of the rendered animation.

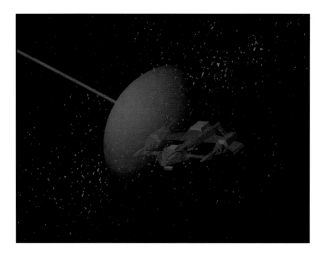

Figure 11.5
A frame from the Energy Shield animation.

A file with the source code for the Energy Shield
AXP is on the CD-ROM with this book, along with
some helpful information for creating your own
IPAS routines. The file is named SHLDSRCE.TXT
and is the \SHIELD subdirectory.

by David Stinnett

Burbank, California

Equipment and Software Used

IBM-compatible 486/66 with 40 MB of RAM

Wacom Tablet

Targa 16/32+ Framebuffer

3D Studio Release 3.0

Aldus Photostyler 2.0

Fractal Design Painter X2 2.0

Yost Group's IPAS Boutique Particle Systems disk

Artist Biography

David Stinnett has spent the past eight years working as a special make-up effects artist and puppeteer for films and television, utilizing skills in prosthetics, sculpting, moldmaking, and animatronics. He has worked on such films as "Terminator 2," "Honey, I Blew Up the Kid," and "Tremors," as well as television shows such as "Tales From the Crypt." He is currently turning his skills toward the digital realm and field of computer effects and is working freelance in that area.

Effect Overview

This chapter details a number of effects that, when used together, give your underwater scenes the illusion of actually being set in the ocean. These include lighting and atmospheric effects that can be done as separate elements in 3D Studio utilizing IPAS modules, or outside 3D Studio in an image processing program. Image programs you can use include Fractal Design Painter, Adobe Photoshop, and Aldus Photostyler, among others. You can then blend these elements together using 3D Studio's Video Post module to create a realistic underwater scene. The final result of the exercise in this chapter is an amazingly realistic still composite image of a humpback whale in a typical ocean scene.

Procedure

Begin by loading the project file that will be used as an example for creating the effect.

1. In 3D Studio, choose **Load Project** from the **File** menu and load the WATERFX.PRJ project file located in the WATERFX subdirectory on the CD-ROM. This is a mesh of a humpback whale that was created in 3D Studio. Figure 12.1 shows the file loaded.

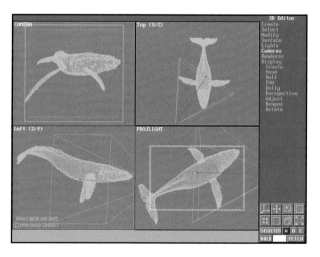

Figure 12.1
The 3D Editor with the WATERFX project file loaded.

Do a preliminary rendering of the scene from the Camera viewport.

2. Choose **Renderer/Render View** and select the Camera viewport.

3. Turn off Anti-aliasing for this exersise to speed rendering times.

4. Choose **OK** to render the scene. You do not need to save it to disk.

5. Look at the resulting image and its background. The best background for this underwater scene is a gradient starting with a bright blue with a little green mixed in at the top and fading to a dark blue/gray at the bottom. You can view the background image, WHLBGND.TGA, by using **Renderer/View/Image** and loading the file from the WATERFX subdirectory on the CD-ROM.

Other than the fact that the subject matter in the foreground is a whale and it is positioned in front of a blue background, there is nothing in the image to suggest it's supposed to be in the water. It will take a bit more than a blue background to bring this scene to life. Here's where the effects come in.

There are some basics to keep in mind when you are creating a realistic underwater scene. Light really doesn't move through water very effectively, so the deeper you go, the less light there is. When only natural light is available, colors tend to disappear in the water. Reds will go first and, as you get deeper, yellow and green go also. By around 60 feet or so, the water absorbs all but blue light. If an artificial light source (such as a flashlight) is introduced at that depth, the colors in an object can be seen again. Try to keep that in mind when creating materials and lighting in your underwater settings.

For example, if the setting is supposed to be fairly deep in the water, you should use very dull colors in your materials and tint the lights in your scene slightly blue. If you have a source for light coming from an object (such as a light on a submarine), you can bring out the colors a bit more under the illumination of those lights.

An effect commonly seen underwater is known as *caustic refraction*. Caustic refractions are the moving light patterns that appear on the tops of objects when they are close to the surface of the water. These patterns are caused by sunlight passing through the water and the light rays being concentrated by the curvature of the waves and ripples in the water's surface. This can be clearly seen by looking at the bottom of a swimming pool on a sunny day. This effect is not always necessary for a believable underwater scene, but when used along with some other effects, it can be extremely effective in creating the illusion.

The easiest way to achieve this in a 3D Studio still image is with a *projector spotlight* and an image of a caustic-refracted light pattern. In 3D Studio, a spotlight can project a bitmap image onto objects in a scene using the Projector function of the light. This can be a scanned image or it can be created in a paint program. The process is the same for an animation, but the projected image should then be a series of frames or an animated moving pattern.

There are many ways to create an animated light pattern. The simplest way is to use an existing one. The World Creating Toolkit CD-ROM that ships with 3D Studio Release 3 contains both a still and an animation of a refraction pattern. You can make one yourself by rotoscoping footage shot on video using a video capture board, a morphing program to create a morph sequence between some stills of light patterns, or even using Video Post to crossfade between some stills and rendering them to an animation.

The resulting animation can then be assigned to the Projector light. The look of the pattern can vary depending on the exact nature of the scene, and some experimentation is usually needed to get

the right look. A good rule of thumb is to decrease the intensity of the light in the caustic pattern as the scene gets deeper. When an object is close to the surface of the water, the light pattern is generally bright and clear, but at greater depths it is dim and softened, sometimes completely. The scene used in this effect uses a still image created in a paint program.

> When creating a caustic pattern to use on a Projector light, it is best to start with a black background and paint light-colored patterns over that. There is a Caustic Refraction pattern included on the CD-ROM. You can view it in 3D Studio using the Renderer/View/Image command and selecting WCAUSTIC.GIF.

6. In the 3D Editor, choose **Lights/Spot/Adjust**, and then click in the PROJLIGHT viewport to bring up the light's settings. Turn on the light, make sure that the Projector button is on, and select the file WCAUSTIC.GIF located on the CD-ROM.

> The bitmap name WCAUSTIC.GIF already appears in the Projector filename slot. If using a release prior to Release 3, click on this button and reset the path to the location of this bitmap on your system. This is true for all bitmaps previously assigned in this chapter. If you are using 3D Studio Release 3, this step is not necessary.

7. Note that the Multiplier for this light is set to 10. Using the light's Multiplier setting can give you more control over the intensity of the effect than just adjusting the color sliders. Leave the value at 10 and click on **OK** to accept the light settings.

8. Render the Camera view again, this time with the Projector light on. This time the image is better, but it still doesn't look like it's underwater, and the whale doesn't look very big.

Adding Underwater Atmosphere

The next step is to add some atmosphere. A common way to add a sense of volume and scale in underwater scenes is to use 3D Studio's Atmosphere Fog feature. This works fine in some cases, but it has its drawbacks.

3D Studio only enables you to use a single color for Fog. If the scene only has a single color as a background, this is not a problem. However, if a color gradient is used for the background, the fog won't match the background. This is especially noticeable during an animation when the camera is moving up or down in the water and the background is getting lighter or darker while the Fog's color over the objects in the scene remains locked at one value. What you need in this situation is a way for the background itself to act as the atmosphere.

Although this is not a feature built into 3D Studio, there is a way to achieve this exact effect using 3D Studio's Video Post module and a *depth matte*. A depth matte is essentially an image containing *alpha* (transparency) information based on the distance of an object from the camera using the camera's ranges. Using this method allows objects in the scene to fade into the background as they get further away from the camera, regardless of whether the background is a solid color, a gradient, or even a bitmap.

1. Because the scene will be put together in Video Post using different elements or layers, you need to render the main element first. This includes all objects in the scene that are to be affected by the atmosphere. Next, add these to other elements to create the final shot. This is refered to as a *composite*.

If you are going to use a depth matte, the background you use when the main layer (in this case, the whale) is rendered is irrelevant, because it will be blocked out by the depth matte. It is a good idea, however, to render the objects in the scene with no background because it will result in smaller file sizes if rendered to compressed Targa files. This can save a lot of disk space when dealing with sequential Targa

files generated for an animation. The one exception to this is if Motion Blur is being used, in which case you should use the background in the final composite for the main layer as well.

2. Choose **Renderer/Setup/Background** and pick **None**. Now choose **Renderer/Render View** and click in the Camera viewport. Normally, if you render an image to be used in a Video Post composite, Render Alpha should be on, but because the alpha information will be coming from a separate image, the Alpha can be turned off in this case.

3. Render the image. This is the main element that is used in the composite. However, you do not need to save the rendered image because the equivalent file is on the CD-ROM. This file is named WHLMAIN.TGA and is located in the WATERFX directory on the CD-ROM.

After rendering, turn off the the Projector light to save memory. It isn't used in later steps.

4. Choose **Lights/Spot/Adjust** and click in the Projlight viewport. Click the **OFF** button and then click on **OK** to exit.

Now you are ready to render the depth matte itself. First you need to make a special material that will be applied to the objects in the scene for the matte rendering. Normally, before starting the next step, you should save the file to disk. This is because some materials are going to be changed and you don't want to accidentally overwrite the file with the original materials. Because this file is on the CD-ROM, however, there is no need for you to save this particular file.

5. Enter the Materials Editor and select an empty material window. Lock the Ambient and Diffuse color values by clicking the **L** button between the two swatches, and then make sure the Ambient or Diffuse color is active.

6. Move the Luminescence slider all the way to the right so that the color values for both the Ambient and Diffuse colors is 255,255,255

(white). Because the material will have 0% Shininess, the Specular color will not be used and can be left alone.

7. Set the Self Illumination slider to 100% and then set the shading mode to Flat.

8. Leave everything else as is and choose **Material/Put To Current** or press the C key to bring up the New Current Material name dialog box. Name the new material **Depth Matte** and click on **OK**.

Refer to figure 12.2 for the Depth Matte material settings.

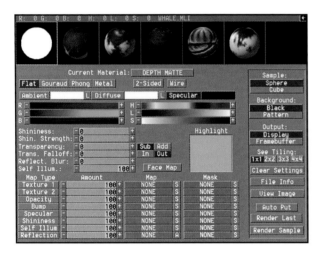

Figure 12.2
The Depth Matte material loaded in the Materials Editor.

9. Press F3 to return to the 3D Editor.

10. Now you need to assign the new material to the objects in the scene. Choose **Surface/Material/Assign/By Name** and select the whale object to assign the new material.

11. Now choose **Renderer/Setup/Atmosphere**, click on the **Distance Cue** button, and then **Define**. Set Near to 0%, Far to 100%, and Dim Background On.

Distance Cue is taken from the Camera's Range settings, which have already been set in this file. This is done with the **Cameras/Ranges** setting in the 3D Editor. You can refer to figure 12.3 to see where the ranges have been set. All objects in the scene should be somewhere between the two ranges. Anything that is between the Camera and the first range will not be affected, and anything beyond the second range will be completely obstructed by the background. By adjusting the Camera ranges and Distance Cue settings, total control of the effect is possible.

Atmosphere is determined by the distance that the camera can see. In clear water you can usually see 100 feet or more, but in cloudy water it is not uncommon to have visibility cut to 15 feet or less. Each scene will require different Camera Range settings, but if your scene is set on a small scale—such as when the camera's view is limited to just a few feet (focused on small fish, for example)—the atmosphere should be barely noticeable, if at all.

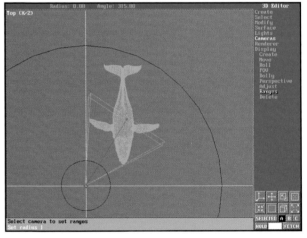

Figure 12.3
Detail of the top viewport showing the Camera's Range settings.

Now you can render the depth matte.

12. Choose **Renderer/Render View** and click in the Camera viewport. Even though the transparency information is being taken from this rendering, it is taken from the color values in the image, so there is no need to turn on Alpha. Click on **OK** and render.

   Once it is done, examine the image. It should be a primarily white silhouette of the whale against a black background. Notice that the further the object is from the camera, the darker it is. Just as in a normal alpha channel, white areas in the image will completely block out the background, while black areas will let it show through completely. All shades of gray in between will have varying degrees of transparency. Figure 12.4 shows the depth matte.

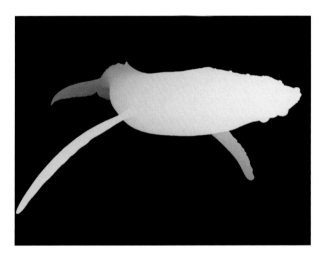

Figure 12.4
The depth matte. This will be used as a mask when placing the whale over the background.

When rendering a depth matte, you must make sure that the viewport and frames rendered are exactly the same as the main object rendering. This means that no camera changes can be made between the time the main frames are rendered and the time the depth mattes are rendered. Anti-aliasing, Field Rendering, and Motion Blur must also be set the same. This is to make sure that both elements line up perfectly when the composite image is created.

There is a pre-rendered depth matte image, named WHLDMAT.TGA, on the CD-ROM, so now you can try creating a composite image.

13. Enter the Keyframer by pressing the F4 key, choose **Renderer/Video Post**, and click in any viewport.

14. In the Video Post dialog box, click on the **Load** button and load the Video Post file WHLCOMP1.VP, which is located in the WATERFX subdirectory of the CD-ROM. There are two entries in the queue. The topmost entry is the blue gradient background and the second is the whale, which is the main element.

15. Choose **Edit** and click in the alpha slot for the lower entry, WHLMAIN.TGA. The **RGB Mask** button is highlighted and the file WHLDMAT.TGA is selected. This is the depth matte and is being used as the alpha for the whale rendering (see fig. 12.5).

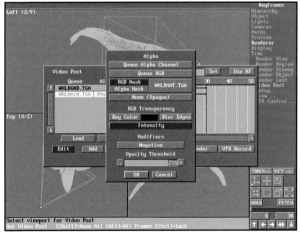

Figure 12.5
The Video Post module in the Keyframer. This screen shows the placement of the depth matte image.

16. Choose **OK** to return to the main Video Post screen.

17. Click the **Render** button in the Video Post dialog box and render a single frame from the Video Post Queue. The whale now looks like it has some scale to it as it fades off into the distance.

18. Press **OK** to exit Video Post.

Depth matte effects can be used for more than just underwater scenes. For example, if you were rendering a blimp flying toward the camera, you could use a picture of some clouds as a background along with a depth matte rendering to give the appearance of the blimp slowly appearing out of the clouds. Adjusting the camera ranges would give you control of where the blimp would appear, and how gradual its appearance (or disappearance) would be.

Adding a Particle Layer

If you examine real footage shot in the ocean, you will notice a lot of little particles floating around. Most of this is plankton—very small organisms that drift in the currents of all the oceans. These organisms exist in such large numbers that they actually cloud the water, which is what causes the usually limited visibility in sea water.

Plankton and other small particles drifting in the water appear as a haze when in the distance, but as they float past the camera at close range you can actually make out the individual particles. These are usually just seen as light-colored specks passing in front of the camera. Adding these to an underwater scene can add yet another level of realism and enhance the overall effect. There are a couple of ways to achieve this.

The best way is with the Yost Group's SNOW.AXP IPAS particle system. Using this, you can make it appear as though hundreds or even thousands of tiny particles are slowly drifting in the current.

This can be set up by placing the AXP stand-in object in front of the camera and have it completely fill the camera's view.

If you have SNOW.AXP, you can create a plankton layer image. First, you'll need to hide the whale.

1. Choose **Display/Hide/By Name** and hide the object named whale.

2. Now choose **Display/Unhide/By Name** and unhide the object partbox.

3. Choose **Object/Attributes**, click on the box and assign SNOW.AXP to it, and then click on **Setup**. Set the Number of Particles to 7500, the Object/Flake diameter ratio to 0.003, the Object/Flake Spiral ratio to 0.1, and the Snowfall period and Random # Seed can be left as is. Make sure the Start, Peak, Hold, and End values are all set to 0, and the Wind and Chaos sliders set between 30 and 100. Leave the Triangle button highlighted. Figure 12.6 shows the settings used for this scene.

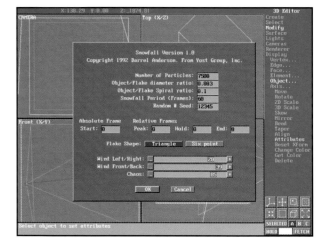

Figure 12.6
The Yost Group's SNOW.AXP particle system IPAS module was used for generating particles floating in the water. The settings shown were used in this scene.

4. Click on **OK** or press Enter to accept these values and exit the Object Attributes dialog box.

5. Render the Camera viewport and look at the results. Because this is the only layer required to have alpha information rendered with the file, make sure Alpha is turned on and the background is set to None.

   If you do not have SNOW.AXP, choose **Renderer/View Image** and select the file WHLPART.TGA in the WATERFX subdirectory of the CD-ROM. This is an image created with SNOW.AXP and is used in the composite later in this chapter. These particles will be combined on top of the scene.

The material used for the particles is important for the look of the composite image.

6. Press F5 to enter the Materials Editor, and then choose **Material/Get From Scene**. You can also press the F key and pick the material Particle from the list.

7. Look at the material settings. The material is flat-shaded to save rendering time, but is also two-sided, required by SNOW.AXP. It also has some transparency and is fully self-illuminated so that the lighting in the scene will not affect it.

   The material will differ depending on the nature of the scene and, as always, a little experimentation is the best way to find the best settings for an individual scene.

8. Leave the material settings as they are and press F4 to return to the Keyframer.

If you don't have the Yost Group's IPAS Particle Systems disk, you can achieve the same type of effect by just making an image in a paint program. The best method is to paint many tiny light specks right on the rendered image. This is impractical for an animation, but you can draw up the particles on a black background and use this as an opacity map in a material.

In an opacity map, dark areas of the map are transparent while light areas are opaque. You could then apply this material to a flat object and place it in front of the camera lens like a sheet of glass with light colored specks painted on it. Then slowly move this object across the screen during the course of the animation to give the appearance of the particles floating in the current. Adding another opacity-mapped particle object or two moving at slightly different speeds and directions would also enhance the effect.

Doing it this way takes a bit of experimentation, but remember to render each particle layer with Alpha on and to hide all other objects in the scene. Then insert each layer as a separate layer for the final Video Post composite.

> **Whether you use SNOW.AXP or create the particles in a paint program, remember to keep the particles small and not too much brighter than the rest of the scene. The effect should be subtle. If the particles stand out too much, they'll start looking more like stars in the sky than particles in the water.**

Now try creating a composite with the particles added.

1. In the Keyframer, choose **Renderer/Video Post** and click in any viewport.

2. In Video Post, click on **Load** and load the file WHLCOMP2.VP from the CD-ROM. This time there is a third entry in the queue. This is the 32-bit particle image with the Queue Alpha active.

> **If this was an animation, IFL files would be listed in the queue instead of the still images. IFL files are text files telling the Renderer to use a series of frames, usually sequentially numbered Targa files, listed in the IFL. Refer to your *3D Studio Reference Manual* for details on how to use IFL files.**

3. Now click on the **Render** button in the Video Post dialog box and render a frame to the screen. You should see the whale fading into

the distance with some particles floating in front of the camera. You would normally save the composite at this time because you need to use it in one last step, but this composite is in the WATERFX subdirectory of the CD-ROM as WHLCOMP.TGA. Figures 12.7 and 12.8 show the scene before and after some of the underwater effects have been applied.

Figure 12.7
The scene rendered without any underwater effects added.

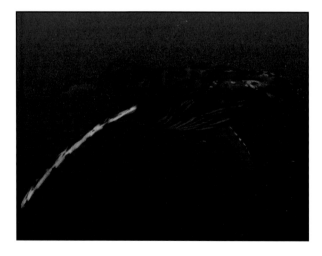

Figure 12.8
The same scene with a combination of several under-water effects.

Softening the Image

Adding one final touch will complete the effect. Things in the ocean have a tendency to look slightly diffused. They are not out of focus, but they have a much softer look. This next step involves blurring a copy of the composite from the last step and blending it into the original so that both images are visible. This will soften the look of the image without losing any of the detail.

1. In the Keyframer, choose **Renderer/Video Post** and load the Video Post file WHLCOMP3.VP located on the CD-ROM.

    The first entry in the Queue is the file WHLCOMP.TGA, which is the composite containing the background, the whale (with the depth matte), and the particles. The second entry is WHLBLUR.TGA, which is the same image, but it was brought into Aldus Photostyler 2.0 and blurred with the Guassian Blur filter set at 9. Any image-editing program with a Guassian Blur filter can be used, or Fractal Design Painter's Soften filter will work also. The exact setting for the filter varies depending on which program is used, the resolution of the image, and the intensity desired for the effect.

    NOTE This effect works best using a standard Guassian Blur filter, but when creating an animation, processing each frame in an image-editing program can be quite time-consuming, if not impossible. There are some programs out that will batch process sequentially numbered image files, and these could be used to blur copies of the composite. The Yost Group's BLUR.IXP IPAS module can also be used in Video Post to process the frames. BLUR.IXP uses a different blur algorithm than a Guassian Blur filter. The Guassian Blur seems to work better for this particular effect, especially for still images.

2. Click in the Alpha slot after the second entry. An RGB Mask is being used to regulate how much of the first entry will show through the second.

The result of the composite should be a slight softening of the image so less of the blurred entry should be visible. The W40GREY.GIF file being used for the mask is a solid gray image created in a paint program. The image is 40% gray, which means that the second entry in the queue is 60% transparent. If an RGB Mask was used that was 70% gray (0% is black, 100% is white), the second image would be 30% transparent, allowing only 30% of the first image to show through, resulting in a much softer final composite. You can gain complete control over the final composite by using different shades of gray for the RGB Mask.

3. Press Enter to return to the main Video Post dialog box.

It is quite common to see bubbles in underwater settings. If done properly, they can add a lot to underwater animations. There are at least two Bubble IPAS routines available commercially. These will let you create and animate bubbles easily—a nice touch for any underwater scene.

4. Render a frame from Video Post. The result of the last step is subtle, but it adds an extra touch of realism to the image that makes it look a little more natural and less like it was created on a computer. This is the final image and is on the CD-ROM as WATERFX.TGA.

Conclusion

The examples and effects listed here are just some of the ways to help create realistic underwater scenes. With all the possibilities 3D Studio has to offer, many other effects can be used to add even more to your images and animations.

When using the procedures outlined here either together or separately, you can achieve many different effects that can enhance a wide variety of images and animations created with 3D Studio.

With a little imagination and experimentation, you can use these effects for more than just underwater scenes.

The key is exploration. The more you use 3D Studio and the more you experiment with different procedures, the more tricks of your own you will discover. Some great tricks have been discovered while just playing around, even by accident. Combining various effects in different ways can generate some truly unique results. Don't be afraid to use your imagination or to use different tools that can be used to enhance your work. But most importantly, have fun!

by Gregory Pyros, AIA

Newport Beach,
California

Equipment and Software Used

Three Sun SparcStation servers

Sixteen networked 486/66 PCs, each with 48 MB of RAM

Sony Beta SP frame-accurate video tape recorder and Sony editor

Sony 3/4" tape decks and Convergence editor

Digital Processing Systems personal animation recorder

Yamaha computer-controlled audio mixer

3D Studio Release 3.0

AutoCAD Release 12

Animator Pro 1.3

Ron Scott HiRes QFX

Altamira Composer 2.0

Adobe PhotoShop 2.5

Custom image processing software developed by Pyros Pictures, Inc.

Artist Biography

Gregory G. Pyros, AIA, founded Pyros Pictures, Inc. (formerly Pyros Partnership) in 1981. He is one of the country's most advanced computer animation and video consultants, providing consulting expertise in all phases of computer graphics operations, programming and configurations, and inter-operability between UNIX and DOS.

Nationally known in the computer industry for integration of computer technology into the architectural and animation fields, Pyros Pictures provides broadcast-quality computer animations for use within the architectural, advertising, broadcast, legal, and corporate presentation fields.

Awards received by Pyros Pictures include First Place in the Autodesk Images Competition, First Place, Second Place, and Third Place in the CADalyst Caddies Awards, and Citation of Excellence in the AEC/Systems Show Awards. Broadcast credits include three CBS prime time specials, plus segments for National Geographic "Explorer" and "Nova."

Greg is the co-author of Inside 3D Studio, *by New Riders Publishing. He has been selected to* Who's Who in California *for the past 10 years.*

Effect Overview

This chapter describes the process for combining computer animations, animated alpha mattes, and live video with perfectly composited edges in a broadcast-quality video production studio. It covers not only what must be done in the animator's studio, but also what happens when the project is sent out to a post-production editing house for final compositing.

Once understood, creating animations with associated animated mattes is extremely easy to accomplish, and is a requirement for creating broadcast quality titles and similar work. When done properly, the titles can be used over and over again, overlaying them on top of different live video footage.

Without a proper alpha matte, the best that can be done with the title is to overlay it with the live footage by electronically removing the animation's background color in the editing studio and replacing it with the live video. There are many problems with this method, however.

The most obvious problem is where there may be shades of the background color in the title, and parts of the live video accidentally show through. Another problem with this method is that the edges of the animation always look rough and jagged when seen against the live video. A third problem occurs when there are parts of the animation that are supposed to be partially transparent, such as a glass effect or a shadow, but they appear totally opaque without a matte. Figure 13.1 shows these problems. The area near the front of the surfboard is completely covered by the text. Also, there is a black line of jagged pixels around each letter where the key color threshold changes.

Figure 13.1
The tell-tail signs of non-alpha matte keying.

To fully understand the principle of a matte, there are a few concepts that you must first understand. They are anti-aliasing, alpha, and A/B/C roll editing.

Understanding Anti-Aliasing

Aliasing occurs whenever a device composed of individual pixels, such as a monitor or television set, displays a non-vertical or non-horizontal edge of an object. If a yellow object is placed on a blue background, the border pixels of the object and background must be either blue or yellow. This results in the familiar *stair step* or *jaggies*. *Anti-aliasing* is the process of creating intermediate colors—in this case, shades of green—where the yellow object meets the blue background to fool the viewer into believing that there is the same perfectly smooth edge as would be seen in real life. Figure 13.2 shows an aliased (upper left) and an anti-aliased (lower right) object.

Figure 13.2
An example of aliasing and anti-aliasing.

Unfortunately, anti-aliasing can work against you, also. If you had created a yellow object against a blue background, with perfectly anti-aliased green edges, and the live video color was later changed to red, the edges of your animation would stick out like a sore thumb with their green tint! No matter how good your animation is, the effect would be totally spoiled. As you see later, creating a traveling alpha matte enables you to change the live video color and always have a perfect edge between the computer graphics and the video image.

Understanding Alpha

Alpha, sometimes referred to as either the *alpha channel*, *transparency channel*, or *alpha matte*, is an 8-bit (256 colors) grayscale representation of your image. If you render an object against a black background, the alpha channel consists of white pixels in areas where the object is opaque; the alpha channel is black in areas with no object. In the alpha channel, areas where anti-aliasing occurs and areas that are partially transparent (such as glass or shadows) render as shades of gray.

Alpha information can be stored as part of a Targa file. Normally, a true-color Targa file consists of 24 bits of color, or 16.7 million colors. Adding the alpha information increases the file to 32 bits. The alpha information is not visible, so a 32-bit file appears no different than a 24-bit file when viewed.

The alpha information can also be stored as a separate 8-bit file. 3D Studio writes this separate file as an 8-bit Targa file, where the file name always starts with A_ as in A_GP0000.TGA. Because it is only 8 bits of information, the separate file could just as easily be a GIF or FLIC file. There are some image-editing programs that cannot read an 8-bit Targa file, so the alpha files must be converted to either 16- or 24-bit Targa files before these programs can process the image.

When an image with alpha information is overlaid on another image, areas of white pixels in the alpha channel cause the upper or foreground image to show. Areas of black pixels in the alpha channel cause lower or background image to show. In the areas where there are gray pixels in the alpha channel, the percentage of gray in the pixel determines what percentage of the upper image color to blend with the lower image. Using the alpha channel to control the blending of foreground image with the background image gives total independence from the colors used in each.

Understanding A/B/C Roll Video Editing

The letters *A/B/C*, when used in context with video editing, refer to the source video devices used in the edit suite. Simple A roll video editing uses one source deck and one record deck, and enables cuts-only editing, giving only a straight cut between images. A/B roll editing utilizes two source decks and enables transitions such as dissolves, fades, wipes, etc. between the two video sources.

A/B/C roll gives all these capabilities, and in addition, enables the use of an alpha channel on one of the decks to control the amount of opacity when one video image is overlaid on another. This is very similar to the process for overlaying one computer image on another as described previously. The A deck is the background live video footage, the B deck is the full-color animation video, and the C deck is for the matte video. When each deck is cued and playing in sync, a perfect composite image results.

Because each element of the composite image is separate, it is an easy matter to substitute other background footage on the A deck and record a number of different composites. This is often used when a show has titles used over one background, and commercial breaks use the same titles with different images behind them.

Procedure

Now that the theory is understood, the actual creation of the matte is almost automatic. Only a few changes from your normal rendering procedure are required. You just need to tell 3D Studio to save separate alpha channel files.

 This chapter assumes you have 30 seconds of recorded video footage and access to A/B/C roll video equipment.

1. Start 3D Studio and open the LOGO.PRJ project file in the \ALPHAMAT directory on the CD-ROM. This file contains the project used to create the logo on the facing page of this chapter. The text objects for LOGO have semi-transparent materials applied to them. The animation set up in the Keyframer is a simple camera dolly.

2. When your animation is ready to render, choose **Renderer/Setup/Options** to display the Render Options dialog box.

3. Set TGA Depth to 24. Alpha information cannot be saved to 16-bit Targa files.

4. Turn on Render Alpha Alpha Split. These settings tell 3D Studio to render the alpha channel and write it to a separate file. See figure 13.2 for the dialog box settings.

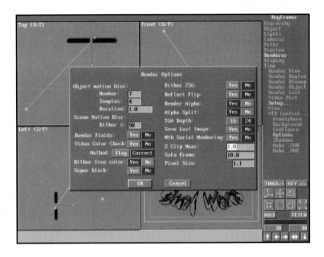

Figure 13.3
The Render Options dialog box settings for creating alpha matte files.

5. Go to the Keyframer, choose **Renderer/Render View**, and select the Camera viewport to render the animation and alpha matte.

 If you have previously rendered the animation frames without the alpha matte and need to create the alpha matte, set 3D Studio to render with the Flat shading limit and with Mapping turned off. These settings render very quickly and, when combined with Alpha Split, create the matte frames. The 24-bit image files can be deleted using a batch file in video post to conserve disk space.

6. Once the animation's image and matte frames are rendered, record the image files on one tape and the alpha files on another tape using a frame-accurate VTR. You must put the images on separate tapes because each tape goes into a separate tape deck for compositing.

7. Review the tapes to view the alpha matte and to check for problems. If you do not have access to a frame-accurate VTR, compile the alpha files into a FLIC and view them on your computer. Figure 13.4 shows a frame from the animation and 13.5 shows the alpha file used for this frame.

8. If you have access to A/B/C roll equipment, overlay the images and alpha mattes on a live video background to see the image quality this process of overlay produces. Look at the figure on the opening page of this chapter and look at the surfboard and wave highlights visible through the logo.

Conclusion

This process can be duplicated in 3D Studio itself using Video Post. You first need to rotoscope the live video background. Rotoscoping is the process of digitizing video frames and saving them as individual files. Once you have the rotoscoped images, you just need two entries in the Video Post queue: one for the rotoscoped frames and one for the Keyframer scene. The high resolution image on this chapter's opening page was created using this method. (Yes, it's cheating, but video doesn't provide the resolution needed for print images.)

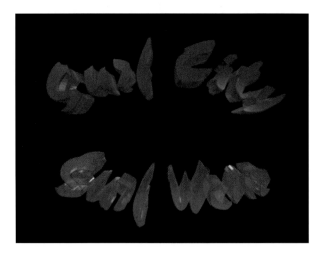

Figure 13.4
The animation image.

Figure 13.5
The alpha channel matte.

by Phillip Miller

San Rafael, California

Equipment and Software Used

IBM-compatible 486/66 with 32 MB of RAM

3D Studio Release 3.0

AutoCAD Release 12

Animator Pro 1.3

Photostyler 2

Artist Biography

Phillip Miller is a registered architect currently working with Autodesk, Inc. as the senior multimedia instructor at their San Rafael, California campus. Most recently he co-authored New Rider Publishing's successful Inside 3D Studio *and has made numerous contributions to* CADENCE *magazine. Before joining Autodesk, Phillip was a project architect and visualization specialist for a full-service architectural and engineering firm in northern Illinois. He graduated from the University of Illinois with a Masters of Architecture and additional concentrations in Painting and Computer Science.*

Effect Overview

Most modelers that use AutoCAD in conjunction with 3D Studio do so by importing their three-dimensional models directly into the 3D Editor. Rules, procedures, and even tricks for making this import smoothly are many, and the complete conversion can be time consuming if the model was not created in AutoCAD with 3D Studio in mind. Although importing meshes can work well, dual users are only utilizing half the potential of the two programs by ignoring 3D Studio's 3D Lofter and 2D Shaper combination.

What eludes most users of both AutoCAD and 3D Studio is how powerful it is to loft their imported DXF shapes along their DXF paths. Such lofts can create intricately modeled pieces that fit perfectly into the remainder of what is probably an AutoCAD model already in the 3D Editor. It is this technique that this chapter explores.

AutoCAD Precision and Coordination

3D Studio and AutoCAD each have their own virtues. Whereas 3D Studio's interface is fluid and intuitive, it does lack the capability to be extremely accurate and interact with databases of additional information. These are capabilities that AutoCAD handles very well, albeit with a more rigid interface. Used together, they form a very precise and powerful modeler that has access to an incredible database of information. The key is in learning some basic techniques to maximize this synergy.

AutoCAD's primary advantage over 3D Studio is it's extreme accuracy. Although this level of alignment is not needed by most animations, it is required for high-resolution still images that can be closely examined and for those professions that use 3D Studio as a visualization tool—studying the resulting model in detail. For these uses, it becomes very important for the modeled components to align precisely with each other.

When beginning a project, it is very common to already have available related information in AutoCAD format that either has been developed or is still in the design process. These could be the shop drawings for furniture, a development's site plan, conceptual drawings for a new product, or proposed architectural plans. Even though such information is two dimensional, they all hold the potential for being valuable sources as future 3D Studio shapes and lofter paths.

Alignment between AutoCAD and 3D Studio

The first thing to grasp is that both AutoCAD and 3D Studio define and store their coordinates for three dimensional space in the same manner:

- AutoCAD's *world axis* of 0,0,0 aligns exactly with 3D Studio's home *global axis* every time. This is regardless of what the current user coordinate system (UCS) may have been in AutoCAD or how 3D Studio's construction planes and global axis have been placed, or even if its axis labels changed in its 3DS.SET file.

- AutoCAD's X,Y plane always relates to 3D Studio's Top viewport (its default X,Z plane), regardless of any AutoCAD UCS realignment or 3D Studio axes re-labeling.

- Paths within the 3D Lofter align exactly with the 3D Editor's coordinate system. This means that an AutoCAD polyline, imported to the 3D Lofter as a path, will create objects that align exactly with the rest of what could be an imported AutoCAD model in the 3D Editor.

- The 2D Shaper's DXF interpretation of two-dimensional geometry is quite different than the preceding rules. Here all imported geometry is projected flat, back to what was AutoCAD's X,Y plane. This means that all AutoCAD geometry intended for use in the 2D Shaper must be drawn, or rotated back, to be parallel to AutoCAD's World UCS X,Y plane *before* exporting DXF files or it will be severely distorted.

- The 2D Shaper's horizontal and vertical coordinates relate directly to AutoCAD's X and Y. Note, however, that objects created from these shapes derive their three-dimensional location from the 3D Lofter's path. The 2D Shaper's coordinates are only relative if an object is created with the 3D Editor's **Create/Object/Get Shape** command.

Knowing these basic rules enables you to import very accurate, or already created, shapes and paths from AutoCAD to 3D Studio for lofting.

The issues dealing with the translation of AutoCAD DXF files into 3D Studio is a subject that is beyond the scope of this chapter. Readers that need detailed information on the procedure should examine Chapter 11 of *Inside 3D Studio,* **from New Riders Publishing.**

3D Lofter Contouring

The 3D Lofter's Contour option is nearly always a given for lofted shapes. As the left side of figure 14.1 shows, contouring means that as the shape travels along the path, it physically rotates to accommodate corners and bends so the resulting extrusion is without severe kinks or flat spots. When used without modification, this feature works great for lofting organic shapes or along gently curving paths. But as you will see, you do need to modify the procedure when lofting exact or rectilinear geometry.

Examining the right side of figure 14.1 shows that the lofted mesh contains sections where the mesh is tapering. This is because the lofted shape maintains the same scale throughout the path, even as it rotates. The more the shape rotates, the thinner the resulting profile becomes. This may not be noticeable at first if the path contains a series of similarly angled corners, because all the shapes will be rotated and the resulting segments will be straight and may appear to be correct. The fact is that these segments have been scaled, they have

just been scaled uniformly. This scaling occurs in figure 14.1's path for vertices 2–5 and 6–9, resulting in what appear to be three straight, correct segments.

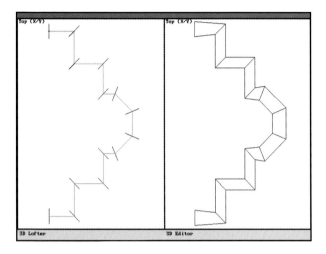

Figure 14.1
A preview of a contoured loft and the resulting mesh in the 3D Editor.

Adjusting for Contour Rotation

A lofted shape is always going to rotate when the Contour option is used. The trick to making a correct loft is to scale the rotated shape so that it forms a correctly sized section and to place these corrected shapes at the transitional corners so the resulting mesh no longer tapers. With Contour on, the shape travels along the path and rotates as it makes turns at an angle that is one half of the path's included angle (a shape making a 90° turn is rotated 45°, for example). Fortunately, the scale decrease caused by this rotation is a basic expression of the included angle

Scale Decrease from Rotation = COSINE θ

where θ is the shape's rotational adjustment (which is one half of the included angle of the path). The correcting ratio by which your shape needs to be increased at a given path corner is the inverse of the preceding scale decrease:

Correction Scale Factor = 1 / COSINE θ

This chapter's discussion assumes you are lofting along two-dimensional paths. Because of this, the shape is only rotating about one axis; thus only its width needs to be corrected. The 2D Shaper can perform this scale quite easily by using **Modify/Polygon/Scale** constrained to the horizontal.

When creating a series of varying scaled shapes for lofting, it is very convenient to place the global axis and the hook at the same location. This enables you to Shift+Scale the original shape and move the iterations to the side by an even snap increment. You then can move all the shapes from side to side as a selection and align the required shape set with the same hook location for their respective export to the 3D Lofter.

After the shapes have been scale-corrected in the 2D Shaper, insert them at each path corner that is a change in angle from the previous path corner, as shown in figure 14.2. The resulting mesh now has a cross section that is constant along the object's entire length—a critical characteristic to many modeling situations.

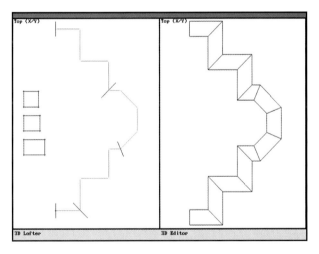

Figure 14.2
Scaled shapes placed at changing path angles and the resulting mesh having a constant cross section.

The extent to which the first, uncorrected loft was distorted is very clear when you compare the resulting meshes side by side. Figure 14.3 points out this difference by overlaying the two meshes. The outer mesh is the result of using the scale corrected shapes, whereas the inner, tapering mesh was formed from lofting one shape across the entire path.

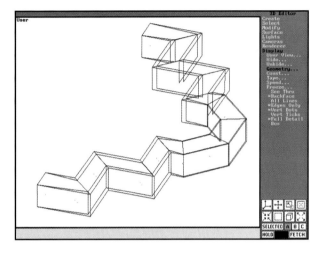

Figure 14.3
Comparing corrected and uncorrected lofts.

Limits to the 2D Shaper's Scaling Precision

The one unfortunate limitation to this method is that 3D Studio's scaling precision in the 2D Shaper is limited to increments of 0.25%—a limit that can hinder the accuracy of the adjustment. Table 14.1 is a quick reference of the correcting scale ratios needed for common angles and the resulting 2D Shaper percentage approximations.

Table 14.1
Scale Ratios for Column Angles

Typical Geometry	Corner Angle	Rotation Angle	Scaling Ratio	2D Shaper's Percentage
Triangle	120°	60°	2.0000000	200.00%
Rectangle	90°	45°	1.4142136	141.50%
Pentagon	72°	36°	1.2360680	123.50%
Hexagon	60°	30°	1.1547005	115.50%
Octagon	45°	22.5°	1.0823922	108.25%
10-sided	36°	18°	1.0514622	105.25%
12-Sided	30°	15°	1.0352762	103.50%

Although the 2D Shaper's 0.25% limit does create a discrepancy, it's only about 1 inch per 100 feet. If this deviation is noticeable or unacceptable, your recourse is to perform the scale within AutoCAD. If you already are modeling the profiling shapes in AutoCAD, it might make the most sense to perform the accurate adjustment there and export the modified shapes directly to the 2D Shaper for lofting.

You could use the 3D Lofter's Scale Deformation feature instead of inserting previously scaled shapes to accomplish the same result. Although the Deform/Scale command has a precision of 0.01%, the placement of the scale change is very difficult to pinpoint and must be repeated individually for every corner location within the path.

Unequal Scaling in AutoCAD

Although AutoCAD is capable of very accurate adjustments, scaling entities about one axis in AutoCAD Release 12 is not nearly as easy as in 3D Studio's 2D Shaper. AutoCAD's SCALE command only enables you to scale a selection uniformly about all three axes. The only way it is possible to perform an unequal scale is to create a block of the selected entities and insert it with different X and Y scale factors. To make this operation as painless as possible, the AutoLISP routine LFTSCALE.LSP is included on the CD-ROM to automate the procedure and make it quite fast and very accurate.

LFTSCALE.LSP contains two utilities—MANGLE for measuring path angles and SCLOFT for creating unequally scaled Blocks. Both are available once you have loaded LFTSCALE by typing (**LOAD "PATH\LFTSCALE"**) from the AutoCAD command line or using AutoCAD's APPLOAD function.

MANGLE calculates what the lofted shape's rotation angle will be for a given path corner. You are prompted for two angle measurements; the routine states the resulting included angle and returns half that angle in the form of a stored variable. To make calculating the angles quicker, you can enter a return at the angle requests to select a line entity or polyline line segment instead and acquire the resulting angle without needing to manually enter it.

For any two line segments there will always be two possible angles—one obtuse and one acute. The correct angle will be dependent on which direction the shape is traveling and which way it is facing. Because of this, two complementary angles are stated and stored for your future use—it is up to you to decide which is appropriate for your particular loft.

SCLOFT creates a block of a selection set and inserts it at a given point, with a Y&Z Scale of 1.0 and an X Scale increased to correct for the given rotation. You are first prompted for an angle to make the adjustment (this angle is the rotation increment for the shape at the given path vertex/corner). You can enter this angle conventionally or, more conveniently, use one of the two angles calculated and stored by MANGLE. These can be retrieved by entering a return at the angle request prompt and then entering the appropriate one (these rotation angles are stored globally as R1 and R2 and can be retrieved by other LISP routines as well).

Next, you are prompted for the entities to be scaled and the point about which to scale them. A block is then created and inserted at the selected point with the correcting X scale ratio. You do not have to make a copy of your selection set because LSCALE leaves the originals undisturbed and inserts a unique block reference. The scale of this operation is to AutoCAD's full 16 decimal places of accuracy.

Reminders When Using DFXFOUT

An overview of some of the AutoCAD's DXFOUT command conventions will make importing the DXF files of the scaled blocks much easier. Of the various DXFOUT options available to you, the Binary option is the most useful for exporting to 3D Studio. This option writes a compact DXF file of the entire drawing to AutoCAD's highest degree of precision.

The most important thing to remember is that, because you are exporting block entities in this procedure, you cannot use the DXFOUT command's Entity option. Using the Entity option writes a file that contains only the Entity section of the DXF format and not the critical Block Table section.

The next thing to remember is that 3D Studio skips any entities that reside on layers that are off or frozen when the DXF file was created. This can lead to some confusion with blocks because they can be composed of entities residing on multiple layers and be inserted on yet another layer. This means that when the insertion layer is off, the block could still display correctly in AutoCAD but be skipped by 3D Studio's DXF interpreter. Although this is not usually a problem, remembering this fact can prevent some confusing situations.

A common method to isolate the required blocks in a complete DXF file is to create a unique layer for the future shape profiles/blocks and turn off all other layers. If the drawing is of significant size, the DXF files can become quite large and loading them into 3D Studio can take time. Alternative methods to reduce DXF file size (and thus translation time) include the following:

Creating a new drawing that contains only the required blocks with the WBLOCK command, loading the smaller drawing, and then use DXFOUT

or

Erase all other entities, use DXFOUT, and then either QUIT or use OOPS to unerase the rest of the drawing.

Procedure: Lofting Cornices and Trim

There often is a need to create the trim work that encircles a room or traces the outlines of furniture or cabinetry. This project involves the visualization of a proposed room that is being concurrently designed and detailed within AutoCAD. Because the base data was in DWG format, and it would be changing often, it made the most sense to model the room in AutoCAD and import it into 3D Studio for materials, lights, cameras, and of course rendering.

Several complex details are critical to the design that make this model quite difficult to complete in AutoCAD alone. The room has ornate cornice and baseboard millwork, in addition to chair and picture rails and wainscot that encircle the room. Although difficult to model three-dimensionally in AutoCAD, they are ideal candidates for the 3D Lofter.

Creating the entire room's millwork with one loft is actually quite easy. Use a 2D polyline to trace the interior of the room at the floor height and save it from AutoCAD as an independent DXF file. Then load this DXF file as a path into the 3D Lofter while the original shape (with equal scaling) is inserted at the door locations—the only points of the path where the shape is perpendicular to the path and thus unscaled. Then place the shapes adjusted for 22.5° at the first two niche vertices and those adjusted for 45° at the remaining transitional corners.

Exporting the AutoCAD Model

1. Begin by starting AutoCAD and loading TRIMBLDG.DWG from the \LOFTING directory of the CD-ROM included with this book. Examine the composition of the model as shown in figure 14.4.

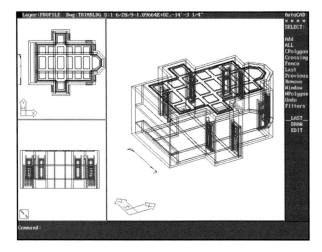

Figure 14.4
The original AutoCAD model.

The drawing includes the basic three-dimensional forms of the finished room: the windows and doors are block entities, the floor and ceiling patterns are made from closed polylines, and the walls are a mixture of closed polylines and 3D faces. To the side of the model is a simple section of the millwork elements made from closed polylines.

2. Export the majority of the model to 3D Studio. Freeze the PATH and PROFILE layers, initialize the DXFOUT command, accept the default file name of TRIMBLDG, and choose the Binary option by entering **B** (note that this option writes the entire AutoCAD file and was chosen because there are block entities that 3D Studio needs to interpret).

3. Reverse the display by thawing the PROFILE layer and making it the current layer, freezing all other layers, and thawing the PATH layer.

Now there should be visible a single polyline that traces the inside perimeter of the room and three smaller polylines for the section profiles of the wall trim. Using the PEDIT command shows that there are only vertices at the room polyline's corners, with an additional pair at the door openings to allow for the lower sections of the trim to be removed.

4. Use the DXFOUT command again to export the path, naming this DXF file **ROOMPATH**. This time choose the Entity option, select the polyline path of the room, and press enter to finish the selection. Complete the command by entering **B** for Binary.

This writes a very small DXF file containing only the description of the single polyline—exactly what is required by 3D Studio for a path description.

5. Now the trim profiles need to be scaled to accommodate their future rotation in the 3D Lofter. Load the LFTSCALE.LSP routine provided on the CD-ROM. Type **MANGLE** and select two adjacent polyline segments at the niche. MANGLE returns the two possible rotation angles of 67.50° and 22.50°. The lesser of these two angles is the correct one because the angle is obtuse.

6. Type **SCLOFT** and enter the correct rotation angle by either typing **22.50** or by pressing Enter and choosing the value returned by MANGLE. Select all three of the trim profiles and then choose one of the profile endpoints as a reference point for the scale operation.

This creates a block of the selected polylines that is slightly elongated to the right of the orignals. It may not look like much of an adjustment, but it is essential for making the trim straight in the final loft.

> When assigning hook locations in the 2D Shaper, it is very convenient if the desired location is on a snap increment. To make this possible, you should ensure that the future hook location (most likely a polyline vertex) be located at a whole number X,Y world coordinate. This will enable you to use an even snap increment to place the hook in 3D Studio. The hook location of this example happens to be at 0,0—a very convenient location to choose because it will also be the hook's default home location in the 2D Shaper.

7. The rest of the corners are 90° right corners, which always results in a 45° rotation angle (you can prove this to yourself by using MANGLE to measure the included angle). Use SCLOFT again, this time entering **45** for the rotation angle. Enter **P** for the selection set (to return your previous selection of the three trim pieces) and then select the same reference point as before.

Another block is created, but with a much greater horizontal scale deformation (as a path's angle becomes more acute, its rotation angle increases and the resulting correcting scale begins to approach infinity).

8. To make selections easier in the 2D Shaper, move the last block to the left 4 feet and the first block to the left 2 feet. Freeze the PATH layer and the profiles are ready for exporting to DXF.

9. With only the PROFILE layer thawed, access the DXFOUT command, give the DXF file the name **PROFILE**, and choose the Binary option. Because SCLOFT creates block iterations, the entire DXF file must be written even though only a small portion will be imported into the 2D Shaper.

10. Begin 3D Studio and load the TRIMBLDG.DXF file into the 3D Editor with the **Load** command. Choose to derive objects from Layers, answer Yes to the Weld Vertices, Unify Normals and Auto-smooth options, and, because the model is rectilinear, give the smoothing angle a value of **0**. The AutoCAD model imports as eleven 3D Studio objects as shown in figure 14.5.

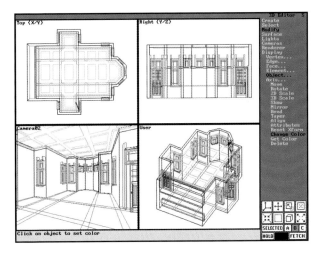

Figure 14.5
The basic AutoCAD model as brought into 3D Studio.

11. Choose **Display/Geometry/Backface** to check how the model's face normals were interpreted (the unavoidable step when importing AutoCAD models).

This model should import with correctly faced normals except for the polylines that make up the floor and ceiling plane. Co-planar entities such as these basically have a 50/50 chance of being faced correctly because they have no depth from which to calculate a centroid. You need to use **Surface/Normals/Entity Flip** to flip those that are facing incorrectly.

12. Enter the 3D Lofter, choose **Path/Get/Disk**, and replace the current path by loading ROOMPATH.DXF. Because the path is recti-

linear and there is no need to tween, choose **Path/Steps** and reduce the value to **0**. Use your Page Up and Page Down keys to make one of the door opening vertices current.

13. Enter the 2D Shaper and load the PROFILE.DXF file. The profiles of the three trim sections appear and are ready for assignment as shown in figure 14.6.

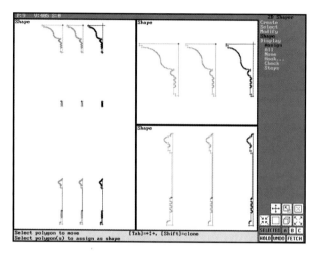

Figure 14.6
The trim's profile shapes, drawn in AutoCAD as polylines and brought into the 2D Shaper by DXF import.

14. Choose **View**, then **Drawing Aids** and change the snap spacing to **1.0**. Activate the snap, choose **Shape/Hook/Place**, and place the hook at the lower right corner of the base trim. Choose **Shape/Assign** and select the three polygons on the right that represent the undistorted profile.

15. Return to the 3D Lofter and choose **Shape/Get/Shaper** to retrieve the shape. Choose **Shape/Put/Level** and select the other door entry path vertex on the other side of the room to quickly copy the just-loaded shape.

16. Return to the 2D Shaper, choose **Shape/None**, then **Shape/Assign**, and select

the middle column of shapes. Choose **Shape/Hook** and place the hook at the same relative position for the new section.

17. Return to the 3D Lofter and use the Page Up key to make one of the first niche vertices current and get the shape from the Shaper. Put this shape to the other first niche vertex on the other side as well.

18. Return to the 2D Shaper, make the left-most polygons the current shape, and move the hook to the same relative position.

19. Return to the 3D Lofter, make one of the 90° corner path vertices adjacent to the niche current, and get the shape from the Shaper. Put this shape to the level on the opposite niche side and to either side of the door entry shapes. You are now ready to loft with 10 shapes on the path as shown in figure 14.7.

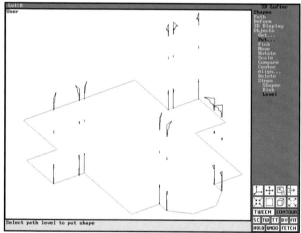

Figure 14.7
Scaled shapes at the transitional corners of the AutoCAD DXF path.

20. Choose **Objects/Make**, make all the choices ON except for Weld Vertices, make Contour active, make Tween inactive, and click on **Create**. For mapping, make sure that Normalize Length is active and that the

Length and Perimeter Repeats are both 1.0. Enter the 3D Editor and examine the lofted trim.

Figure 14.8 shows how the resulting loft fits the remainder of the AutoCAD model perfectly, without adjustment, because the 3D Lofter's path was originally an AutoCAD polyline from the same base model. This technique is especially useful when making changes to the millwork. Correcting such a mesh using the modeling tools traditionally available within AutoCAD would have been quite a task. Adjusting the profiles of the mesh and performing additional lofts is quite fast and easy in comparison.

to think of this as a standard option when lofting. With its Normalize Length option, and the ability to manipulate the repeat of any bitmap with material map parameters, giving any loft the default value of 1.0 for length and perimeter repeat is extremely easy.

The millwork in this example was given a normalized repeat of 1.0, and the material's texture map was given a U-Scale repeat of 0.05—thus repeating 20 times through the length of the room (note that these values will vary depending upon the nature of your bitmaps). The faces comprising the wainscot were given a different material with the appropriate repeat. The result can be quite convincing, as shown by the finished rendering in figure 14.9.

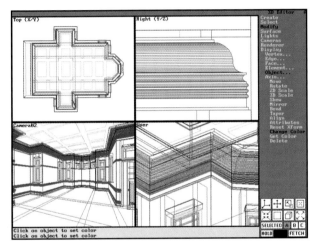

Figure 14.8
The lofted mesh aligning exactly with the remainder of the original AutoCAD model.

Figure 14.9
Lofted millwork using lofted mapping coordinates.

21. You can now select and deselect the faces that interfere with the door openings. You can also assign materials of your choosing to the model.

Lofted Mapping Coordinates

An additional advantage when lofting geometry is the opportunity to apply lofted mapping coordinates along the length of the mesh. Considering the cohesive mapping that results, you might want

Procedure: Lofting Complex Building Forms

Many people often overlook how easy it can be to loft the majority of what could be a very complex building. Perhaps this is because the lofting operation is more akin to an extrusion than actually building a mesh. But once you are comfortable with the concept of lofting, the same techniques used for creating the trim can be repeated to create very detailed and accurate building profiles—you are just facing the shapes to form the outside, rather than the inside, of the object's perimeter.

One drawing that can be found within nearly all architectural documents is the typical wall section that the building's construction is based on. This drawing is a cross section through the building, showing how the structural members, enclosures, and finishes relate to one another. When the perimeter of this drawing is defined as a closed polyline, it becomes the perfect shape source for the 2D Shaper.

 AutoCAD's BPOLY command is very useful for tracing the outline of complex drawings such as wall sections with one polyline.

1. Begin by loading LOFTBLDG.PRJ from the CD-ROM. The vertical elements located in the 3D Editor began as AutoCAD blocks and closed polylines, the current path in the 3D Lofter was formed from the column center lines, and the shapes in the 2D Shaper are the profile of the building section (formed from 2D polylines).

This project is just a portion of what was originally a very large architectural model, but it will serve to show the concept of lofting the majority of a building's form. Note that AutoCAD is not required for this exercise, because all the required components have already been imported to 3D Studio.

2. Enter the 2D Shaper and examine the collection of shapes. This wall section (see fig. 14.10) was imported into the 2D Shaper from an AutoCAD DXF file. The original AutoCAD entities had all been closed polyline outlines.

This is a fairly complex wall section and is complete with railings, mullions, drapery pockets, drips, and roof flashing. Remember that you can loft as many shapes concurrently as your shape limit allows. You can detach the varying elements

into different objects later if you want. Optionally, you can assign the distinct pieces separately and loft them as individual objects. For this procedure, the choice will be to loft the entire wall section at once.

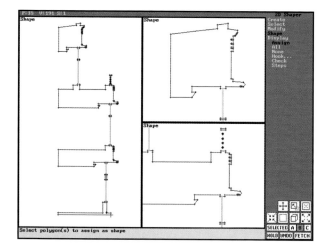

Figure 14.10
The AutoCAD building section after importing it into the 2D Shaper.

Notice that the hook is located at the lower right corner of the wall section. This location was selected because it represents the wall section's correct relationship to the column center line path that currently resides in the 3D Lofter.

3. Select all of the polygons by pressing Alt+A, choose **Select/Polygon/Single**, and deselect the three thin rectangles of glass. These polygons representing the glass will need to be lofted later because they intersect the mullions and thus produce an invalid shape.

4. Choose **Shape/Assign** and assign the selected polygons as the current shape.

5. Enter the 3D Lofter and make the first vertex of the curve active. Get the shape from the 2D Shaper and then put the shape to the similar path level on the other side of the path's quarter circle with **Shapes/Put/Levels**.

The path formed from the column center lines is composed entirely of 90° corners, with the notable exception being the quarter circle in the middle. If it was critical for this loft to be absolutely accurate, the angle formed at the first and second arc vertices would be calculated and the resulting scale percentage applied to shape in the 2D Shaper. Because this scale increment is very small (about 0.064%) it is considered unscaled for this procedure. If such accuracy was required, the scale adjustment would need to be done in AutoCAD using the procedure described in the preceding room trim exercise.

6. Return to the 2D Shaper, choose **Modify/Axis/Place**, and place the global axis at the same location as the hook.

7. Choose **Modify/Polygon/Scale**, press Tab until sure your multi-directional arrow is constrained to the horizontal, and scale the current selection by 141.50% while holding down the Shift key. This creates an enlarged clone of the wall section with the same hook location as the original shape.

Note that this scale increment is just an approximation of the actual percentage required of a 45° angle. The resulting shape will taper slightly at the transitional corners of the lofted mesh.

8. Choose **Select/Invert** to select the new scaled section and then use **Select/Polygon/Single** to deselect the three unwanted glass sections.

9. Choose **Shape/None** to clear the old shape and then use **Shape/Assign** to select the current selection set.

10. Return to the 3D Lofter, make one of the 90° corner vertices next to the arc current, and get the shape from the 2D Shaper.

11. Put the current shape to the similar path level on the other side of the arc, as shown in figure 14.11. The building section is now ready for lofting.

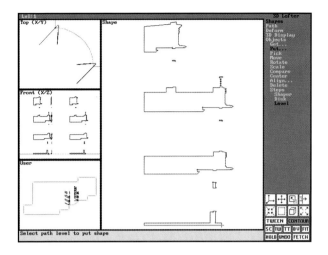

Figure 14.11
The scale-corrected shapes at the required corners of the building's perimeter path.

12. Choose **Objects/Make** and loft the building section using the same options as for the trim loft in the previous example.

The resulting mesh that is created from this loft forms a substantial portion of the building and fits precisely into the vertical elements of the original AutoCAD model, as shown in figure 14.12. Once lofted, the components of the building can be detached as objects according to material (railings, glass, mullions, and so on). The short amount of time required for this sorting in the 3D Editor is far less than lofting all the components individually and also ensures that all the pieces have the same scale and relationship to one another.

The finished model pictured in figure 14.13 shows how nearly all the horizontal components of this model were lofted. The section for this particular building proved to have enough detail and interest to make mapped materials seem unnecessary—all of the building's elements in the final rendering are of simple materials.

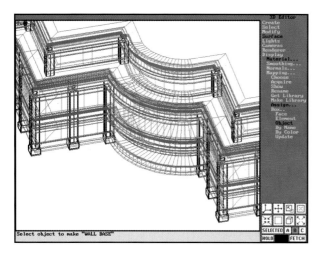

Figure 14.12
The resulting building section loft in the 3D Editor.

Figure 14.13
The finished building model with nearly all horizontal features created by lofting a complex building section.

Figure 14.13 also shows how this chapter's modeling effect was used in creating the continuous curbs that encircled the facility. Normally, this is a modeling detail conveniently overlooked or faked—it is often considered too difficult to do quickly by conventional methods. When done correctly, however, it provides that extra element of

realism needed to be especially convincing. In this case, the roadway's perimeter found on the AutoCAD site plan formed the perfect Lofter path for the simple curb profile drawn in the 2D Shaper.

Special Concerns When Importing DXF Arcs and Circles

The modeling effect described in this chapter does point out some anomalies in how 3D Studio Release 3 interprets DXF arc entities. Because the included AutoLISP routines make what was a difficult procedure easy, you may not have experienced these translation situations.

Although the 2D Shaper imports all manners of DXF arcs and circles, you need to understand that it does so differently for various iterations of the entities. The following is a quick list of how the 2D Shaper interprets the basic AutoCAD arc entities:

- **Circles**—interpreted as the 2D Shaper's traditional four-arc-segment curved polygon

- **Arcs**—interpreted as the 2D Shaper's traditional three-segment curved polygon

- **Polyline Arcs of 1–180°**—interpreted as a one-segment curved polygon

- **Polyline Arcs of +180°**—interpreted as a one-segment curved polygon that is no longer circular (this is an improper translation, and polylines containing arcs over 180° should be avoided)

Because SCLOFT.LSP makes it easy for you to create unequally scaled blocks, it suddenly becomes important to learn how 3D Studio interprets arc and circle entities that are unequally scaled, and thus become elliptical:

- **Unequally Scaled Circles**—interpreted as a true, four-segment ellipse

- **Unequally Scaled Arcs**—interpreted as fairly elliptical arcs that are somewhat pointed at their endpoints

- **Unequally Scaled Polyline Arcs of 1–90°**—interpreted as somewhat elliptical arcs that are noticeably pointed at their endpoints (this effect is worsened as the arc segments approach 90°)

- **Unequally Scaled Polyline Arcs of 90–180°**—these are converted into circular arc segments (no elliptical translation)

- **Unequally Scaled Polyline Arcs of +180°**—these are distorted as before and somewhat scaled

If these anomalies of arc interpretation are disturbing to your particular model, you must either import the original, undistorted shapes into the 2D Shaper and scale them there, or convert the troublesome arc entities into segmented polygons before using SCLOFT.

Conclusion

Often, it is the inclusion of convincing models that makes a particular image or animation particularly eye catching or convincing. This chapter shows how using 3D Studio's basic modeling procedure with a bit of sophistication and accuracy can create those vital objects.

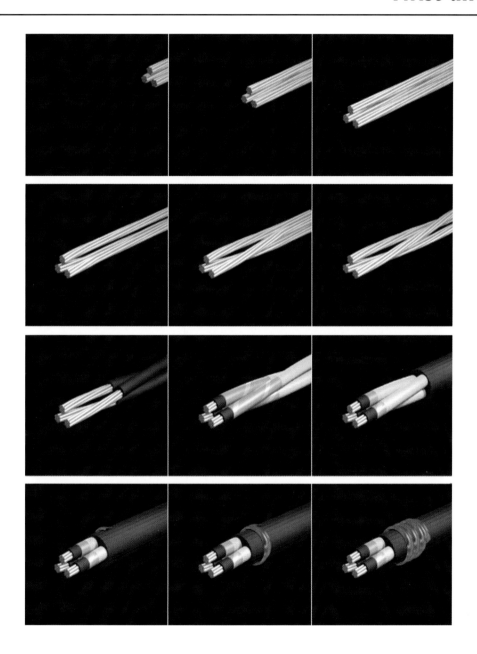

by Tim Forcade

Lawrence, Kansas

Equipment and Software Used

LANtastic networked IBM PC compatibles

3D Studio Release 3.0

Yost Group's TWIST IPAS application

Artist Biography

Building on an education in traditional fine arts that stressed drawing, painting, sculpture, and graphic design, Tim Forcade's artwork has advanced through optical, kinetic, and digital electronic media. This has resulted in numerous works utilizing photography, electronics, and video as well as the invention of electronic image-processing systems of his own design.

Concurrent with his artwork, Tim has over two decades of practice as a commercial artist, designer, and photographer. In 1978 Tim formed Forcade & Associates as a graphic resource to the commercial and professional communities. His project experience extends from illustration and publication design through photography and 3D visualization to computer animation and multimedia.

Tim's work has been exhibited in the U.S., Canada, Europe, and Japan. He has written and presented extensively on the subjects of applied 2D and 3D computer graphics and animation. He is a contributing editor to Computer Graphics World *and* Computer Artist *magazines. He can be reached via CompuServe at* 72007,2742 *or via Internet at* tforcade@falcon.cc.ukans.edu

Working with Tim at Forcade & Associates are Terry Gilbert and Perry Robinson, who provided invaluable assistance to Tim in creating and documenting this effect.

Effect Overview

The Twist and Shout procedure was used to create the twisted cable animation illustrated on the opening page of this chapter. The animation smoothly builds a cutaway view of a multi-layered oil well power cable. Figure 15.1 shows a frame from the twist animation in TWIST.FLI on the CD-ROM. There are three twists that make up this procedure. A primary twist is applied to the stranded metal conductors during lofting. A secondary (IPAS) twist is used to twist the black insulation, tape, and braid layers into a helical pattern. Finally, a manual twist is used to create the morph objects used to animate the stranded conductors into the same helical pattern.

Figure 15.1
A frame from the TWIST.FLI animation.

The animation opens with three tinned-copper conductors slowly twisting (the primary twist) and extruding on-screen from right to left. Each conductor consists of six individual strands that are twisted around a central conductor.

As the conductors come to a stop, all three twist again (the secondary twist), this time around each other, forming a helix of three stranded wires. This helix defines the motion for the next three layers—a black insulation layer, a translucent tape layer,

and a white braided layer. Each of these spins on-screen, sliding along each conductor's 3D path, while maintaining exact alignment with the conductors. As each layer spins in, it stops short of the end, enabling each inner layer to remain visible and creating an overall cutaway view of the cable.

Finally, a black ribbed jacket spins into place and the steel armor wraps itself around the remaining cable, completing the animation.

The multiple twisting effect for this animation relies heavily on several variations of twist deformations that were applied and reapplied to the geometry. The process, by necessity, uses both procedural and manual twisting methods, as well as a good deal of empirical monkey business and tweaking. The twisting effects are accomplished by using a combination of 3D Studio's modeling and animation tools along with TWIST.PXP, an IPAS application.

IPAS applications are add-on programs that work only with 3D Studio. There are currently six categories of IPAS processes. These enable you to perform a range of functions from image processing to procedural modeling. 3D Studio Release 3 ships with 26 IPAS applications, including STARS.IXP—a starfield generator—and DENTS.SXP—a *solid pattern external process* (SXP) that generates dented looking surfaces.

TWIST.PXP is a *procedural modeling external process* (PXP) available from Yost Group, Inc. After installation, you can access the program using the PXP Loader located in 3D Studio's **Program** drop-down menu. As the name implies, TWIST twists geometry along any axis, enabling you to smoothly deform the geometry to suit your needs.

TWIST.PXP is essential to reproducing the overall effect. Although it is possible to accomplish it using only 3D Studio's tool set, TWIST enables the effect to be produced quicker and with a smoother and more predictable result. Furthermore, it enables you to avoid the tedium associated with manually setting numerous keyframes and repeatedly aligning complex geometry.

Table 15.1
The Shape, Loft, and Project Files Used in Twist and Shout

Object	Shape File	Loft File	Project file
all shapes	ALL.SHP	—	—
conductor	STRANDED.SHP	STRANDED.LFT	CABLE_A.PRJ CABLE_B.PRJ
insulation	INSUL.SHP	INSUL.LFT	CABLE_B.PRJ
tape	TAPE.SHP	TAPE.LFT	CABLE_B.PRJ
braid	BRAID.SHP	BRAID.LFT	CABLE_B.PRJ
jacket	JACKET.SHP	JACKET.LFT	CABLE_B.PRJ
armor	ARMOR.SHP	ARMOR.LFT	CABLE_B.PRJ

Procedure

Table 15.1 lists the 3D Studio Shape, Loft, and Project files located on the CD-ROM in the \TWIST directory. Also included is TWIST.FLI, the complete animation. The project files contain all cameras, lighting, and materials to produce the animation.

The project files CABLE_A.PRJ and CABLE_B.PRJ both contain the conductor model, but in two separate states. CABLE_A.PRJ contains the conductors with the primary twist applied. CABLE_B.PRJ contains the conductors, as well as all other scene objects, in their final state (with both twists applied).

Also note that CABLE_C.PRJ contains all scene objects prior to having the secondary twist applied. All scene objects have been lofted and require the helical twist via the IPAS application TWIST. This project should be used for the TWIST.PXP tutorial in step 11.

The cable model consists of three groups or copies of four layers: the conductors, the insulation layer, the tape layer, and the braid layer. Around these layers is the jacket layer and the armor. All the shapes needed to create the cable are in the file ALL.SHP and are shown in figure 15.2. This view in the 2D Shaper of ALL.SHP shows the 14 circles comprising the stranded conductor's section highlighted in yellow.

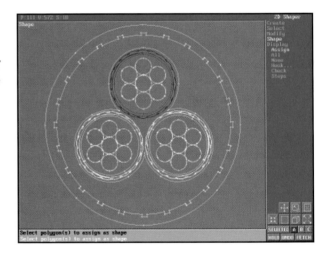

Figure 15.2
All of the shapes needed to create the final twisted cable model.

1. Load the ALL.SHP file and examine the construction of the shapes. The shapes were created using a combination of Line, Circle, and Arc tools along with **Create/Outline** and **Modify/Polygon/Rotate** with **Clone**. They were copied, scaled, and positioned relative to the layout of the final model.

2. Load the STRANDED.LFT file in the 3D Lofter and examine the loft path. Each conductor consists of a circular array of six circles

centered around a seventh. The circles for the conductors are lofted using **Deform/Twist** deformation to create the seven individual twisted cylinders that form the stranded conductors. This produces the primary twist in the conductors. The additional circles positioned inside each strand's circular section are used to create a chamfer on the end of each strand. The cable's 3D Lofter path was created manually using **Path/Insert Vertex**.

The second loft path vertex is placed very close to the first. Another 11 vertices are placed evenly along the path. Setting Pathsteps to 1 produces a path with the 25 path levels necessary to assure a smoothly twisting model. The inner conductor circles are placed onto path level 1 and the larger outer circles are placed on the path at levels 2 and 14. This is done to allow a slight chamfer to be modeled on one end of each conductor strand.

3. Loft the stranded conductor using STRANDED.LFT with **Deform/Twist** set to 135 degrees, as shown in figure 15.3.

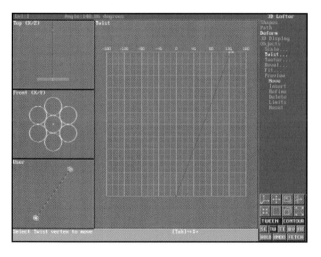

Figure 15.3
The shapes and the **Deform/Twist** *settings used to loft the three twisted conductors. This is the primary twist that opens the animation.*

4. Create the tape layer using the file TAPE.LFT. Lofting this file creates a 3D cylinder with overlapping geometry that, when used with a semi-transparent material, simulates the translucent tape wrap of the cable.

5. Use the same 3D Lofter settings as in the previous step, without deformation and using a standard path to create the insulation and jacket layers from their respective shapes in INSUL.SHP and JACKET.SHP.

6. Create the armor using ARMOR.LFT. The armor shape is created from a circle and the **Deform/Scale** settings in ARMOR.LFT.

The braid layer poses an interesting problem. The model's requirements dictate that a layer of white braided material be created to resemble the thick fibrous layer in the real-world cable. Although this could be accomplished by painstakingly weaving its component parts together in 3D space, there is a simpler and considerably faster method that results in a reasonable approximation. The braid can be simulated by lofting a helix of strands in one direction, and then overlaying a mirrored copy to create the strands for the opposite direction.

7. Load the BRAID.SHP file and look at the braid shape. The series of small closed arcs around the center of each conductor group were created using **Create/Arc** to make a shallow arc and then outlined using **Create/Outline** with a thin outline width. A circular array of these arcs was manually created using **Modify/Polygon/Rotate**.

 Setting Angle Snap to 18 degrees in the Drawing Aids dialog box speeds exact placement of each copy of the outlined arc.

8. Load the BRAID.LFT file and examine the 3D Lofter settings. Once again, **Deform/Twist** is used to loft the first part of the braid object. After you are done, create the object.

9. In the 3D Editor, use **Modify/Object/Mirror** with **Clone** (across the vertical axis only) to create the second part of the braid layer. Align the mirrored copy with the original braid object. Close examination reveals the braid layer's imperfections where the woven elements do not actually weave above and below each other. In spite of this, when rendered and animated, the braid layer works surprisingly well.

To make placing the mirrored braid **object easier and more accurate, select the** braid **and turn on Snap before creating the mirrored** braid. **The mirrored** braid **object will be perfectly aligned with the original.**

10. With a single set of cable objects complete, create the additional two sets. First, select the conductors, insulation, tape, and braid objects and move them up about .27 units. If you want, you can use **Create/Object/Get Shape** to bring several of the shapes from ALL.SHP into the 3D Editor to act as a template for more exact alignment. With the conductors, insulation, tape, and braid layers still selected, choose **Modify/Object/ Rotate/Clone**, and place the copies at about 120 degree increments around the axis. The axis should be positioned at the cable center. Remember to click on Local Axis in the Icon Panel to turn it off, and copy the objects to multiple.

Then, separate the three cable bundles into their respective layers. For instance, select all three insulation objects and use **Create/Face/ Detach** to create a single object insul. Follow the same procedure for the conductors, tape, and braid layers.

The completed model CABLE_C.PRJ is shown in figure 15.4 and is ready for you to apply the TWIST IPAS application. TWIST.PXP is applied only to the insulation, tape, and braid layers. The conductors are manually twisted later.

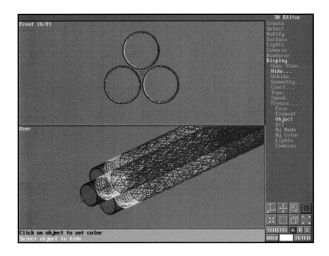

Figure 15.4
The completed cable model layers ready for the TWIST IPAS application.

The TWIST.PXP works like this: You first create a Twist template object and align it to the geometry you wish to twist. Then you set up the Twist parameters and apply TWIST to the object that creates a twisted copy of the original. The key to getting the most from Twist is to be sure that the original object is built from enough evenly distributed faces to conform to the desired parameters. This can be handled either by supplying ample path steps during lofting, as was done for the cable model, or by using **Create/Object/Tessellate** to create additional geometry.

11. Load the CABLE_C.PRJ file and hide all the objects in the scene except insulation. This object will be used to demonstrate how TWIST works. Load TWIST using the PXP Loader from the 3D Editor's **Program** pull-down menu. When the Twist Options dialog box displays, click on **Create Template**, the first step in the twisting process. The Twist Template Orientation dialog box shown in figure 15.5 enables you to set the axis along which twist will be applied to the geometry. If you wish, you can also select a template material from your current materials library.

This is rarely necessary, however, as the template is not often rendered. For our purposes, choose **Front** as the template axis and then choose **OK**.

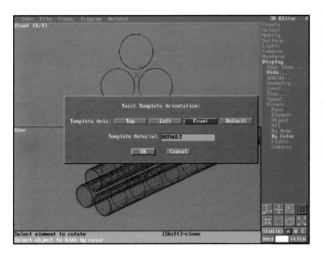

Figure 15.5
The template orientation settings used for the Twist process.

12. Next, select insulation as the target object. The TWIST.PXP builds a template object consisting of an octagonal base at one end and a smaller octagonal dial at the other (see fig. 15.6). The twist travels from the base to the dial. Because TWIST creates the template at the center of the insulation's bounding box, not at the geometric center of the object, you must move the template so that the line that runs between the twist template's base and dial is aligned with an imaginary line that runs down the center of the insulation's geometry.

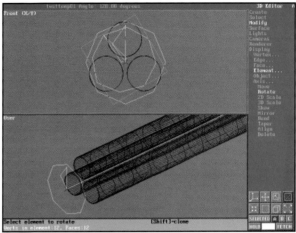

Figure 15.6
The TWIST template.

13. Use **Modify/Element/Rotate** to set the twist angle by rotating the Dial portion of the template. Use angle snap and set the rotation angle to –120 degrees (counterclockwise).

14. Reload TWIST using the PXP loader. This time, click on **Set Parameters**. From the Parameters dialog box, set the Twist Extent to Template. This assures that the object will be modified based on the length of the template and holds the twist effect consistent for each twisted object, per unit of length, regardless of the overall object length. You will use this same template for twisting the other objects. Set Twist Direction to Counter Clockwise and set both the number of full twists and Bias to zero. Leave the number of morphs at 1 and enter a four-character Name Prefix. When you have made these settings, click on **OK**. The result appears in figure 15.7.

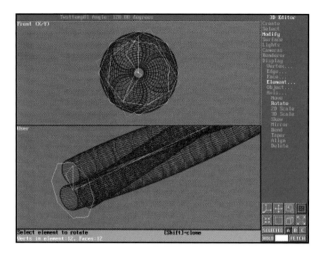

Figure 15.7
The result of applying a 120-degree counterclockwise twist to the insulation.

15. Apply the TWIST IPAS program to the tape and braid layers using the same parameter settings and template.

All the necessary actors for the animation are now complete, except for two sets of morph objects: one for the three stranded conductors and a second set for the armor wrap sequence.

The animation storyboard requires a secondary twist be applied to the conductors after they spin and extrude into the frame. Furthermore, the twist is required to move like a wave, starting at one end and affecting the conductors as it moves back from left to right (see CONDUCT.FLI on the CD-ROM). Unfortunately, TWIST.PXP morphs cannot be used here because their effect is applied generally over the entire template or object length. Using TWIST to create the morph target would result in an effect more resembling wringing water out of a wet cloth rather than the required localized effect. This means that you need to manually create a series of morph objects.

16. Load CABLE_A.PRJ and look at the conductor object. This file contains the completed morph targets. You may need to turn on Fastdraw and set **Display/Speed/Set Fast** to

50 to speed up the display of the objects. Each conductor strand consists of 25 vertex levels.

The manual twisting process begins by selecting 24 of the vertex sets, leaving the first set deselected on all of the strands. These vertex level sets are rotated 5 degrees around the cable center and the result is copied as the first morph object, CONA01. Then 23 vertex sets are selected, 5 degrees of rotation applied, and the result copied as the second morph object, CONA02. This process continues until 120 degrees of rotation is applied to the original object, and a total of 24 morph objects are created. The 120-degree value matches the TWIST IPAS rotation value applied to the insulation, tape, and braid layers. This is essential to be certain that the last morph object, CONA24, aligns perfectly with the three twisted layers. The full set of the morphs is in CABLE_A.PRJ. Figure 15.8 shows the conductor object (highlighted in blue) before the manual twist process; three morph objects at different stages of the process are highlighted in yellow.

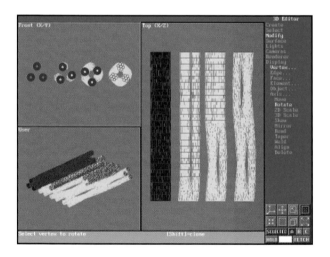

Figure 15.8
Original conductor *object and three stages of morph targets.*

17. Load the CABLE_B.PRJ file and examine the armor morph targets (see fig. 15.9). These targets were created by taking the lofted armor segment (created in an earlier step) and skewing it slightly in the 3D Editor to resemble the real-world armor's wrap angle. One set of faces was then deleted from the side opposite the camera view. This allowed four morph objects to be created by selecting groups of vertices and rotating them around the circumference of the armor segment. This process compressed and distorted part of each segment. However the distorted segments are positioned opposite the camera view and thus do not appear in the finished animation.

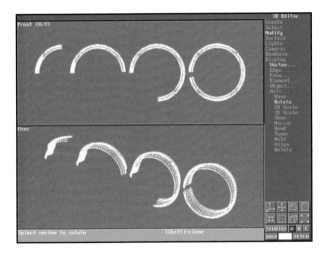

Figure 15.9
The four morph objects used to create the armor wrap sequence.

With the actors prepared, all that remains is to structure the animation in the Keyframer. To reduce file size and simplify the animation, it is separated into two project files on the CD-ROM: CABLE_A.PRJ, the stranded conductor sequence; and CABLE_B.PRJ, the remaining animation.

18. Load the CABLE_A.PRJ file and examine the Track Info settings in the Keyframer (see fig. 15.10). The animation in frames 0–138 consists of two essential moves: the conductor primary twist and the conductor secondary twist.

The primary twist, where the strands appear to twist into the frame, was accomplished in the following way. First, in the 3D Editor, the three stranded conductors were broken into three individual groups by first selecting each group and using **Create/Face/Detach**. The resulting individual objects were saved as cond-a, cond-b, and cond-c.

Next, because the conductors' positions, as seen through the camera view, is where they should be at the end of their move on-screen, this position was copied to frame 60 in the Keyframer. Then, at frame 0, all three objects were moved off-screen and rotated 140 degrees counterclockwise about each strand's axis. This is the same as the rotation value applied in the Lofter to create the primary twist in the conductors. The match in rotation value makes the cables twist rather than rotate on screen. If you play back the TWIST.FLC animation on the CD-ROM from frames 0 to 60, you will see the three conductors twist into view and freeze until frame 90.

For the first 90 frames, the morph target (the conductor object) is keyed to hide (highlighted in blue in figure 15.10). The three conductor groups (cond-a, cond-b, and cond-c) highlighted in yellow, were keyed to be visible until frame 90.

The secondary twist starts at frame 90 where the three stranded conductors (cond-a, cond-b, and cond-c) are hidden and the object conductor, the morph target, is made visible. From frame 90 to 138 a morph keyframe is set every two frames.

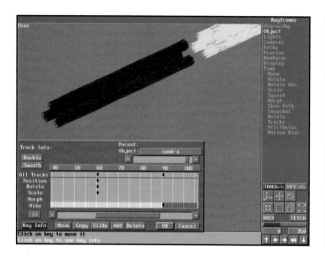

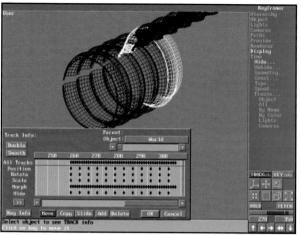

Figure 15.10
The Track Info dialog box and keyframes for the stranded conductors' twist on-screen.

Figure 15.11
The twelve sets of four morph keys set to create the sequential armor wrap.

19. The remainder of the animation in frames 139–350 is rendered separately and uses CABLE_B.PRJ. The insulation, tape, braid, and jacket are keyed to spin into place through 120 degrees of rotation. This value matches that used to produce the manual and IPAS twists and assures that everything lines up as expected.

20. The armor wrap segment uses the armor morphs (armora, armorb, armorc, and armord) that were explained and created previously. The armord object is used as the morph target, and eleven copies or instances are offset to make the wrap appear to be sequential (see fig. 15.11).

Conclusion

The key to understanding and applying this procedure is a clear picture of the three twists that are applied to the cable model. These are Lofter twist, IPAS twist, and Manual twist.

The Lofter twist refers to **Deform/Twist** as used in the 3D Lofter. It is used here for the initial twist that is applied to the stranded conductors, tape, and braid.

The IPAS twist refers to twist applied using the TWIST.PXP IPAS application. It is used to create the secondary twist in the insulation, tape, and braid layers.

Manual twist refers to the process of twisting geometry by selecting and rotating vertex sets. This technique is used to create the morph objects of the stranded conductors' secondary twist.

The relationship of the three is as follows. The rotation value applied by the 3D Lofter twist is relevant only when animating the stranded conductors. If you want them to appear to twist into view, you will need to match the rotation key to the Lofter twist rotation value. The Manual twist, IPAS twist, and rotation key values applied to the `conductors`, `insulation`, `tape`, and `braid` must have the same rotation and the same linear speed to insure proper alignment.

by Keith A. Seifert

Castle Rock, Colorado

Equipment and Software Used

IBM-compatible 486/66 with 32 MB of RAM

3D Studio Release 3.0

3D Studio IPAS Toolkit

Metaware High C compiler

PharLap DOS Extender Software Development Kit

Artist Biography

Keith A. Seifert is V.P. of Engineering in charge of program development at Schreiber Instruments, Inc. He has created a series of visual design programs for use with and within 3D Studio and AutoCAD. This series of programs brings true 3D design and modeling to the engineering, architectural, and animation professions. He has an extensive background in engineering problem solving using computer-aided modeling and simulation. He enjoys adding the forces of chaos to mechanical geometries to model the unpredictable 4D geometries of nature. He creates programs that have a functional blend of hard geometry and aesthetics.

Effect Overview

The Pastel Filter creates an effect often used in titling. Using the Pastel Filter, you can fade out the colors in an image to produce a uniform, low-contrast backdrop for foreground titles or objects. This lets the foreground objects or titles stand out from the background.

Procedure

The Pastel Filter runs as an *image processing external process* (IXP) in Video Post in 3D Studio version 2.0 or later. This process is a very powerful feature of the 3D Studio IPAS extensions. The IXP process enables you to write a program that can alter the appearance of the current rendered image. An IXP is added to the Video Post rendering queue. Video Post enables you to create a final image by combining image elements, processing them with an IXP, adding other elements, and then rendering Keyframer geometry and combining its image with the other elements. Video Post controls to the frames of an animation to which an IXP is applied and the sequence in which the scene is rendered.

To use the Pastel Filter included on the CD, you need to transfer the PASTEL_I.IXP file to the process subdirectory.

1. Copy the PASTEL_I.IXP file from the CD-ROM \PASTEL subdirectory to your 3D Studio process directory, usually called \3DS3\PROCESS.

2. Start 3D Studio as you normally do.

3. Load the project file PASTEL.PRJ from the \PASTEL subdirectory on the CD-ROM. Figure 16.1 shows the 3D Editor with the PASTEL project file loaded.

4. The Pastel example project file contains the bird and sphere objects from the BIRDWLK3.3DS file that ships with 3D Studio. Change to the Keyframer module by pressing F4 or by choosing Keyframer from the program pull-down menu. Figure 16.2 shows the PASTEL project in the Keyframer.

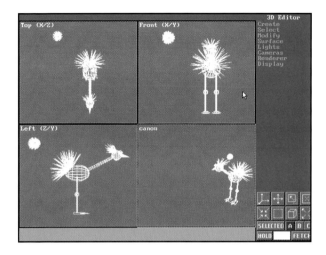

Figure 16.1
The PASTEL.PRJ project file in the 3D Editor.

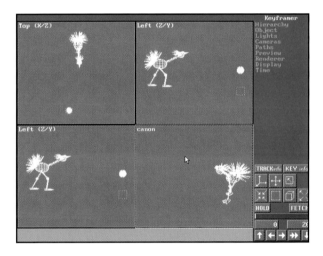

Figure 16.2
The PASTEL.PRJ project file in the Keyframer.

To achieve the greatest effect from an IXP process it is important to understand how an IXP affects the rendering process.

The Pastel Filter is added as a process to the Video Post rendering queue. The Pastel Filter processes the image buffer according to its place in the queue. The settings of the Pastel Filter are changed from the Video Post dialog box.

1. Choose **Renderer/Video Post** and then select the canon viewport. Video Post already contains entries in the queue from the PASTEL project file.

2. Click on the **Edit** button to highlight it, and then select the PASTEL_I.IXP queue entry to display the Queue Entry dialog box for the entry. Figure 16.3 shows the Queue Entry dialog box with the PASTEL_I.IXP loaded.

Luminance-Saturation (HLS) values, and then the Color Fade percentage value is applied to the saturation value.

The Brightness slider controls the brightness of each processed pixel of the image buffer. The Brightness slider bar affects the luminance value of processed pixels using the HLS color model. The Hue value of the HLS color model remains unchanged by the Pastel Filter.

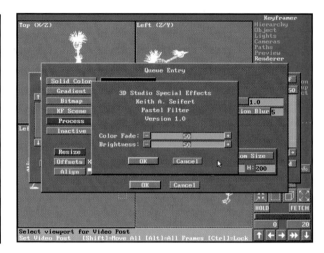

Figure 16.3
The Queue Entry dialog box for the PASTEL_I.IXP Video Post queue entry.

Figure 16.4
The Pastel Filter Settings dialog box.

3. Click on the **Setup** button next to the PASTEL_I.IXP name box to display the Pastel Shader dialog box. Figure 16.4 shows the Pastel Shader dialog box.

The Pastel Filter Settings dialog box has two slider bars that control the effect: Color Fade and Brightness.

The Color Fade slider bar controls the amount of color in each processed pixel of the image buffer. The slider controls the percentage of color removed from each pixel. A higher Color Fade percentage removes more color, making the final colors grayer. The Red-Green-Blue (RGB) values of the pixels in the image buffer are converted to Hue-

4. Click on **OK** to accept the settings and exit the Pastel Shader setup dialog box. The settings are saved with the current queue entry.

To do test renderings of your scene without the Pastel Filter, you can turn off the effect by clicking on the **Inactive** button in the Queue Entry dialog box. The Inactive button causes the Video Post queue entry to skip the step during rendering. All of the settings controlling the effect are retained when the Inactive option is activated. Figure 16.5 shows PASTEL.PRJ rendered with the Pastel Filter inactive or turned off.

Figure 16.5
Rendered PASTEL.PRJ image with the Pastel Filter turned off.

Figure 16.6
The original background image.

5. Click on **OK** to exit the Queue Entry dialog box and save the settings.

You can have more than one Pastel Filter entry in the Video Post queue. Each occurrence in the Video Post queue can be set up differently. The time segments may overlap or occur over completely separate frames.

The example project for this chapter is set up with three entries in the Video Post queue. The first entry is the background image and loads the background into the image buffer. Figure 16.6 shows what the image buffer looks like after loading the background.

The second Video Post queue entry is the Pastel Filter. The Pastel Filter processes the current image buffer (containing the background image only) and changes its colors according to the slider settings. Figure 16.7 shows the image buffer after processing by the Pastel Filter.

Figure 16.7
The background after image processing.

The third entry in the Video Post queue is the Keyframer scene. The scene is composed on top of the current image buffer. Figure 16.8 shows the rendered scene without the background.

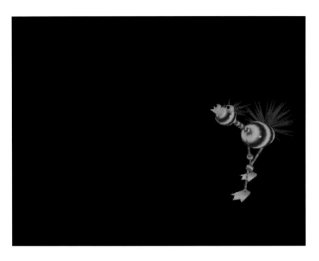

Figure 16.8
The rendered Keyframer scene without the background.

6. Click on the **Render** button in the Video Post dialog box to display the Render Video Post Animation dialog box and set up the rendering. Determine the rendering options you want to use. The Pastel Filter is not an animated effect, so this example project only renders a single still image. Choose the image size and the output file type you want to use.

7. Choose **Render** to begin rendering the example project. If you do not want to save the rendered image, click on **OK** when prompted `Render to screen only?`

8. If you saved the rendered image to disk, you can view it by choosing **Renderer/View /Image** and selecting the file you just rendered. Click on **Resize** if the image size is larger than your display resolution. If you have the Save Last Image option set to Yes in the render Options dialog box (which you can reach by choosing **Render/Setup/Options**), you can also see the last image you rendered by choosing **Renderer/View/Last**.

Figure 16.9 shows the image buffer after the last queue entry has been processed. The image shows the bird object rendered in full brilliance on top of the background faded to pastel by the Pastel Filter.

You can add an IXP at any point in the Video Post rendering queue. Try moving the Pastel Filter Video Post entry so it is the last process and see how that effects the final image. The IXP enables you to use your creativity in your animations.

On the CD-ROM is a file with the source code for the Pastel Filter IXP, along with some helpful information for creating your own IPAS routines. The file is named PSTLSRCE.TXT and is in the \SHIELD subdirectory.

Figure 16.9
The completed image.

by Martin Foster

Laguna Hills, California

Equipment and Software Used

LANtastic network of three IBM PC compatibles: 486/66, 486/33, and Pentium 60, each with 32 MB of RAM

Sony Beta SP frame-accurate video tape recorder

Sony Laserdisk Video Recorder

3D Studio Release 3.0

Yost Group, Inc. IPAS3 Disk #6

Animator Pro 1.3

Photostyler 2.0

Artist Biography

Martin Foster is a 3D artist and owner of Animatrix in Laguna Hills, California. He works predominantly with 3D Studio to create all kinds of animation and graphics for a broad client base. Martin worked on the award-winning architectural animation project "Port de Plaisance" for the Pyros Partnership; the pre-visualization of stunts and special effects for the feature films "My Life" and "Wolf" for Sony Pictures; and the award-winning, CD-ROM–based game "Rebel Assault" for LucasArts. Other samples of his work can be found on the 3D Studio Siggraph 1993 tape and on the 3D Studio World Creating Tool Kit CD-ROM. He is currently working on 3D game development for a next generation video game platform.

Effect Overview

This chapter demonstrates how to use IPAS plug-in effects to help prevent seams in the joints of characters such as human models. This is a common problem with polygon-based 3D packages because, up until now, you either had to break your characters into relatively small parts (upper arm, lower arm, thigh, shin, foot, and so on) to animate them effectively, or you had to morph between versions of the larger model. With models divided into small pieces, you often had to work around ugly gaps or seams at these joints. Although morphing gave good results, it was very awkward to animate.

Two new IPAS routines from the Yost Group, Inc., called SLICE.AXP and SKIN.AXP, enable skinning with smooth spline-based surfaces over cross-sections of regular polygon geometry created in the 2D Shaper and 3D Lofter. This lets you use the powerful 2D Shaper and 3D Lofter tools, such as the Deform/Fit tool, and create complex characters with skinning across the joints of major limbs. The lofted body parts are sliced up into cross-sections using SLICE.AXP in the 3D Editor, and then can be hierarchically linked in the Keyframer for easy animation. SKIN.AXP handles the job of creating a skin surface during rendering. These new routines provide you with new freedom for character animation.

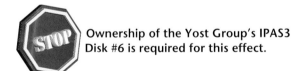 Ownership of the Yost Group's IPAS3 Disk #6 is required for this effect.

To render the animation in this chapter, it is recommended that your computer have 32 MB or more of RAM to avoid 3D Studio having to swap to the hard drive. Swapping can drastically increase rendering times.

Procedure

Start 3D Studio and examine the items necessary for the effect.

1. Choose **File**, then **Load Project**. Select SKIN-A.PRJ from the CD-ROM included with this book.

2. Choose **Info/Configure**, click on Map Paths in the program configuration menu and add the CD-ROM map path *n*:\maps\meshmaps1 to access the images and maps necessary for this exercise. (Substitute the drive letter your CD-ROM uses for *n*.)

If you need to access any materials used in this chapter that are not in the current project, just choose Surface/Material/Get Library and load SKIN.MLI from the CD-ROM.

Familiarize yourself with the objects, processes, and materials that together will be used to create this modeling effect (see fig. 17.1).

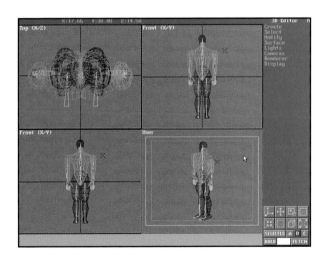

Figure 17.1
Sample construction of a male figure with skeleton.

3. If you are not already in the 3D Editor, press the F3 key to go there. Examine the male mannequin model. It is composed of 18 objects created using the 3D Lofter Deform/Fit tool using shapes from the 2D Shaper. The names of each object are as follows:

M-Head

M-Torso-

M-LegR-

M-LegL-

M-ArmL-

M-ArmR-

M-HandL-

M-FngL1-

M-FngL2-

M-FngL3-

M-FngL4-

M-FngL5-

M-HandR-

M-FngR1-

M-FngR2-

M-FngR3-

M-FngR4-

M-FngR5-

4. Move to the Keyframer by pressing the F4 key. In the Keyframer, all of the body objects are hidden, and the skeleton objects are displayed (see fig. 17.2). Also displayed is a master dummy object, Body-dummy, that can be moved to move the entire skeleton (and later the entire skinned body). The skeleton objects are named as follows:

Sk-torso-U

Sk-torso-M

Sk-torso-L

Sk-neck

Sk-arm-UR

Sk-arm-LR

Sk-hand-R

Sk-arm-UL

Sk-arm-LL

Sk-hand-L

Sk-thigh-R

Sk-shin-R

Sk-foot-R

Sk-thigh-L

Sk-shin-L

Sk-foot-L

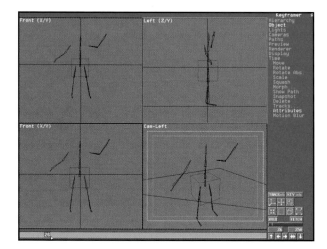

Figure 17.2
Skeleton objects in the Keyframer.

5. Move the frame slider at the bottom of the screen, or click on the double arrow icon in the icon panel, to play the animation.

6. Choose **Hierarchy/Show Tree** and examine the links shown. You will see that the skeleton parts are all linked together for you, but the body parts are not linked to the skeleton. Remember that these body parts are going to be sliced up and the resulting cross-sections

skinned using SLICE and SKIN. The cross-sections will be linked to the skeleton rather than the body parts you saw in the 3D Editor.

7. Press F1 to go to the 2D Shaper and examine the shapes there. The shapes used to create the torso are in the lower right portion of the 2D Shaper screen (see fig. 17.3).

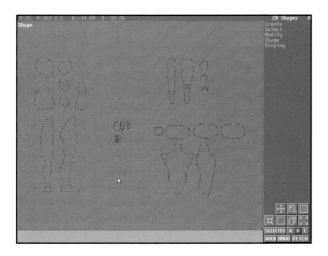

Figure 17.3
Fit shapes in the 2D Shaper

8. Press F2 to move to the 3D Lofter. The shapes used to create the torso are in the 3D Lofter.

9. Select **Deform/Fit** to see how the fit shapes are used. Typically, you need a front and side view (x and y) of the object you want to create and one or more shapes used to define the cross-section through the object.

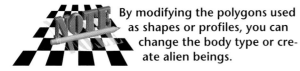

By modifying the polygons used as shapes or profiles, you can change the body type or create alien beings.

10. From 3D Lofter, choose **File,Load** and load T-ARM.LFT from the CD-ROM. This is the prototype arm object.

11. Using **Deform/Fit**, examine how the shapes go together to create the arm object. Note that the path has irregularly positioned vertices. This was created by using the **Deform/Fit/Gen Path** command to customize the path for each set of fit shapes.

To ensure that the fit path has enough vertices in the right places to create the object you want, and to minimize the excess or misplaced vertices, always use Gen Path after getting both fit shapes.

12. Load each of the following files in turn: T-FINGER.LFT, T-HAND.LFT, T-LEG.LFT, and T-TORSO.LFT. These are the prototype finger, hand, leg, and torso objects. You can use these files in your own projects to define typical body parts.

13. After loading each 3D Lofter file, preview the resulting object by using **Object/Preview**. Keep Path Detail Low and Shape Detail High to minimize the number of cross-sectional objects produced using SLICE. SKIN, with its spline surfacing, will produce nice smooth surfaces from just a few cross-sections.

If you want to experiment with making some of these body parts from the LFT files, you can. However, all of the necessary objects for this project are already in the 3D Editor.

To create an object, choose **Object/Make** and name the object appropriately (`arm`, `finger`, `hand`, `leg`, `torso`, and so on). Don't use more than eight letters for each name because SLICE uses at least two when it creates cross-section objects. Again, keep Path Detail Low and Shape Detail High to minimize the number of cross-sectional objects produced using SLICE.

Once you have created a single protoype object of each, use the 3D Editor's cloning power with **Modify/Object/Move**, Rotate, Mirror, and 2D and 3D Scale to produce a complete body with two legs, two arms, two hands, and ten fingers.

Slicing up the Body

Next, use SLICE to create cross-sectional objects from the prototypes created using the 3D Lofter.

SKIN can actually create a spline-surfaced object from a non-SLICEd object created using the 3D Lofter, but it is extremely difficult to animate. Using cross-sections lets you freely rotate portions of an arm or leg.

Press F3 to go to the 3D Editor, if you're not there now, and repeat the following steps for every object except the head.

1. From the Program menu, choose the PXP Loader and then choose SLICE.

2. Click on the **Pick** button in the Source Object panel of the SLICE dialog box, and then pick the left arm object, M-armL-.

3. In the Output Object(s) panel, click in the Prefix: field to the right of the Create Slices button and enter an appropriate prefix. In this case, it should be **armL-** (see fig. 17.4).

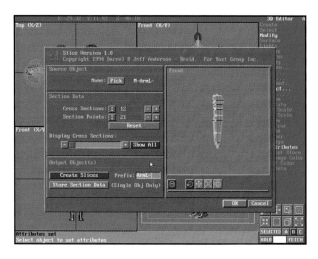

Figure 17.4
The SLICE dialog box with the left arm object ready to process.

4. Accept the default values and click on **OK**.

When SLICE has completed its work, you are returned to the 3D Editor with a number of new objects in the same 3D space as the source object. These new objects are sequentially numbered, such as armL-01, armL-02, and so on. The original object is left intact.

5. Repeat the previous four steps for each of the other master objects in the scene. (These are the objects with the M- prefix.) See figure 17.5.

Rather than using the mouse to select SLICE from the Program menu each time, press F12 and then press Enter. This automatically selects the last PXP process you used.

It may seem that there are an inordinately large number of objects to deal with, but you will probably find it easier to edit slices when refining your model than a whole, unsliced limb. For example, if you want to make the calf more muscular, just scale the appropriate section of the leg. This will smoothly stretch the skin at rendering time to create the effect you want.

If you feel you have too many cross-sections, you can manually delete sections you feel are superfluous, but you will have to rename the remaining slices so that you have an uninterrupted sequence. For example, if you delete armL-04 from the sequence of armL-01 through armL-06, you must rename armL-05 and armL-06 to armL-04 and armL-05. Use Modify/Object/Attributes to accomplish this.

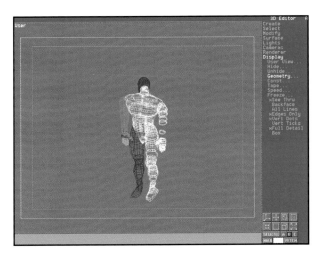

Figure 17.5
The mannequin in the 3D Editor with his left side parts sliced.

Applying the Skin Attributes

To assign the SKIN attribute to the left arm, you use the **Modify/Object/Attributes** command.

1. Choose **Modify/Object/Attributes** and press **H** to bring up the Click on Object by Name dialog box.

2. From the scrolling list, select armL-01.

3. When the Object Attributes dialog box appears, click on the **External Processes** button to the right of the Name: label.

4. Select SKIN from the scrolling list of AXP processes available.

5. Click on the **Settings** button to bring up the SKIN dialog box.

6. In the SKIN dialog box, make sure the settings match those shown in figure 17.6. In particular, make sure that the Spline Type is B-Spline (the skin will pass through the cross-section control points) and the Template Objects is set to Use Prefix (tells the process to extract the prefix from the object name and apply skin to all similarly named objects).

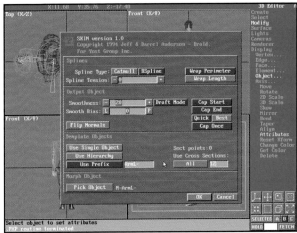

Figure 17.6
Suggested settings for skin objects.

7. Click on the **OK** button to return to the Object Attributes dialog box, and then click on **OK** again to return to the 3D Editor.

Repeat these seven steps for each body part with the 01 suffix.

Applying Materials

You only need to assign a material to the the first numbered object of each set—that is, the object numbered 01.

1. To assign the SKIN material, select **Surface/Material/Choose** and select SKIN from the list of materials loaded with the project.

2. Select **Surface/Material/Assign/By Name** and tag each object that has a suffix of 01, such as armL-01 (assuming that armL- is the prefix you chose for the left arm in the SLICE dialog box). Don't select the Torso, which uses a different material.

3. Click on **OK**, and then click on **OK** again in the confirming dialog box.

4. Assign the SKIN-TORSO material to the Torso by again using **Surface/Material/Choose** to select the material, and **Surface/Material/Assign/By Name** to assign it to Torso-01.

Linking the Slices to a Skeleton

To make animation of these cross-sectional objects easier, link them to the skeleton shown earlier in the Keyframer, and then you only need to manipulate the skeleton to create the movement you want. Link each cross-section to the closest skeleton part using **Hierarchy/Link** in the Keyframer.

Getting the skin to look good takes a great deal of trial and error, scaling and adjusting cross-sections. To avoid going through this, load the second project file from the \SKIN sub-directory on the CD-ROM.

1. Press Ctrl+J to load the project file named SKIN-B.PRJ.

2. Press F4 to go to the Keyframer. There you will find a sliced body already set up and linked to the skeleton.

Some simple animation keys have been set up and applied to the skeleton objects. Slide the frame slider back and forth to examine the motion. The slices move along with the skeleton quite nicely. You can preview this quite effectively using **Preview/Make**.

Rendering the Animation

Now render a few sample frames to see how the skinning looks in practice.

1. If you want to render the pre-defined camera view, named Cam-Left, you can replace the active viewport with this camera view by pressing the C key.

2. Choose **Renderer/Render View** and then click in the viewport of your choice. If the viewport is not active, click twice—once to make it active, and a second time to render it.

3. Configure the output file by clicking on the **Configure** button in the Render Animation dialog box.

4. Choose an appropriate resolution and output file type for your equipment. This could be 320×200×0.82 or 640×480×1.0 flics for computer playback, or 752×480×0.85 and Targa files for video output to a personal animation recorder.

5. After setting the output, try rendering every 30th frame as a test to make sure everything is in order.

6. After rendering, examine the output using **Renderer/View/Image** or **Renderer/View/Flic**, as appropriate. Note how the skin stretches across joints, except where the legs and arms join the torso.

7. When you are satisfied that everything is set up correctly, render all frames and save the sequence with a name of your choice.

8. Take a look at the sample image which uses this technique as a basis. Choose **Render/View Image** and examine SK-HEROS.JPG. This image is a composite of three characters that use extensive texture and bump mapping to enhance the skin objects.

Conclusion

Edit the polygon shapes in the 2D Shaper to produce different types of humans. With these shapes as a basis you should be able to create taller, shorter, stockier, or skinnier males.

Try creating a female by editing the polygons in the 2D shaper.

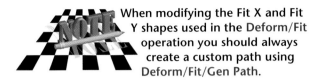

When modifying the Fit X and Fit Y shapes used in the Deform/Fit operation you should always create a custom path using Deform/Fit/Gen Path.

Add clothing or accessories to the body using **Hierarchy/Link** to ensure that these new objects move correctly with the appropriate part of the skeleton.

Explore some different texture mapping and bump mapping possibilities. You can create new texture maps quite easily with 2D paint and animation software such as Animator Pro. Examine the texture and bump maps in the SKIN subdirectory as a guide.

by Tim Forcade

Lawrence, Kansas

Equipment and Software Used

LANtastic networked IBM PC compatibles

Storm Technology PhotoDSP board

Sony Hi-8 Video camera

Macintosh ColorOne scanner

Macintosh computers

VideoVision Studio

Adobe Photoshop

HiRes QFX

3D Studio Release 3.0

Autodesk Animator

Adobe Premiere 3.0 Mac

DeBabelizer

Image Alchemy

Kai's Power Tools Mac & PC

Aldus Gallery Effects

Xaos Alchemy Mac

Artist Biography

Building on an education in traditional fine arts that stressed drawing, painting, sculpture, and graphic design, Tim Forcade's artwork has advanced through optical, kinetic, and digital electronic media. This has resulted in numerous works utilizing photography, electronics, and video as well as the invention of electronic image-processing systems of his own design.

Concurrent with his artwork, Tim has over two decades of practice as a commercial artist, designer, and photographer. In 1978 Tim formed Forcade & Associates as a graphic resource to the commercial and professional communities. His project experience extends from illustration and publication design through photography and 3D visualization to computer animation and multimedia.

Tim's work has been exhibited in the U.S., Canada, Europe, and Japan. He has written and presented extensively on the subjects of applied 2D and 3D computer graphics and animation. He is a contributing editor to Computer Graphics World *and* Computer Artist *magazines. He can be reached via CompuServe at* 72007,2742 *or via Internet at* tforcade@falcon.cc.ukans.edu

Working with Tim at Forcade & Associates is Terry Gilbert, Mark Anderson, and Joel Flory (see above left group composite: mutant.rastermonkey.tractorcity) who provided invaluable assistance to Tim in creating these maps.

Overview

For a number of years as a painter, I worked long hours in the studio creating monumental abstract canvases in mixed media, including charcoal, oil, collage, enamel, and encaustic. The media were applied to stretched canvases and paper using a combination of application techniques ranging from carefully drawn or brushed to thrown, dripped, rolled, and splattered. The results were paintings that combined two-dimensional geometric and organic forms into eccentric pictures of three-dimensional images and patterns.

Many of these techniques share compelling similarities with those we used to create the images and animations you will find on the CD-ROM. Here the brushes, palette knives, and other standard trappings of traditional media were replaced with a video camera, scanner, non-linear editing software, and numerous image processing programs.

In spite of a reliance on applied automata such as arithmetic difference or edge detection filters, much of what went into these map images and animations was created using manual techniques: the computer-aided equivalent of brushing, dripping, and spattering.

The objective was to create rich and detailed images that rely as little as possible on real-world surfaces or objects. For those instances where a map was created using an object, any visual cues that might suggest the source object or objects have been minimized. We wanted to create a series of non-objective images largely with the intent of exploring the use of color, texture, form, and space.

The assumption was that real world materials such as wood or marble have been exhaustively produced and are commonly available through numerous means including CD-ROM libraries and on-line services. Also assumed is that many of you have found yourselves in the position of needing a surface look that offers more than mere concrete and plywood, perhaps even reaching to "eleven" or beyond. In any case, what there does not ever seem to be enough of are map images that are strange, zany, or bizarre.

This is what this collection attempts to provide you; some unusual images and animation clips. These are static and moving pictures that are useful for either direct application as any of 3D Studio's maps or masks or as points of departure to create your own custom effects. Furthermore, many of these will work well along with the special effects described elsewhere in this book.

The CD-ROM contains some 135 MB (195 images) of static maps and 135 MB (22 animations) of animated maps. The static maps are all 24-bit color or 8-bit grayscale at an average resolution of 600×600 (see table A.1).

Table A.1
A Complete List of the Static Maps Located on the CD-ROM in the \NRPTEX Directory

File Name	Resolution	Color/Gray	Tileable
BEEBEE1	579×600	color	tile
BEEBEE2	525×600	color	tile
BEEBEE3	600×413	color	tile
BEEBEE4	600×413	color	tile
BEEBEE5	525×600	grayscale	tile
BEETLES	600×600	color	tile

continues

File Name	Resolution	Color/Gray	Tileable
BENDOID	600×600	grayscale	
BIZARRO1	600×600	grayscale	
BIZARRO2	600×600	grayscale	
BIZARRO3	600×600	grayscale	
BIZARRO4	600×600	grayscale	
BLOB	600×600	color	
BLOBB	600×600	color	
BLOBBY	600×600	color	
BLOBEBW	600×600	color	
BLOBEM	600×600	color	
BLOBOID	600×600	color	
BROCADE1	600×600	color	
BROCADE2	600×600	color	
BRUSHD2	600×600	grayscale	
BUBLCITY	600×600	color	
BUBLSTK2	600×600	color	
BUBLSTK3	600×600	color	
BUBLSTK4	600×600	color	
BUBLSTK5	600×600	color	
BUBLSTRK	600×600	color	
BUBULAR	600×600	color	
CELLOFAN	600×600	color	
CHPSUIT	600×600	color	
CHROMPOK	600×600	color	
CIRC01	600×600	color	
CIRC03	600×600	color	tile
CIRC04	600×600	color	
CIRCULA2	600×600	color	
CIRCULA3	600×600	color	

File Name	Resolution	Color/Gray	Tileable
CIRCULAR	600×600	color	
COLRCRET	600×600	color	tile
CONFETTI	600×600	color	
CRACKS01	600×600	grayscale	
CRACKS02	600×600	color	
CROCHET	600×600	color	
CRUSTY	600×600	color	
CRYSTL01	600×600	color	
CURVNOVA	600×600	color	
DEMONS1	600×600	color	
DEMONS2	600×600	color	
DEMONS3	600×600	color	
DIRT01	600×600	grayscale	
DIRT02	600×600	grayscale	
DIRT03	600×600	grayscale	
DIRT04	600×600	grayscale	
DIRT05	600×600	color	
DIRT06	600×600	grayscale	
DIVAN	600×339	color	tile
DOTTED	600×600	color	
DOTTED1	600×600	color	
DOTTED2	600×600	color	
DOTTED3	600×600	color	
DRIBBLE	600×600	color	
DYED1	600×600	color	
DYED2	600×600	grayscale	
DYED3	600×600	grayscale	
EROD1	600×600	color	
EROD2	600×600	color	

continues

File Name	Resolution	Color/Gray	Tileable
ESHEROI2	600×600	color	
ESHEROI3	600×600	color	
ESHEROI4	600×600	color	
ESHEROID	600×600	grayscale	
EXBLODE	600×600	color	tile
FIREOID	600×600	color	
FIREOID2	600×600	color	
FIREOID3	600×600	color	
FIREOID4	600×600	color	
FLECKS1	600×600	color	
FLECKS2	600×600	color	
FROGEGGS	600×600	color	
GALV1	600×600	color	
GALV2	600×600	color	
GALVMSK1	600×600	color	
GALVMSK2	600×600	color	
GALVMSK3	600×600	color	
GAUZOID	600×600	color	
GRADED	600×600	color	
GRAIN01	600×600	grayscale	tile
GRAIN02	600×600	grayscale	
GRAINY	600×600	color	
HAIR01	600×600	color	
HAIR02	600×600	color	
HAIR03	600×600	color	
HAIR03B	600×600	grayscale	
HATCHED	600×600	color	
JAGSPIN	600×600	grayscale	
JOELSOUL	600×600	color	

File Name	Resolution	Color/Gray	Tileable
LEOPARD	600×600	color	
LINEAR	600×600	color	
LINEAR2	600×600	color	
LINEAR3	600×600	color	
LINEAR4	600×600	color	
LINEGRAY	600×600	grayscale	
LINES01	600×600	color	
LINES02	600×600	color	
LINES03	600×600	color	
LINES04	600×600	color	
LINES05	600×600	color	
LINES06	600×600	color	
LIZSKIN1	600×600	grayscale	
LIZSKIN2	600×600	color	
LOOPS1	600×600	color	
LOOPS2	600×600	color	
LOOPS3	600×600	color	
MOLECULE	600×600	grayscale	
NOVA	600×600	color	
ODDFOSIL	600×600	color	
OILWATER	600×600	color	
PLADOID3	600×600	color	tile
PLAIDOI2	600×600	color	
PLAIDOID	600×600	color	
PLASMA	600×600	grayscale	tile
PLASMA-C	600×600	grayscale	
PLASMA-E	230×600	grayscale	
PLAZBOLT	600×600	color	
POLAR01	600×600	color	

continues

File Name	Resolution	Color/Gray	Tileable
POLAR02	600×600	color	
QUILTED	600×600	grayscale	tile
ROK_HC	600×600	grayscale	
ROKSURF	600×600	grayscale	
ROX	600×600	color	
RUFNEON	600×600	color	
SCRAPIT	600×600	grayscale	
SCRAPIT2	600×600	grayscale	
SCRAPIT3	600×600	color	
SCRAPIT5	600×600	grayscale	
SCRATCH1	600×600	grayscale	
SCRATCH2	600×600	grayscale	
SCRATCH3	600×600	grayscale	
SCRATCH4	600×600	grayscale	
SOFTGRID	600×600	color	
SPAGET	600×600	color	
SPATERD	600×600	color	
SPINDOT2	600×600	color	
SPINDOTS	600×600	color	
STARANIS	600×600	color	tile
STARFLD	600×394	color	
STONE01	600×600	grayscale	tile
STONE02	600×600	color	
STONE03	600×600	grayscale	
STRCGRID	600×600	color	
STREAKD	600×600	color	
STRING01	600×600	grayscale	
STRING02	600×600	color	
STRINGY	600×600	color	

File Name	Resolution	Color/Gray	Tileable
STRIPEBW	600×600	grayscale	tile
STUCCO	600×600	grayscale	
SWIRL	600×600	grayscale	tile
SWIRL3	600×600	color	tile
SWIRL4	600×600	color	
SWIRL5	600×600	color	tile
SWIRL6	600×600	color	tile
TAPRGRID	600×600	color	
TEX	600×600	color	
TEX2	600×600	color	
TI_DI	600×600	color	
TISSUE	600×600	color	
TISSUE2	600×600	color	
TISSUE3	600×600	color	
TURBUL1	600×600	color	
TURBUL2	600×600	color	
TURBUL3	600×600	color	
TURBUL4	600×600	color	
TURBUL5	600×600	color	
TURBUL6	600×600	color	
WARPBLUE	600×600	color	
WARPGRID	600×600	color	
WARPMUL2	600×600	color	
WARPMUL3	600×600	color	
WARPMULT	600×600	color	
WARPYELL	600×600	color	
WATRCOL2	600×600	color	
WATRCOLR	600×600	color	
WAVES01	600×600	color	
WAVES02	600×600	color	

continues

File Name	Resolution	Color/Gray	Tileable
WAVES03	600×600	color	
WIGGLE01	600×600	grayscale	tile
WIGGLE02	600×600	color	
WIGGLE03	600×600	color	
WIGGLE04	600×600	color	
WIGGLE05	600×600	color	
WOBLGRID	600×600	color	
WORM01	600×600	color	
WORM02	600×600	color	
WORM03	600×600	color	
WORM04	600×600	color	
WORM05	600×600	color	
WORM06	600×600	color	
WORMMUD	600×600	color	
WOVEN	600×600	color	

Procedure

1. From the Keyframer, using **Preview/View Flic**, load CATALOG.FLC from the \NRPTEX directory on the CD-ROM. Press the spacebar immediately after clicking on the file name to stop the FLIC and display the first frame of the FLC file. Each frame of the FLIC displays twelve map images. The corresponding file name for each map is printed at the upper left of each sample image.

2. Press the right arrow to step through the FLC file and view the remaining images. Some of the images have three or more variations in characteristics such as the color palette. You can use any of the static maps in the Materials Editor as any map type or any mask. You can also use them as background images using **Renderer/Setup/Background** or projector spotlights.

If you use the map image directly off the CD-ROM, be sure to add \NRPTEX to 3D Studio's Map Paths so 3D Studio can find the map images at render time.

The animated maps average 320×240 and are all in 24-bit JPEG format. There are two categories of animated maps (or *animaps*) on the CD-ROM: videotaped and constructed. The former originated as real-world phenomena that were first videotaped on location or in our studio, and then captured to a hard disk for editing and image processing. They are designed to be used with their accompanying IFL files as maps in 3D Studio's Materials Editor, as background sequences, or with projector spotlights for lighting effects. These maps average approximately 10 seconds or 300 frames each.

Examples of the video type include CAUSTIK, which depicts continuously varying water caustics, or SMOKE, which consists of a sequence of swirling smoke that fades in from black.

The constructed animaps were created as animations in 3D Studio and rendered to disk in JPEG format. These are designed primarily for use in transition effects or as wipes. However, they are also suitable for use as maps, masks, or in projector spotlights. As with the videotaped animaps, each comes with its own .IFL file.

Examples of the constructed animaps include MOLS or CRKS, which are grayscale pattern transitions from black to white. There are eight constructed animaps that are two seconds each and consist of two second intervals of four different black-and-white patterns. Each pattern was animated using two methods. The first is an orthogonal move on the pattern that produces an overall pattern shift from black to white. The second method is a transverse with the pattern moving from left to right—black to white.

The animated maps are located in the /ANIMAPS directory on the CD-ROM. Table A.2 lists the map file names, the name of its IFL file, and the name of its preview FLIC.

Table A.2
Animated Maps on the CD-ROM

Animap Frames, IFL, and Preview	Total Frames	Resolution	Description
Animap Files			
BOIL*.JPG BOILED.IFL &.FLC	217	320×240	boiling water (rolling)
BUBL*.JPG BUBBLES.IFL &.FLC	226	320×240	boiling bubbles
COST*.JPG CAUSTIK.IFL &.FLC	360	320×240	pool caustics
CORO*.JPG CORIDOOR.IFL &.FLC	31	320×240	optical effect
CRIS*.JPG CRISCROS.IFL &.FLC	300	320×240	criss-crossing streaks
SDYE*.JPG DYEJOB.IFL & .FLC	240	320×240	swirling dye in water
FS*.JPG FIRESNAK.IFL &.FLC	263	320×240	burning torched snakes
HPNO*.JPG HYPNO.IFL &.FLC	31	320×320	optical effect
FILZ*.JPG IRONFILE.IFL & .FLC	300	320×240	abstract iron filings

continues

Animap Frames, IFL, and Preview	Total Frames	Resolution	Description
SMOK*.JPG SMOKE.IFL & .FLC	360	320×240	smoke
SPRK*.JPG SPARKS.IFL & .FLC	164	320×240	sparks
SPNB*.JPG SPINBALL.IFL & .FLC	301	320×240	moving balls
SFIR*.JPG SPINFIRE.IFL & .FLC	270	320×240	spinning sparks and smoke
STRK*.JPG WATRSTRK.IFL & .FLC	300	320×240	streaks on water
WORM*.JPG WORM.IFL & .FLC	360	320×240	box of worms

Transitions and Wipes

Animap Frames, IFL, and Preview	Total Frames	Resolution	Description
CIRS*.JPG CIRS.IFL & .FLC	60	320×320	circular pattern
CIRT*.JPG CIRT.IFL & .FLC	60	320×320	circular pattern, transverse
CRKS*.JPG CRKS.IFL & .FLC	60	320×320	cracks
CRKT*.JPG CRKT.IFL & .FLC	60	320×320	cracks, transverse
GRNS*.JPG GRNS.IFL & .FLC	60	320×320	serpentine grain
GRNT*.JPG GRNT.IFL & .FLC	60	320×320	serpentine grain, transverse
MOLS*.JPG MOLS.IFL & .FLC	60	320×320	irregular balls
MOLT*.JPG MOLT.IFL & .FLC	60	320×320	irregular balls, transverse

1. In the Keyframer, choose **Preview/View Flic**, and load CATALOG2.FLC from the \NRPTEX directory on the CD-ROM. Press the spacebar immediately after clicking on the file name to display the first frame of the .FLC file and stop the FLIC . Each frame displays four frames from one of the animated maps. The corresponding file name for each map along with the resolution and frame count is printed in the upper left of each sample image.

2. Press the right arrow to step through the FLC file and view the remaining sequences. The CATALOG2.FLC is provided as a quick reference. To see a complete thumbnail of each complete animap, view its corresponding FLC file.

Any of the animaps may be used in the Materials Editor as any map or mask type to create animated materials. They may also be used as background images by choosing **Renderer/Setup/Background** dialog or using the animated map with projector spotlights.

If you use the animated maps directly off of the CD-ROM, be sure to add the \NRPTEX to 3D Studio's Map Paths so 3D Studio can access these images at render time.

Remember that editing the animation maps' IFL files in your text editor can produce some remarkable variations in the animaps. This technique makes it simple to produce ramps, rhythmic variations, reverses, and loops from these sequences.

Conclusion

As you would expect, the key to getting the most from these maps is taking the time to experiment with them. Although they are certainly suitable for use singly as texture or opacity maps, try various combinations of still maps or still and animation maps on the same material.

Also try using the maps, particularly the animaps, as starting points to create unique moving textures with your paint or special effects programs.

GALLERY

OF IMAGES

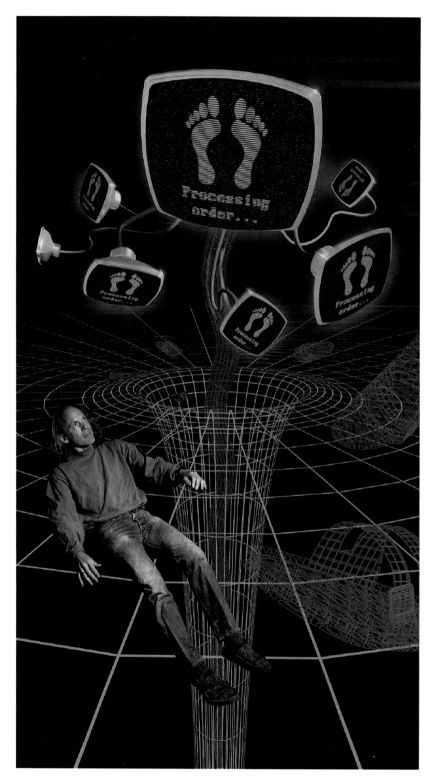

ILLUSTRATION COURTESY OF FORCADE AND ASSOCIATES

ILLUSTRATION COURTESY OF FORCADE AND ASSOCIATES

ILLUSTRATION BY MARTIN FOSTER

ILLUSTRATION BY MARTIN FOSTER

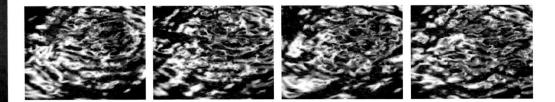

BOILED.TIF

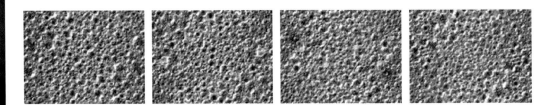

BUBBLES.TIF

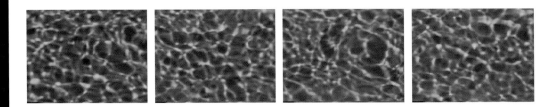

CAUSTIC.TIF

CIRS.TIF

   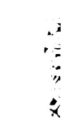

CIRT.TIF

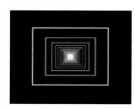   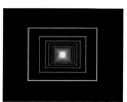

CORRIDOR.TIF

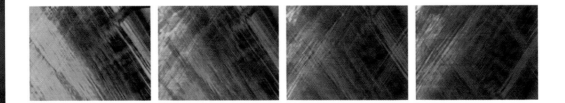

CRISCROS.TIF

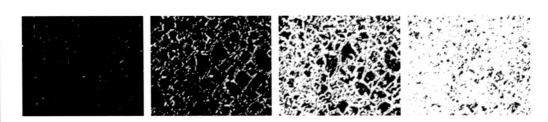

CRKS.TIF

CRKT.TIF

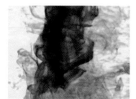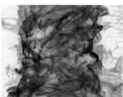

DYEJOB.TIF

FIRESNAK.TIF

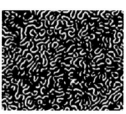

GRNS.TIF

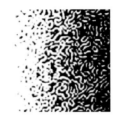

GRNT.TIF

HYPNO.TIF

IRONFILE.TIF

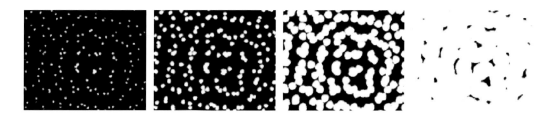

MOLS.TIF

MOLT.TIF

SMOKE.TIF

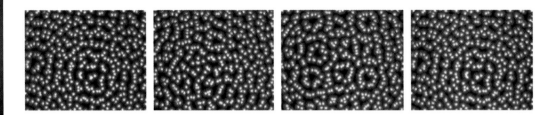

SPINBALL.TIF

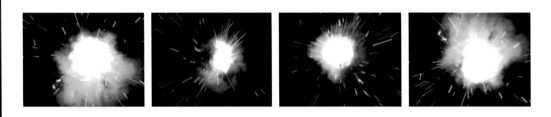

SPINFIRE.TIF

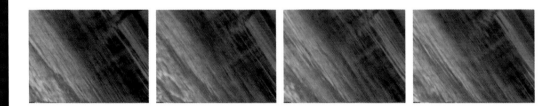

WATRSTRK.TIF

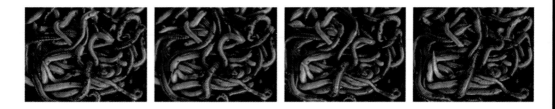

WORMS.TIF

BEEBEE1.TIF

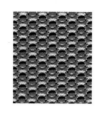

BEEBEE5.TIF

BIZARRO2.TIF

BEEBEE2.TIF

BEETLES.TIF

BIZARRO3.TIF

BEEBEE3.TIF

BENDOID.TIF

BIZARRO4.TIF

BEEBEE4.TIF

BIZARRO1.TIF

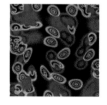

BLOB.TIF

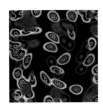

BLOBB.TIF

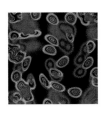

BLOBOID.TIF

BRUSHD2.TIF

BLOBBY.TIF

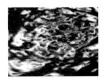

BOIL0200.TIF

BUBL0100.TIF

BLOBEBW.TIF

BROCADE1.TIF

BUBLCITY.TIF

BLOBEM.TIF

BROCADE2.TIF

BUBLSTK2.TIF

WORMMUD.TIF

BUBULAR.TIF

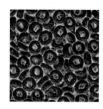

CIRCO1.TIF

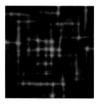

WOVEN.TIF

CELLOFAN.TIF

CIRCO3.TIF

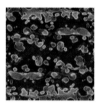

BUBLSTK5.TIF

CHPSUIT.TIF

CIRCO4.TIF

BUBLSTRK.TIF

CHROMPOK.TIF

CIRCULA2.TIF

CIRCULA3.TIF

COLRCRET.TIF

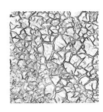

CRACKS01.TIF

CIRCULAR.TIF

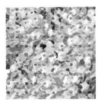

CONFETTI.TIF

CRACKS02.TIF

CIRS0030.TIF

CORO0029.TIF

CRIS0200.TIF

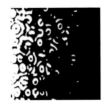

CIRT0030.TIF

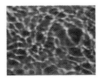

COST0200.TIF

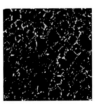

CRKS0030.TIF

CRKT0030.TIF

CURVNOVA.TIF

DIRT01.TIF

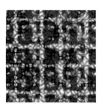

CROCHET.TIF

DEMONS1.TIF

DIRT02.TIF

CRUSTY.TIF

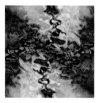

DEMONS2.TIF

DIRT03.TIF

CRYSTL01.TIF

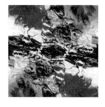

DEMONS3.TIF

DIRT04.TIF

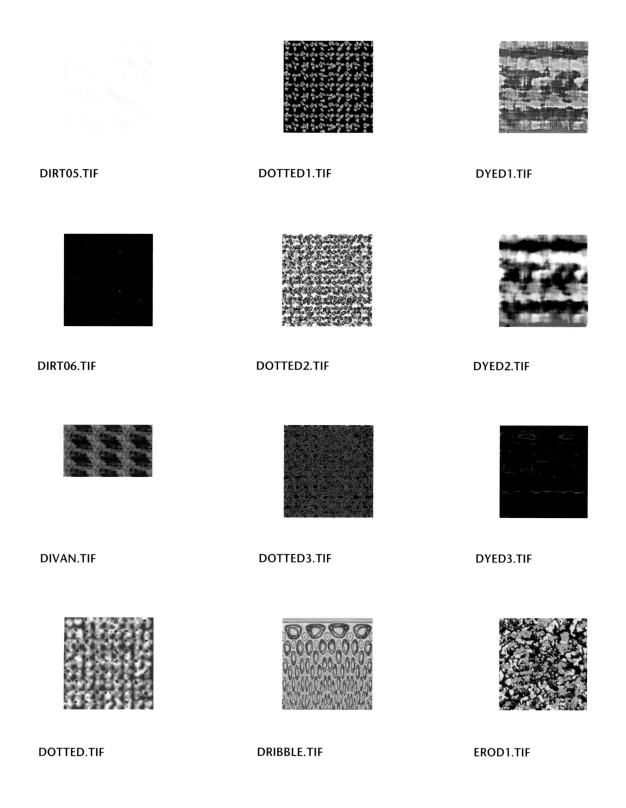

DIRT05.TIF

DOTTED1.TIF

DYED1.TIF

DIRT06.TIF

DOTTED2.TIF

DYED2.TIF

DIVAN.TIF

DOTTED3.TIF

DYED3.TIF

DOTTED.TIF

DRIBBLE.TIF

EROD1.TIF

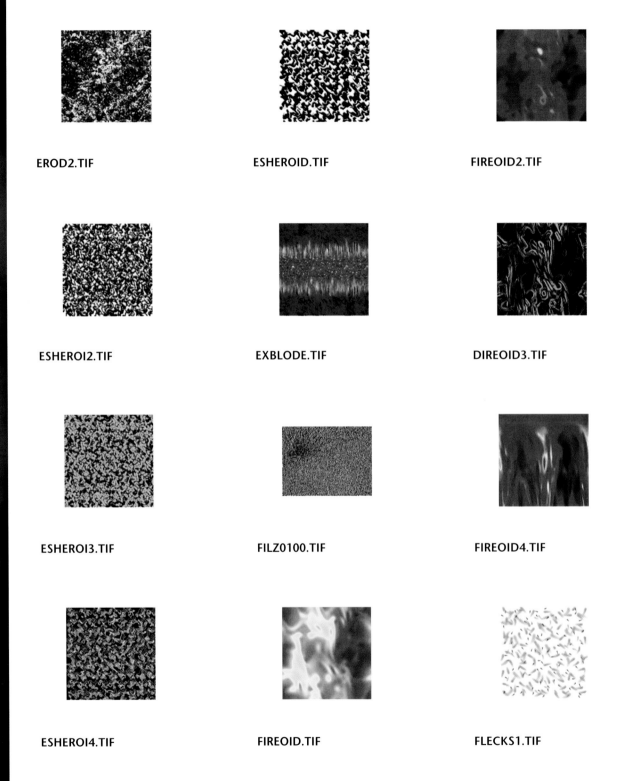

EROD2.TIF

ESHEROID.TIF

FIREOID2.TIF

ESHEROI2.TIF

EXBLODE.TIF

DIREOID3.TIF

ESHEROI3.TIF

FILZ0100.TIF

FIREOID4.TIF

ESHEROI4.TIF

FIREOID.TIF

FLECKS1.TIF

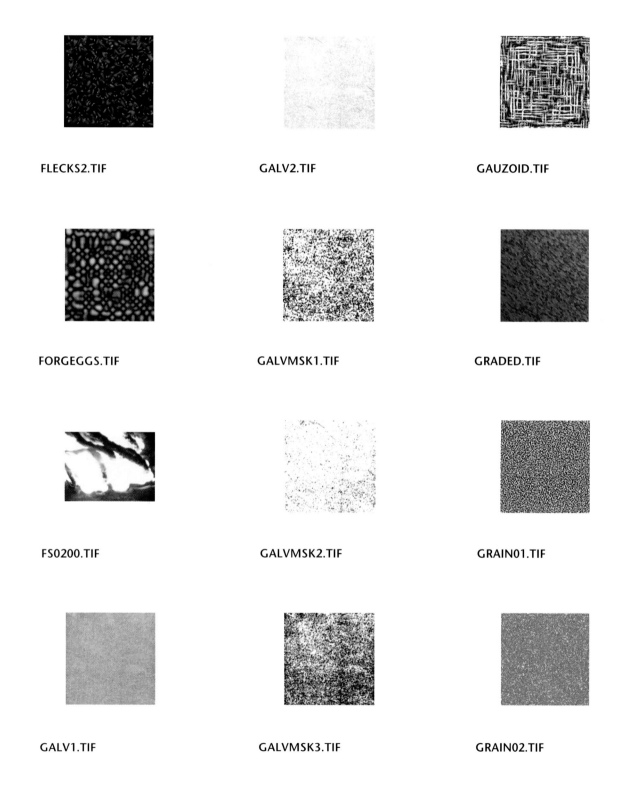

FLECKS2.TIF

GALV2.TIF

GAUZOID.TIF

FORGEGGS.TIF

GALVMSK1.TIF

GRADED.TIF

FS0200.TIF

GALVMSK2.TIF

GRAIN01.TIF

GALV1.TIF

GALVMSK3.TIF

GRAIN02.TIF

GRAINY.TIF

HAIR02.TIF

HPNO0030.TIF

GRNS0030.TIF

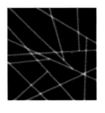

HAIR03.TIF

JAGSPIN.TIF

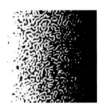

GRNT0030.TIF

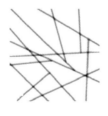

HAIR03B.TIF

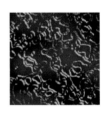

LEOPARD.TIF

HAIR01.TIF

HATCHED.TIF

LINEAR.TIF

LINEAR2.TIF

LINES01.TIF

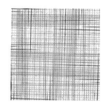

LINES05.TIF

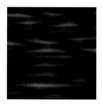

LINEAR3.TIF

LINES02.TIF

LINES06.TIF

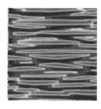

LINEAR4.TIF

LINES03.TIF

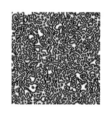

LIZSKIN1.TIF

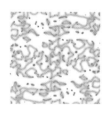

LINEGRAY.TIF

LINES04.TIF

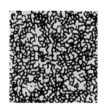

LIZSKIN2.TIF

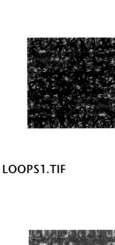

LOOPS1.TIF

MOLS0030.TIF

ODDFOSIL.TIF

LOOPS2.TIF

MOLT0030.TIF

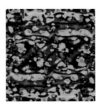

OILWATER.TIF

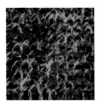

LOOPS3.TIF

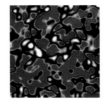

MYSOUL.TIF

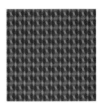

PLADOID3.TIF

MOLECULE.TIF

NOVA.TIF

PLAIDOID12.TIF

PLAIDOID.TIF

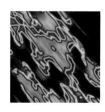

PLAZBOLT.TIF

ROKSURF.TIF

PLASMA.TIF

POLAR01.TIF

ROK_HC.TIF

PLASMA_C.TIF

POLAR02.TIF

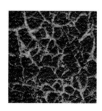

ROX.TIF

PLASMA_E.TIF

QUILTED.TIF

RUFNEON.TIF

SCRAPIT.TIF

SCRATCH1.TIF

SDYE0200.TIF

SCRAPIT2.TIF

SCRATCH2.TIF

SFIR0200.TIF

SCRAPIT3.TIF

SCRATCH3.TIF

SMOK01.TIF

SCRAPIT5.TIF

SCRATCH4.TIF

SOFTGRID.TIF

SPAGET.TIF

SPNB0200.TIF

STONE01.TIF

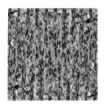

SPATERD.TIF

SPRK0025.TIF

STONE02.TIF

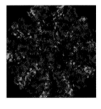

SPINDOT2.TIF

STARANIS.TIF

STONE03.TIF

SPINDOTS.TIF

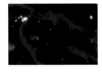

STARFLD.TIF

STRCGRID.TIF

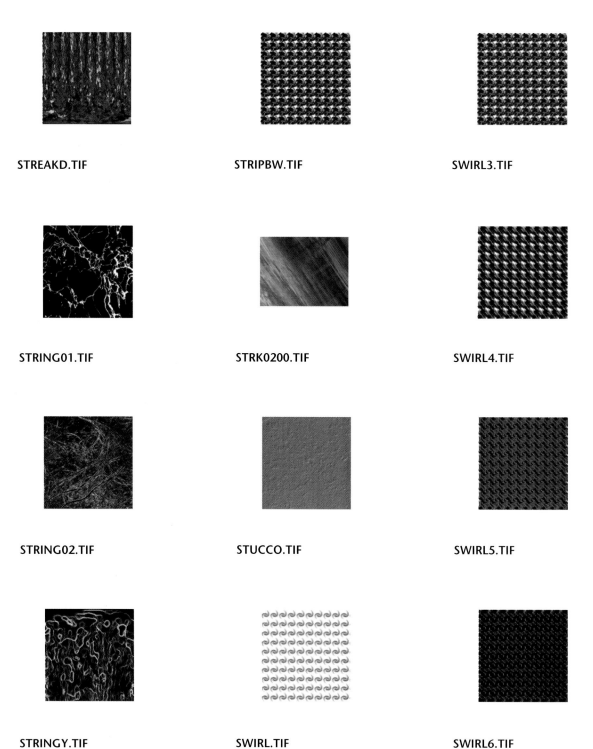

STREAKD.TIF

STRIPBW.TIF

SWIRL3.TIF

STRING01.TIF

STRK0200.TIF

SWIRL4.TIF

STRING02.TIF

STUCCO.TIF

SWIRL5.TIF

STRINGY.TIF

SWIRL.TIF

SWIRL6.TIF

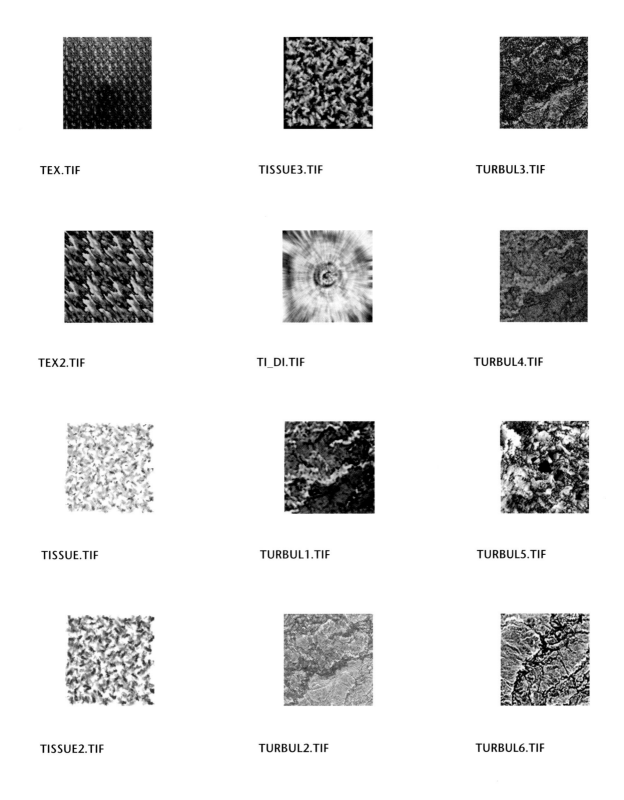

TEX.TIF

TISSUE3.TIF

TURBUL3.TIF

TEX2.TIF

TI_DI.TIF

TURBUL4.TIF

TISSUE.TIF

TURBUL1.TIF

TURBUL5.TIF

TISSUE2.TIF

TURBUL2.TIF

TURBUL6.TIF

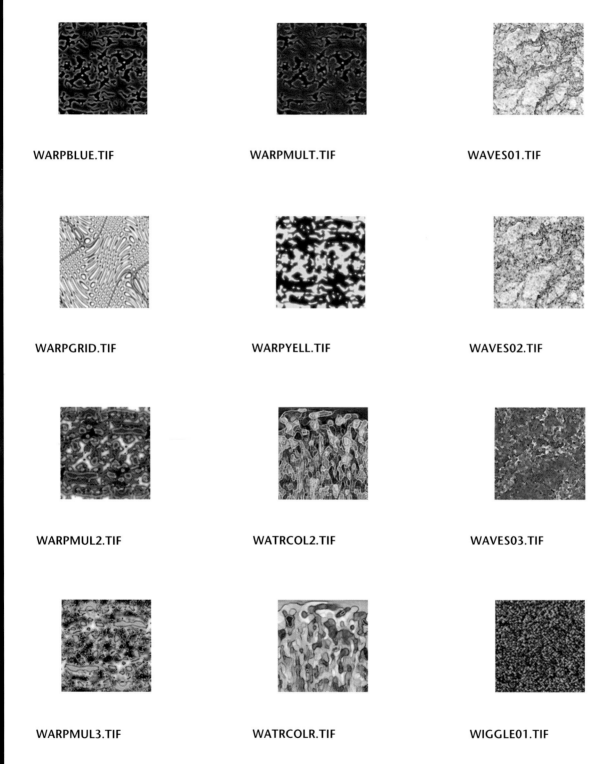

WARPBLUE.TIF WARPMULT.TIF WAVES01.TIF

WARPGRID.TIF WARPYELL.TIF WAVES02.TIF

WARPMUL2.TIF WATRCOL2.TIF WAVES03.TIF

WARPMUL3.TIF WATRCOLR.TIF WIGGLE01.TIF

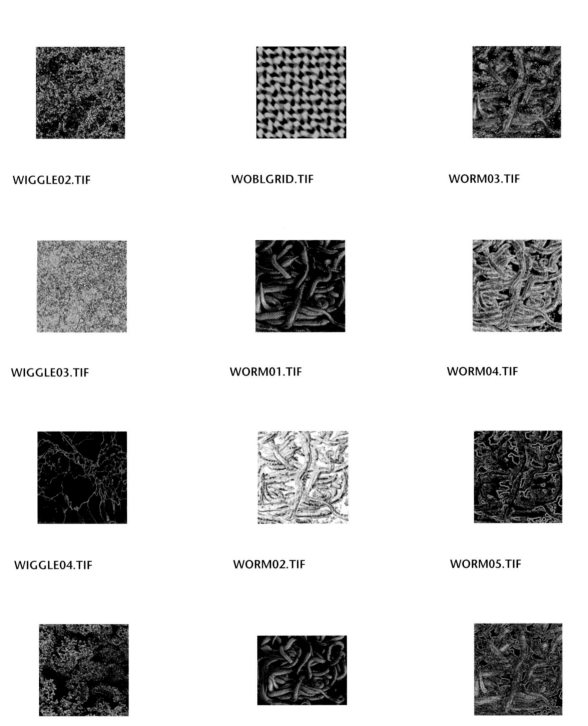

WIGGLE02.TIF

WOBLGRID.TIF

WORM03.TIF

WIGGLE03.TIF

WORM01.TIF

WORM04.TIF

WIGGLE04.TIF

WORM02.TIF

WORM05.TIF

WIGGLE05.TIF

WORM0200.TIF

WORM06.TIF

WORMMUD.TIF

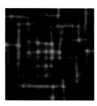

WOVEN.TIF

Index

Symbols

2D Scale function, 69
2D Shaper command (Program menu), 90
3D Display menu commands
   Choose, 18
   On, 18
3D Lofter command (Program menu), 18

A

A/B/C roll video editing (mattes), 130-132
Adjust command (Mapping menu), 55
aliasing
   anti-aliasing, 130
   mattes, 130
aligning views (refraction mapping), 57
alignment templates, 11
Alpha dialog box, 85
alpha mattes, 130-132
Ambient command (Lights menu), 9, 39
ambient lighting, 39
Anim Cel command (Cel menu), 73
animated maps, 186-189
animating, 61
   background shadows, 37-48
   cattails, 29-33
   chromakeying, 37
   energy shield effect, 113
   frames, 13, 25
   glow effect, 108
   highlighting, 83-85
   images on background, 38-44

   live video, 129
   objects (skin attributes), 175
   paths, 17-25
   shadow maps, 12, 13
   shadows, 8-13, 44
   twisting, 151-159
anti-aliasing, 130
Apply menu commands, 71
Apply Obj command (Mapping menu), 71
Arc command (Create menu), 153
artists
   Bell, Jon A., 68
   Elliott, Steven D., 16
   Forcade, Tim, 6, 50, 100, 150, 178
   Foster, Martin, 36, 88, 168
   Miller, Phillip, 134
   Phillips, Greg, 60
   Pyros, Gregory, 128
   Seifert, Keith A., 28, 110, 162
   Sher, Richard, 80
   Stinnett, David, 116
Assign menu commands (Shape menu), 90
Attributes command (Object menu), 42
Attributes dialog box, 29
AutoCAD, 144
   3D Studio, 135-140
   coordinates, 135-136
   DFXFOUT commands, 140
   exporting to 3D Studio, 135-136
   importing
      DFX arcs, 148
      DFX circles, 148

G

Geometry command (Display menu), 75, 142
Get command (Path menu), 23
Get command (Shape menu), 90
Get from Scene command (Material menu), 124
Get Material command (Material menu), 70
Get Materials from Scene command (Materials menu), 63
glow effect, 77-78, 105-108
grayscale (alpha mattes), 130
Guassian Blur filter, 125-126

H

helical paths, 18-21
    moving, 19
    rotating, 19
Helix Path Definition dialog box, 18-19
Hide command (Display menu), 37
hiding objects, 9
Hierarchy menu commands
    Create Dummy, 13
    Link, 13, 175
    Links, 97
    Show Tree, 170
high resolution, 33
highlighting, 81
    animating, 83-85
    background, 81-82
    HILITE IPAS filters, 84
    rendering, 84
    saving, 86
    texture maps, 82-83
    textures, 73
Hilite Filter dialog box, 84
HILITE IPAS filters, 84
Hook command (Shape menu), 90

I

IFL files, 13
illuminating images, 77-78
Image menu commands, 74
images
    composite, 119
    cropping, 74-75
    Guassian Blur filter, 125-126
    illuminating, 77-78

masking, 101-105
transparencies, 45-46
twisting, 151-159
importing
    AutoCAD, DFXFOUT commands, 140
    DFX arcs, 148
    DFX circles, 148
    objects from AutoCAD, 135-136
Info menu commands, 89
Insert Vertex command (Path menu), 20
inserting vertices (paths), 20
installing cattail generator, 29
intermediate colors, 130
Invert command (Select menu), 147
IXP Selector dialog box, 84

J-K-L

jaggies (aliasing), 130

Keyframer command (Program menu), 21
Keyframer Hierarchy commands, 12

laser effects, 93
layers
    image transparency, 46
    underwater effect, 122-126
letters
    detaching, 17-18
    paths, 21
lighting, 61-62
    ambient, 39
    backlighting, 10-11
    burn-in effect, 97
    Omni-fram, 39
    projector spotlights, 118
    refraction mapping, 54
    shadows, 37-38
    spotlights, 39
    underwater effect, 118-126
    wind tunnel, 62
Lights menu commands
    Ambient, 9, 39
    Cameras, 72
    Omni, 38
    Spot, 9, 38
Link command (Hierarchy menu), 13, 175
Links command (Hierarchy menu), 97

N-O

None command (Shape menu), 90
Normals command (Surface menu), 142-143

Object Attributes dialog box, 29
Object by Name dialog box, 22
Object command (Apply menu), 71
Object command (Create menu), 11, 91
Object command (Modify menu), 18, 29
Object menu commands
  Attributes, 42
  Make, 90
  Morph, 64
  Motion Blur, 64
  Preview, 90, 171
  Rotate, 24
  Rotate Abs, 64
  Tracks, 24
objects
  black-box, 42
  cross-sections, 171
  hiding, 9
  refraction mapping, 53
  rotating, 13, 23, 24
  skin attributes, 175
  stand-in
    AXP (animated stand-in external processor), 31
    mapping coordinates, 32
  texture maps, 32
  widths, 22
Omni command (Lights menu), 38
Omni lighting, 39
On command (3D Display menu), 18
opacity map (wooden text), 92
Open command (File menu), 74
Outline command (Create menu), 152

P

paint programs, texture mapping, 72-73
Parameters dialog box, 155
Paste command (Cel menu), 73
Pastel Filter, 163-166
Pastel Filter Settings dialog boxes, 164
Path menu commands
  Delete Vertex, 91
  Get, 23

Insert Vertex, 20
  Move Path, 19
  Move Vertex, 20, 91
  Rotate, 19
  Steps, 143
paths
  animating, 17-25
  helical, 18-21
  letters, 21
  lofting, 136-137
  moving, 19
  rotating, 19
  seamlessness, 171
  vertices, inserting, 20
Perspective command (Cameras menu), 55
Phillips, Greg, 60
Polygon command (Modify menu), 137
Polygon command (Select menu), 146-147
Position menu commands, 73
Preview command (Object menu), 90, 171
Preview menu commands, 186
Program menu commands
  2D Shaper, 90
  3D Lofter, 18
  Keyframer, 21
projector spotlights, 118
Put command (Material menu), 83
Put to Current command (Material menu), 120
Put to Scene command (Material menu), 75
Pyros, Gregory, 128

Q-R

Queue Entry dialog box, 84, 164

Ranges command (Cameras menu), 120
ratios, scaling, 138
reflection masking, 102-105
reflections
  rendering, 42
  shading, 42
refraction mapping, 51
  aligning views, 57
  files, 52
  lighting, 54
  marble, 56
  objects, 53

X-Y-Z

3D Studio
Special Effects
REGISTRATION CARD

Fill out this card to receive information about future 3D Studio books and other New Riders titles!

Name _____ **Title** _____

Company _____

Address _____

City/State/ZIP _____

I bought this book because: _____

_____

I purchased this book from:

☐ A bookstore (Name _____)

☐ A software or electronics store (Name _____)

☐ A mail order (Name of Catalog _____)

I purchase this many computer books each year:

☐ 1–5   ☐ 6 or more

I currently use these applications: _____

_____

_____

_____

I found these chapters to be the most informative: _____

_____

I found these chapters to be the least informative: _____

_____

Additional comments: _____

_____

☐ I would like to see my name in print! You may use my name and quote me in future New Riders products and promotions. My daytime phone number is:_____

New Riders Publishing 201 West 103rd Street • Indianapolis, Indiana 46290 USA

Fold Here

PLACE
STAMP
HERE

New Riders Publishing
201 West 103rd Street
Indianapolis, Indiana 46290
USA

WANT MORE INFORMATION?

CHECK OUT THESE RELATED TITLES:

	QTY	PRICE	TOTAL

Inside AutoCAD Release 12. Completely revised for AutoCAD 12, this book-and-disk set is your complete guide to understanding AutoCAD. You won't find another book about AutoCAD as comprehensive, detailed, and easy to use. That is why *Inside AutoCAD Release 12* is the world's no. 1 selling AutoCAD title—successfully teaching more people to use AutoCAD than any other AutoCAD title!
ISBN: 1-56205-055-9.
(Also available for AutoCAD for Windows, ISBN: 1-56205-146-6, $37.95)   _____ $37.95   _____

Maximizing AutoCAD Release 12. Filled with expert techniques for customizing AutoCAD, including demonstrations of how to create a complete, customized AutoCAD system. Extensive coverage of menu and macro creation, including DIESEL. Also includes information on how to customize support files.
ISBN: 1-56205-086-9.   _____ $39.95   _____

Maximizing AutoLISP. Learn ways to take advantage of AutoLISP, AutoCAD's built-in programming language. This comprehensive reference and tutorial explains every AutoLISP function. The text carefully introduces and explains programming concepts and demonstrates those concepts with annotated sample programs. If you want to learn AutoLISP, you need this book.
ISBN: 1-56205-085-0.   _____ $39.95   _____

AutoCAD Release 12: The Professional Reference, 2nd Edition. This reference offers detailed examples of how each command works, and its effect on other drawing entities. *AutoCAD: The Professional Reference* takes you beyond menus and commands to learn the inner workings of essential features used every day for drawing, editing, dimensioning, and plotting. Covers releases 11 and 12.
ISBN: 1-56205-059-1.   _____ $42.95   _____

Name _____   *Subtotal*   _____

Company _____   *Shipping*   _____

Address _____   *$4.00 for the first book and $1.75 for each additional book.*

City _____ State ____ ZIP _____

Phone _____ Fax _____

☐ Check Enclosed ☐ VISA ☐ MasterCard   *Total*   _____
Indiana residents add 5% sales tax.

Card #_____Exp. Date _____

Signature _____

Prices are subject to change. Call for availability and pricing information on latest editions.

New Riders Publishing   201 West 103rd Street • Indianapolis, Indiana 46290 USA

Orders/Customer Service: 1-800-428-5331
Fax: 1-800-448-3804

Fold Here

PLACE
STAMP
HERE

New Riders Publishing
201 West 103rd Street
Indianapolis, Indiana 46290
USA

GO AHEAD. PLUG YOURSELF INTO
MACMILLAN COMPUTER PUBLISHING.

Introducing the Macmillan Computer Publishing Forum on CompuServe®

Yes, it's true. Now, you can have CompuServe access to the same professional, friendly folks who have made computers easier for years. On the Macmillan Computer Publishing Forum, you'll find additional information on the topics covered by every Macmillan Computer Publishing imprint—including Que, Sams Publishing, New Riders Publishing, Alpha Books, Brady Books, Hayden Books, and Adobe Press. In addition, you'll be able to receive technical support and disk updates for the software produced by Que Software and Paramount Interactive, a division of the Paramount Technology Group. It's a great way to supplement the best information in the business.

WHAT CAN YOU DO ON THE MACMILLAN COMPUTER PUBLISHING FORUM?

Play an important role in the publishing process—and make our books better while you make your work easier:

- Leave messages and ask questions about Macmillan Computer Publishing books and software—you're guaranteed a response within 24 hours

- Download helpful tips and software to help you get the most out of your computer

- Contact authors of your favorite Macmillan Computer Publishing books through electronic mail

- Present your own book ideas

- Keep up to date on all the latest books available from each of Macmillan Computer Publishing's exciting imprints

JOIN NOW AND GET A FREE COMPUSERVE STARTER KIT!

To receive your free CompuServe Introductory Membership, call toll-free, **1-800-848-8199** and ask for representative **#597**. The Starter Kit Includes:

- Personal ID number and password

- $15 credit on the system

- Subscription to CompuServe Magazine

HERE'S HOW TO PLUG INTO MACMILLAN COMPUTER PUBLISHING:

Once on the CompuServe System, type any of these phrases to access the Macmillan Computer Publishing Forum:

GO MACMILLAN   **GO BRADY**
GO QUEBOOKS   **GO HAYDEN**
GO SAMS   **GO QUESOFT**
GO NEWRIDERS   **GO ALPHA**

Once you're on the CompuServe Information Service, be sure to take advantage of all of CompuServe's resources. CompuServe is home to more than 1,700 products and services—plus it has over 1.5 million members worldwide. You'll find valuable online reference materials, travel and investor services, electronic mail, weather updates, leisure-time games and hassle-free shopping (no jam-packed parking lots or crowded stores).

Seek out the hundreds of other forums that populate CompuServe. Covering diverse topics such as pet care, rock music, cooking, and political issues, you're sure to find others with the same concerns as you—and expand your knowledge at the same time.

GRAPHICS TITLES

INSIDE CORELDRAW! 4.0, SPECIAL EDITION

DANIEL GRAY

An updated version of the #1 best-selling tutorial on CorelDRAW!

CorelDRAW! 4.0

ISBN: 1-56205-164-4

$34.95 USA

CORELDRAW! SPECIAL EFFECTS

NEW RIDERS PUBLISHING

An inside look at award-winning techniques from professional CorelDRAW! designers!

CorelDRAW! 4.0

ISBN: 1-56205-123-7

$39.95 USA

CORELDRAW! NOW!

RICHARD FELDMAN

The hands-on tutorial for users who want practical information now!

CorelDRAW! 4.0

ISBN: 1-56205-131-8

$21.95 USA

INSIDE CORELDRAW! FOURTH EDITION

DANIEL GRAY

The popular tutorial approach to learning CorelDRAW!...with complete coverage of version 3.0!

CorelDRAW! 3.0

ISBN: 1-56205-106-7

$24.95 USA

To Order, Call 1-800-428-5331